W9-BKK-119

THE DEATH OF THE
IMPERIAL DREAM

BOOKS BY EDWARD GRIERSON

The Death of the
IMPERIAL DREAM

The British Commonwealth &
Empire   1775–1969

Edward Grierson

DOUBLEDAY & COMPANY, INC., GARDEN CITY, NEW YORK
1972

LIBRARY OF CONGRESS CATALOG CARD NUMBER 72–186024
COPYRIGHT © 1972 BY EDWARD GRIERSON
ALL RIGHTS RESERVED
PRINTED IN THE UNITED STATES OF AMERICA
FIRST EDITION IN THE UNITED STATES OF AMERICA

909.0917
G848d

ACKNOWLEDGEMENTS

My grateful thanks are due to the following for their kind permission to quote from books, periodicals and newspapers:

To — Associated Book Publishers, Ltd. for an extract from *William Lyon Mackenzie King* by R. Dawson and H. B. Neatby.

— George Allen and Unwin, Ltd. for an extract from *India and the Commonwealth* by S. R. Mehrotra.

— Doubleday and Company, Inc., Mrs. George Bambridge, and Macmillan and Co., Ltd. for poems by Rudyard Kipling. (The poem "The Jubilee" appears in the collected works under the title, *What the People Said.*)

— Ernest Benn, Ltd. for an extract from *History of the English People in the Nineteenth Century* by Elie Halévy.

— Doubleday & Company, Inc. and Jonathan Cape, Ltd. for an extract from T. E. Lawrence's *Seven Pillars of Wisdom.*

— Harper & Row, Publishers, Inc. for an extract from Joyce Cary's *Mister Johnson.*

— Oxford University Press for an extract from *Survey of British Commonwealth Affairs, 1937-42* by W. K. Hancock.

— George Weidenfeld and Nicolson for an extract from *The Colonial Empires* by D. K. Fieldhouse.

— Associated Newspapers, Ltd. for extracts from the *Daily Mail.*

— The Bulletin, Sydney, for extracts and verse from *The Bulletin.*

— The Economist for an extract from *The Economist.*

— John Fairfax and Sons, Ltd. (Associated Newspapers, Ltd.) for an extract from the *Sydney Morning Herald.*

— Illustrated Newspapers, Ltd. for an extract from *The Illustrated London News.*

38943

— The Daily Times of Nigeria, Ltd. for an extract from the *Daily Times of Nigeria*.

— The New Statesman for extracts and verse from *The New Statesman and Nation*.

— Punch for extracts and verse reproduced by permission of *Punch*.

— The Spectator for extracts from articles in *The Spectator*.

— The Statesman, Ltd., Calcutta, for extracts and verse in *The Statesman*.

— The Times of India for an extract from *The Times of India*.

— Times Newspapers, Ltd. for extracts from *The Times*.

CONTENTS

We are the music-makers,
And we are the dreamers of dreams,
. . . .
With wonderful deathless ditties
We build up the world's great cities,
And out of a fabulous story
We fashion an empire's glory:
One man with a dream, at pleasure,
Shall go forth and conquer a crown;
And three with a new song's measure
Can trample an empire down.

—*Arthur O'Shaughnessy, ODE.*

Men are we, and must grieve when even the Shade
Of that which once was great is pass'd away.

—William Wordsworth

I

Empire and Nation in 1914

A WEEK-END WORTH LIVING FOR

> "The best week-end of the year," was the general verdict of
> holiday-makers as they returned to London last night from the
> seaside, the river and the road. . . . The golden sunshine and the
> elastic quality of the air stimulated athletic endeavours . . . "You
> could not go wrong, you felt so full of life," was the explanation
> of an athlete modestly depreciating his success.

On another page of this edition of the London *Daily Mail* for June
29, 1914, the assassination of an Austrian archduke and his wife
at the hands of student terrorists filled several columns. "We cannot
yet estimate the full consequences of yesterday's tragedy at Sarajevo
upon the future of the Austro-Hungarian empire," commented *The
Times* in an informed article on the "Political Aspects" of the crime.
That the consequences would affect the British Empire and engulf
the whole world would have occurred to few readers of those lines.
In any case, there were happier things to enjoy:

Frocks were never prettier than on Church parade in Hyde Park [noted the *Mail*]. The most conspicuous costume was worn by a lady, the grey horses of whose carriage matched her grey side ringlets. She wore a crinoline gown of marvellously flowered yellow silk, her coal-scuttle bonnet was as bright as a geranium bed, and she shaded her face from the sun with a parasol like a pagoda.

Nor were foreign affairs on the most sensitive of all fronts less euphoric. In Kiel, the officers of the visiting squadron of the Royal Navy had been entertained to lunch in the town hall, where the German Grand Admiral had proposed toasts to "the imperishable Nelson," the *beau ideal* of every sailor. And if any fears might have been entertained in England about the dangers lurking in the world, there were certainly no doubts in Scotland. Had the 28th not been the six hundredth anniversary of Bannockburn!

For those of us brought up in a comparable era before the launching of Hitler's war, when every day on the moving staircase took us visibly nearer to catastrophe, the insouciance of the generation of 1914 will always remain something to marvel at.

It was not a generation immune from shocks. The Boer War, the Syndicalist unrest that had been rising to a climax since 1910, the antics of the suffragettes and the Irish problem in its potentially most critical stage, threatening civil war and the breakdown of the whole process of democratic government, had all excited on electoral platforms and in the press jeremiads as anguished as any in British history. Nor had incidents of the most dramatic and shattering kind been lacking—a Home Secretary directing a siege of foreign anarchists in the heart of London; a young woman hurling herself in front of the Derby field; strikers looting a Welsh village. In the mother of Parliaments, Mr. Winston Churchill had been struck on the head by a well-directed copy of bound Order Papers. Could sensationalism go further?

Nor was it a generation that had not been warned of the Pandora's box that Europe had become, only waiting for someone to let loose the demons inside. As early as 1904, at the time of the formation of the *Entente* with France, Lord Rosebery had prophesied that it would mean war with Germany in the end, and other figures as eminent as Lord Esher and Lord Roberts had for long been sound-

ing the alarm. No very acute perceptions were needed: the perils involved in the interlocking alliances of two rival power blocks—Triple
Alliance and Triple *Entente*—facing one another across Europe
were there for all to see. Perhaps the crises which for over a decade
had arisen one after the other from these rivalries, only to subside
into *détente,* had devalued the sense of danger. In Morocco the
Germans had twice forced the pace against France and her partner
Britain, only to draw back. In 1908–09 Russia, faced with the direct
threat of war with Germany, had similarly accepted diplomatic defeat over the Austrian annexation of Bosnia/Herzegovina. Even the
storm that had been raging over German naval expansion had begun
to blow itself out with the realisation that the Royal Navy was still
incomparably the greatest power on the seas. There was a general
feeling abroad in the world that war was too archaic and unprofitable
a thing to be possible in an enlightened age. After surviving the Bos-
nian crisis and Agadir, Europe seemed to be getting the measure of
its problems. In fact, the spring and summer of 1914 had been remarkably quiet and pacific. And though the situation on the home
front in Britain, with its endemic strikes and violence, was explosive
enough to have charmed the conference of anarchists due to meet in
London that August, that was not how ordinary people saw it, to
judge from the popular press, the newsreels and the faded sepia
photographs of the time. For them the world was a more restful
place: not quite the "Long Garden Party" of our modern fantasy
about the era, but at least a walk along the "prom" in the sunshine
of that blissful summer.

How evocative those old snapshots are—the men in their straw
boaters and high collars wilting in the heat (*The Times* had a whole
article devoted to man's incredible masochism); the girls in their
floral dresses; the bathing machines; punts moored along the booms
at Henley; the intrepid aviators. In all directions life was bursting at
the seams. DOCTOR'S LOVE CODE: KISSES FOR A PATIENT deserved
its full column. The *Mail's* Woman's Page, always solicitous for the
welfare of its readers, was concerned with the probably insoluble
problem of "The Frivolous Husband." And on a deeper level, under
headlines A SOCIETY OF SPIRITS, a Dr. Schiller was encouraging those
interested in psychical research with his assurance that, whatever the
shortcomings of the living, the dead "on the other side" were definitely beginning to co-operate.

By July 3 the assassination at Sarajevo had vanished from the headlines. That day the panic leader, DRIFTING TO DISASTER, referred to the crisis in Ireland. On the 9th a very small column announced that the Austrian press had called Serbia "a nest of plague rats," but no one was alarmed. After all, it was the Silly Season. In the park a lady had been photographed with her pet piglet on a lead. Five thousand fans had created "amazing scenes" in greeting Georges Carpentier, "the Prince of Pugilism," when he arrived at the Savoy to fight Gunboat Smith. The headmasters of Eton and Harrow, giving evidence before a commission on venereal disease, had expounded on the problem of whether schools should give sex education to their boys. On the whole they were against it, prescribing "hard exercise, hard work, wholesome society and moderation in diet and drinking" as the best safeguards against indulgence. Clearly, the permissive society was on the wing and after inspecting the cadets of the Eton O.T.C. the inspecting general had commented very sourly: "There is a great deal too much long hair about." Yet if one really desired to know more of the sterner world existing over the horizon of the summer holidays, there was the great naval review at Spithead, and, with increasing insistence, in headlines a little larger with each succeeding day, the Irish crisis which by mid-July had come to dominate the political news to the virtual exclusion of everything else. THE KING AND THE CRISIS. DANGER OF CIVIL WAR. Should Protestant Ulster be coerced into a shot-gun wedding with the Catholic "South" at the altar of Home Rule? *Could* it be coerced? Ireland has always posed insoluble problems; indeed it asks them still. In Dublin and Belfast, rival political leaders, with armed forces in support, had taken up extreme positions. At Westminster the Liberals and Unionists were equally divided. Even the King's anguished intervention could do nothing to heal the self-inflicted and perhaps mortal wound from which the nation was suffering.

In face of so grave and so near a crisis, the distant rumblings from Europe fell into a kind of vacuum. On July 21, when its headlines were concerned with the Buckingham Palace Conference which George V had called to try and knock his statesmen's heads together over Ireland, the *Mail* devoted a mere thirty lines to UNEASY VIENNA: STRAINED AUSTRO-SERBIAN RELATIONS; and when next day *The*

Times took up the call with a leader, A DANGER TO EUROPE, it was only a second leader.

Suddenly on July 25 the curtain began to rise for Englishmen on a more fateful drama. EUROPEAN CRISIS. GRAVE GERMAN SUGGESTIONS. RUSSIA INTERVENING. Over that week-end the tension mounted, and by Monday, July 27, the fat was really in the fire. In the *Mail* huge banner headlines reported PANIC-LIKE SELLING ON THE BOURSES; and EUROPE AND THE CRISIS had reached first-leader status in *The Times*.

Yet such was the climate bred in England by a century free of major wars, that as late as August 3 eight thousand watched the Bank Holiday "Roses" cricket match between Yorkshire and Lancashire at Old Trafford and seventeen thousand were at The Oval to acclaim Hobbs's double century against Notts. "The War and Racing" was the subject of a *Times* article on August 4. "No curtailment at present." If not sensible, it was at least a magnificent display of nerve. As late as July 31 a plaintive article had dealt with the sufferings at the hands "of solitude and of servants" of husbands whose wives had basely deserted them to take the children to the seaside. But on August 5 (though the Brighton race card was published) some of the largest banner headlines ever used were proclaiming that Britain had at last declared war on Germany. "Rainy: fair later" was the Met forecast for the day.

     *   *   *

In Britain this life and death struggle against the greatest military power on earth was accepted without undue misgivings as something unavoidable, for the German invasion of Belgium had made the path of duty very clear. A Liberal cabinet, sincerely pacific and elected on a platform of social justice, was swept with only two resignations into war, and huge crowds, fresh from the cricket fields and the seaside, gathered to cheer the death sentence that had been passed on them as heartily as their fellows in Vienna, Paris and Berlin. "The nations slithered over the brink into the boiling cauldron of the war," wrote Lloyd George, "without any apprehension or dismay."

Britain was far from being a socially harmonious or balanced state. Quite apart from the Irish problem, the suffragettes and the dangerous social unrest in the mines and factories, she presented a somewhat tarnished image. Inequalities were rife. Compared with her chief rival, Germany, she was a laggard in the field of education, which claimed no more than 1 per cent of the national income. Children left school at thirteen. One per cent of the population owned two thirds of the national wealth. Only three million workers in certain specified heavy industries were protected by unemployment insurance. The nation which had launched the Industrial Revolution on the world had fallen industrially behind the United States and Germany and no more than held its own against France and Tsarist Russia. A deep-seated dislike of standing armies—supposedly a folk memory of sufferings under Cromwell's Major Generals but more probably the result of laziness and insularity—had limited Britain's planned contribution to any continental war to the derisory figure of 185,000 men; and to raise and commit even so many had taxed the ingenuity of the few realists in Asquith's Liberal cabinet to the full. Loud and anguished had been the cries of the majority of its members when they were at last acquainted with the terms of the staff talks with France which had been going on for years.

Yet none of this visibly marred the general impression of strength and well-being so vividly portrayed in the photographs and writing of the time. Britain's free-trade economy suited her industrialised and maritime state. Fuel for the factories and fleets was coal, and Britain was an exporter of coal. Even industrial strife could not hide the fact that things were improving for the growing and increasingly articulate working class. Expenditure on the social services had doubled since the Liberal government had come in.

And it was a government of giants—Asquith, Grey, Haldane, Lloyd George, Churchill. Few more talented administrations have ruled anywhere. The King—new to his job but earnest and high principled—was a fervent advocate of social peace and justice for all his subjects. In the arts there was Hardy, Conrad, Wells, Shaw (to borrow one Irishman), Yeats (to borrow another), Elgar, Vaughan Williams, Delius, D. H. Lawrence, Kipling, Arnold Bennett, Belloc, Sickert, Augustus John.

What a disputatious, self-confident group they make in retrospect, even the mavericks among them. And in this they perfectly mirrored the man in the street, "the man on the Clapham omnibus," those old open-to-the-skies top-deckers that speak of a less cramped and sunnier world. Was not Britain the moral tutor of Europe, its trend-setter and exemplar? English social customs had everywhere been gaining ground. The "week-end" was about to become a continental institution: even tea was becoming acceptable. The craze for sport had crossed the Channel, but the great social occasions still took place on British soil. Fashion gathered at Cowes for the yachting, at Henley for the regatta, at Ascot and Goodwood to see the ladies' hats. Association football had begun its triumphant march across the world. Only cricket remained a fairly general mystery, though Australians and South Africans embraced it and West Indians were about to follow suit.

This robust, sport-loving society, cradled in peace behind the shield of the Royal Navy, accepted the challenge of war with alacrity, almost as another game to be played. Germany as a rival was resented but not feared. Among the volunteers hurrying to answer Kitchener's call on behalf of King and Country there was apprehension that the war, most provokingly, would be won without them, before Christmas, before they could "do their bit." This is not legend, it is fact, and it was a spirit which affected not only the products of the public schools but hundreds of thousands from all walks of life who hastened to the recruiting stations to take the King's shilling. To them it was not only a duty but a glorious adventure. And even in government circles, where the facts were known and thoughtless patriotism was strictly at a discount, there was a residual belief that a just war must be a successful one. Lord Kitchener's sombre prediction that it would be at a minimum a three-year ordeal was received, if not with derision, at least with astonishment. In the last resort, even statesmen as experienced and pacific as Grey, even as radical as Lloyd George, were at one with the mood of the people they represented and entered the arena of death with the same clear conscience and with just as little thought for the morrow.

For the timorous, there was always the Royal Navy to fall back on. That July, only a fortnight before the old order of the world and the *Pax Britannica* collapsed together into ruin, forty miles of warships had lain in Spithead for the royal review of the fleet—certainly the most formidable concentration of naval strength which had ever been assembled. The newspapers went into rhapsodies about it, as well they might. The weather was overcast and the *Daily*

Mail's correspondent reported "a wilderness of ships with the smoke of a great town drifting above them. Ship after ship till the eye grew dizzy." "A business-like rather than a ceremonial occasion," was how *The Illustrated London News* saw it with prophetic insight. But when darkness fell the viewers witnessed a truly apocalyptic scene:

> The searchlight men worked in concert great long white blinding lines. They were thrown on the city and every nook of it was unveiled; then into the sky where they feathered into plumes of light. . . . It was like a firmament gone mad. They rose and fell like saluting comets.

That Germany had chosen to challenge this invincible array on the high seas was a matter for some wonder. And Britain—quite apart from her continental allies—was not alone in the world, one small offshore island. In his message—proudly printed in the entire colonial press—King George had set the tone in suitably sober words:

> I shall be strengthened in the discharge of the great responsibility which rests upon me by the confident belief that in the time of trial my Empire will be united, calm and resolute, and trusting in God.

"My Empire." How archaic it sounds: almost as remote from us as the chivalry of Agincourt. And what indeed was it, this peculiar entity which almost without consultation and with one stroke of the pen had been hurled by "the King in Parliament"—a United Kingdom parliament—into a war which hardly one in a million of its citizens could have dreamed of a month earlier?

Few more illogical structures could be conceived than this far-flung array of coral atolls and sub-continents which had become linked together under one crown. Even on a map, with all the relevant pieces coloured red, the haphazard shape of the organism was striking. What relevance had Newfoundland for Natal, Fiji for Tobago? What community of interest could exist between a French-speaking politician in Quebec, a Boer farmer on the veldt, a tribal chief in Nigeria, a sadhu by the banks of the Ganges, a New Zealand sheep farmer, a Bengali peasant?

In the Roman Empire a similar motley of cultures had existed but at least there had been an ideal of equal citizenship behind it, a single code of laws, an administrative structure that was substantially the same from Hadrian's Wall to the Pyramids. The British Empire gloried in its disparities—French *droit administratif* in Quebec, Roman-Dutch law at the Cape, Scottish law in Edinburgh, tribal customs in incredible profusion. The Judicial Committee of the Privy Council as a supreme appellate court in London and the existence of the Colonial Laws Validity Act, rendering null and void colonial legislation repugnant to the dictates of the mother of parliaments, kept some kind of order in the nursery. But what a grand old jumble it was—full representative government in what were coming to be called "dominions"; Crown Colony rule in the smaller territories; indirect rule by tribal chiefs along the Niger; the glittering apparatus of Viceregal court and Council by which India was administered.

Very grand indeed it looked, at least on Mercator's Projection which blew up Baffin Land to the size of the United States. One fifth of the world's population lived within its boundaries; its subjects practised all known religions and many unknown ones. Its Christian monarch was the successor by treaty and conquest of the Mogul Emperors and commanded more Muslims than any Muslim ruler, not to mention three hundred million Hindus. Since he was also by title the Defender of the Faith, which his ancestors had shed several centuries earlier, there was nothing particularly illogical in all this; the whole Empire seemed illogical, an anachronism, a sport of nature.

But for good or ill, there it lay: the pieces of a jig-saw never properly assembled but nonetheless vast in scope and size. Britain owned the Indian sub-continent with its appendages in Burma, Malaya and Ceylon. Her will was paramount in the Persian Gulf. Japan was her admiring and hopeful imitator. She had contained the mighty power of Russia and planted merchant communities on the coasts of China. She owned most of the railways in South America. Her missionaries and explorers had played a leading part in opening up Africa and she had established herself at key points around that continent, on the Niger, on the Nile, at the Cape. She owned a commanding block of shares in the Suez Canal. Egypt was in pawn to her. She had created Australia where she had intended to provide a convict settlement. She had bred New Zealand in the bone.

This was the Empire on which the sun never set—perhaps because, as the cynics said, even God could not trust it in the dark.

Fifty years later almost all of it had gone, bar the homeland and a few islands. And Dean Acheson had said that Britain had lost an empire and had failed to find a role. Was this fair comment? And, if it was, how had it all come about?

II

Project for an Empire

Of every empire one might ask certain questions. What brought it into being? What sustained it? What brought about its end? Were these factors related? What did it leave behind? In the course of this book we shall apply these questions to Britain's empire and try to answer them.

Some empires have owed their birth to a population explosion or other economic causes which sent men out to find *lebensraum* abroad. The empires of Jenghiz Khan and Hitler were of this kind. Sometimes the aggressive power is prodded from behind by other predatory states. The Ottoman Turks started their career of conquest from such a cause and it took them to the gates of Vienna. Sometimes the dynamic is religious as with the Arabs and Islam.

All these were land empires of the Eurasian land-mass. Sometimes sea empires are similarly affected. The Vikings are a case in point, and so in a lesser way are the Saxons, Jutes and Angles who broke up Romanised Britain. But normally sea empires are not thrust forward by *force majeure* or lust of conquest: they are drawn by greed and the adventuring sense that inspires people who live by the ocean. In early times such empires were limited in scope because of the rudimentary nature of their ships, though we should do well to remember the astonishing force behind the Viking in-

vasions which reached as far south as Sicily, as far north as Green-
land, if not to America itself. With the coming of the galleon and
then the man-o'-war the potential of such empires naturally rose.
The exploits of the sea-going Portuguese, Spaniards and Dutch led
to something far more durable than had gone before.

The British Empire was a perfect illustration of the sea-borne
empire. It depended on the one element it happened to have mas-
tered. Frequently defeated on land by Frenchmen, Germans, Americans, Boers and inhabitants of Afghanistan, the British have seldom
lost a sea battle. The Dutch occasionally beat them there, but then
the Dutch are a sea-going people too. If you live on a sandbank
or on an island where you cannot get more than sixty miles from
the sea, the national genius is apt to be salty. So it was with Athens,
with the Vikings, with the Portuguese of Henry the Navigator's time.
It was a fact of life, for the sea is a radical element which draws
men out of themselves.

Britain was late in the field. Her seamen were brought into the
business by a combination of daring, greed, envy, godliness and
revengeful feelings. Her first trading ventures on the waters were in
human flesh—the slaving voyages of John Hawkins to the Caribbean
which led to Spanish reprisals against the trespassers and, in turn,
to a sense of Protestant outrage at the punishment meted out at the
Inquisition's hands. Thus, the first probings towards overseas empire
developed into near piracy and acts of war against the Spanish
masters of the New World, and when in the next reign the notion
of settlement along the American mainland began to grow, the
Crown's and government's role was minimal, the real protagonists
being either court favourites on the make, chartered companies in
search of profits, or protesting groups looking for sanctuary. "The
Treasurer and Company of Adventurers and Planters of the City of
London for the First Colony in Virginia"—the very title taken from
the charter of 1609 granted to one of the most favoured of the
colonies tells its tale.

This amateurism, this individualism, was to remain a permanent
feature of British colonialism down to the days of the white rajahs
of Sarawak and Raffles' foundation of Singapore. It was seldom
directed from the centre but arose through the daring and imagination of a number of far-sighted men or out of the arbitrament of
war. Just as Drake and Hawkins were drawn into the Caribbean

through rivalry with Spain, so the British conquest of Quebec came out of the struggle with France, a by-product of victory. Similarly, there was at first no conscious aim to rule India. The government was finally driven to assume sovereign powers when it became evident that a trading company (which had in fact ceased to trade there) was incapable of administering a sub-continent. In South Africa the home government, under the spur of a brief spell of inflamed Jingoistic sentiment, was driven to bail out Rhodes and the settlers of English blood who had dreamed dreams beyond the imagination of Whitehall. In Egypt the British appeared in the guise of bailiffs put in to assure the payment of debts due to them. In Australia a continent was colonised where the intention had been to dump a few convicts. Large sections of Africa were swallowed in the wake of missionaries. Later, other tracts of the same continent and certain Arab territories across the Red Sea fell into the kitty as a result of the defeat of Germany and Turkey in 1918. It was a kind of lucky dip.

* * *

Now at first sight this piecemeal agglomeration, this Empire picked up as Sir John Seeley said "in a fit of absence of mind," seems to have been devoid of ideological backing or even of rational structure. Some of the most sensitive and able leaders at home were either lukewarm or temperamentally opposed to it. Mr. Gladstone, if he had been in power at the time, would have bought no shares in the Suez Canal. He would have shed the Sudan, just as he tried to disencumber himself of Ireland; he dubbed Disraeli's romantic elevation of their sovereign into a Queen-Empress "theatrical bombast and folly." Many of the greatest of the proconsuls were deplored by their governments when they were not being actively persecuted or abandoned. One remembers Clive, Warren Hastings, Marquis Wellesley, Gordon at Khartoum.

The truth is that in these sensible but not always logical islands imperialism and anti-imperialism (to use words not coined till the 1870s) have always existed side by side and sometimes in the same person—as witness that alleged arch-imperialist, Disraeli again, who in his middle days had dubbed the colonies "millstones" round Britain's neck. Sometimes the one interest was in the ascendant, sometimes the other. The same three decades that saw British imperialism at its height saw also what many took to be a conscious attempt by Mr. Gladstone's government to dismantle the whole apparatus and send the colonies packing.

In fact, when we come to examine the fully developed system of Victorian imperialism we shall see that the closer we look, the more clearly it appears that what distinguished it from other empires was not too little ideology but, perhaps, too much. Gibbon Wakefield's schemes for the settlement of virgin territories, the doctrines of the radical-imperialists in the mid-nineteenth century, of the Liverpool School and the Imperial Federation League towards its end, Kipling's concept of the white man's burden and, much earlier and more fundamental, Edmund Burke's insistence that all political power was a Trust—were there ever so many theories at work on one topic over so long a period of years?

What is more, the theorists came from every sector of political opinion and had widely different views of what empire should be about. Some wanted to keep it, some to abolish it for one reason or another, but all felt the need to change it to keep in tempo with a changing time. It was the least static of empires, the most responsive to pressures both among the rulers and the ruled. And, therefore, since all empires like other organisms decline as their parts atrophy or become entities of their own, so in the British Empire the symptoms of dissolution became visible at a very early stage, and changed and multiplied, always with the consent and often under the active inspiration of the imperial government or of powerful groups within its establishment. All kinds of conflicting desires and impulses can be detected—commercial greed, enlightened self-interest, the pure milk of humanitarianism, often fascinatingly interwoven. Was Mr. Gladstone an imperialist? Was Disraeli? What, and indeed what on earth, was Richard Cobden? But the net result was certainly an empire which from a very early time had forged the machinery for dissolving itself, even if it had not yet formed the corresponding intent. Even the word Commonwealth in a surprisingly exact and prophetic sense had been used of it a full century and a half before the transformation happened. An ideological empire? It was incontestably a jumble of ideologies.

But this is to speak of the nineteenth-century development, the organism some people call the Second British Empire, the one that arose like a phoenix out of the ashes of the lost American colonies. For the moment, it is of the First British Empire that we must speak, and here it is clear that the builders had not many ideologies, but one —the welfare and enrichment of the mother country (and to a lesser extent of her colonial offspring) through a mercantile system which aimed to create one viable economic unit.

Mercantilism as a theory is now discredited. Adam Smith gave it a mortal blow, but it died hard. For over a century before the publication of his *Wealth of Nations* it had seemed to provide the structure on which the national prosperity had been built, and half a century after his death it was still alive and kicking. The indispensable base had been laid in the famous Navigation Acts of 1651, 1660 and 1696 and in the Staple Act of 1663.

Seldom can a theory have been subscribed to so wholeheartedly or practised more remorselessly. Since England was part of a small and comparatively poor group of islands whose defence rested on the seas and whose commerce had to cross the seas, then the two prime needs were ships and seamen. Commerce was not only good in itself: it also trained the sailors who would defend the country in time of war. Therefore, the marine must at all costs be petted, encouraged and built up in every way. The nation's trade as far as possible must be carried in English ships manned by English crews, while within the Empire it must be rigorously confined to them.

Thus, under the provisions of the Navigation Acts foreign shipping was excluded from the "plantations," from lucrative dealings with the mainland colonies in America and the English Caribbean islands. Certain "enumerated" commodities on which great store was set—notably sugar and tobacco—could be traded by the colonies only into English ports. Some concessions were made—trading even of enumerated goods was permitted direct from the colonies to southern but not to northern Europe, and the West Indian sugar islands were eventually allowed still greater leeway—but the grand design was plain: to channel these commodities through English ports and to deny them to rivals except at a price. For the aim of mercantilism was not only to benefit oneself but to damage one's competitors.

Similarly, by the Staple Act of 1663 almost all foreign imports into the plantations had to be off-loaded in England en route. It was our hope to create in our fortunate island a vast *entrepôt* of trade, a clearing house for the goods of half the world. Nothing must be permitted to prevent it. It was not our aim to build up colonies beyond what was reckoned in London to be good for them, and for us. They were not exactly milked, for they were granted compensations, privileges, an assured market. But the ideal that lay behind the whole conception was of a manufacturing, warehousing, exporting, ship-building England, nourished by the raw materials supplied by colonies which should dutifully remain for ever in that state of grace unto which it had pleased God to call them, without too many industries of their own, and never, *never,* aspiring to be competitors.

* * *

For nearly a hundred years this system, modified and made palatable by a judicious amount of smuggling, worked on the whole extremely well. England supplied the ships, the capital, the mart, the protection of her all-powerful navy and to a lesser extent of an army when required, and the colonies duly delivered the raw materials in return for the manufactured goods and luxuries of the metropolis. There were some disappointments on both sides—the mainland colonies for some reason never succeeded in providing the naval stores with the timber and cordage which a hopeful government in London demanded of them in order to rid itself of too great a dependence on the Baltic trade, where these indispensible articles had to be bought on Swedish or Russian terms. Also, the colonies themselves were often irked by the existence of trade regulations which denied them markets in Europe and in the French- and Spanish-owned islands of the Caribbean. But the colonies knew themselves to be weak and almost defenceless; very sensibly they understood that a price had to be paid for their security in an uncertain world, and in any case their commerce was paying handsome dividends under the system, restrictive though it was.

The West Indian islands were to remain weak and dependent, part of an archipelago that included territories under Spanish, Dutch and French control. Their only real advantage was the sugar lobby in the Westminster Parliament which made itself loudly heard whenever West Indian interests seemed to be threatened.

But on the American mainland it was quite another story. By the middle of the eighteenth century the thirteen colonies had come to number nearly two million energetic, thrustful, individualistic people by no means inclined to regard themselves as cyphers or pawns of a distant government. What would happen when such a people felt their own strength and their *difference* from the motherland was bound to be the crucial question for the British mercantilist Empire, but the causes of the clash were as much moral as commercial and produced effects which continued long after both the mercantilist system and the constitutional links between Britain and her mainland colonies had passed away. The War of American Independence was a catalyst for Britain as well as for the rebellious states, and it is as such that we must study it in relation to the very different empire that arose out of the ruins.

The problem did not at once arise. Just so long as the aggressive power of the French in Canada was feeling its way down past the Great Lakes, along the Ohio, towards the Mississippi and the other French possessions at its mouth, aiming to cut off the "Old Thirteen" and pen them between the Appalachians and the sea— just so long as that situation existed, the mainland colonies looked to Britain to save them. By the end of the Seven Years War the genius of the elder Pitt had worked the miracle: Canada was no longer French and the threat from the north and along the western frontier had disappeared.

The ensuing gratitude was heartfelt and widespread. Statues to the hero and liberator were voted up and down the land and the captured Fort Duquesne on the Ohio was renamed Pittsburgh in his honour.

But there the gratitude tended to stop. The past threat from the French was forgotten: the grievances against Britain revived. All this was natural enough. The causes of the War of American Independence have been endlessly debated. Grenville's Stamp Act was certainly among them, as was Townshend's budget of 1767 and the system of the Navigation Acts which Burke in his great speech on American taxation in 1774 castigated as "wholly restrictive" and as leading to a "condition of as rigorous servitude as man can be subject to." But these were only symptoms of a fever which Burke himself never clearly comprehended. Unknown to him and unrealised as yet by its thirteen component parts, a nation had been born and had reached

the age of indiscretion. The mainland colonies had altogether outgrown their apron strings: the fundamental cause of their estrangement from Britain lay in this simple and inescapable fact.

It is one of the oddities of history that in the Age of Reason itself
hardly anyone in Britain had realised this. For a century earlier, at
the height of Cromwell's arbitrary rule, James Harrington in the pref-
ace to his *Oceana* had laid it down that colonies, though in his time
still "babes that cannot live without sucking the breast of the mother
cities," would be sure to "ween themselves": an aphorism which in
Burke's day had been trenchantly repeated on the far shores of the
Channel in Turgot's more famous dictum that colonies were like
fruits which as soon as they had ripened must fall from the parent
tree. Furthermore, in *The Wealth of Nations* Adam Smith had gone
much further than this and had attacked the whole system of monopoly which he saw as harmful not only to the colonies but to Britain's
own commercial well-being, an interference with trade in its natural
and free state which he held to be the lifeblood of any commercial
organism, and in fact "unwholesome," a potential blood clot in the
veins and arteries—using another simile he saw it as "a dead weight
upon the action of one of the great springs which put into motion a
great part of the business of mankind." His final verdict was unequivocal:

> Under the present system of management, therefore, Great Britain
> derives nothing but loss from the dominion which she exercises
> over her colonies.

Yet if only the lesson could be learned, if only Britain could free
herself from the burdensome expense of supporting her colonies in
peace and war, then better days would dawn for everyone. In a famous passage he looked prophetically into the future of Anglo-
American relations:

> By thus parting good friends, the natural affection of the colonies
> to the mother country . . . would quickly revive. It might dispose

them not only to respect, for whole centuries together, that treaty of commerce which they had concluded with us at parting, but to favour us in war as well as in trade, and, instead of turbulent and fractious subjects, to become our most faithful, affectionate and generous allies.

Such a concept was so far in advance of its time that nearly two centuries were to pass before the dream finally became reality. Even so great a friend of America as the elder Pitt could not shed his belief in Britain's right to do almost anything to the Americans except tax them without their consent, and in the passionate advocacy of this belief he spent the last fully conscious moments of his life. Even such convinced lovers of toleration and magnanimity as Burke and the Earl of Shelburne believed implicitly in the preservation of the union between mother country and colonies, and such rudimentary public opinion as there was in Britain heartily supported them. There was intense pride in an Empire which had been built up from small beginnings to include the whole eastern seaboard of America from Hudson's Bay to Florida, the vast and still largely unexplored territories of inland Canada as far as the Great Lakes, a number of important sugar islands in the Caribbean, the Mediterranean bases of Gibraltar and Minorca, staging posts along the route to India, and the East India Company's growing possessions in that sub-continent—the presidency of Bombay, the more important one of Madras, and a huge slice of Bengal—not to mention various mysterious islands or continents in the south seas lately visited by Captain Cook. Did it not seem that the vision of Samuel Daniel in his *Musophilus,* written in Queen Elizabeth's accession year, nearly half a century before this colonisation had even begun, had already come to pass?

And who (in time) knows whither we may vent
The treasures of our tongue? To what strange
        shores
This gain of our best glory shall be sent
T'enrich unknowing nations with our stores?

Foremost among these nations were the Old Thirteen. They were the "jewel" in King George's crown, as speaker after speaker remorselessly insisted. Only Adam Smith had dared to be unrespectful of this galaxy:

> The rulers of Great Britain have, for more than a century past, amused themselves with the imagination that they possessed a great empire on the west side of the Atlantic. This empire, however, has hitherto existed in imagination only. It has hitherto been, not an empire, but the projection of an empire; not a gold mine, but the projection of a gold mine; a project which has cost, which continues to cost, and which, if pursued in the same way . . . is likely to cost, immense expense, without being likely to bring any profit.

To the London and Bristol merchants and to the hordes of placemen and bureaucrats from state governors to customs officials who crossed the Atlantic in the King's service, this was self-evident nonsense; the Old Thirteen were as sacrosanct as the flag they lived under. When the fatal steps were taken that put the brew of revolution to the boil even the most apprehensively liberal minds in Tory England had failed to recognise the danger. "There has been nothing of note in parliament but a slight day on the American taxes," reported that prince of gossips, Horace Walpole, of Grenville's Stamp Act. Not till Louis XVI wrote the one word *"Rien"* in his diary on the day the Bastille was taken by the mob was there to be another such misunderstanding of a climactic event. Only George III showed a true awareness of what was at stake, and on receiving news of the rebellious reactions in America towards the Act (of which, to his credit, he had disapproved) called it with singular prescience "undoubtedly the most serious matter that ever came before Parliament."

The Stamp Act was repealed. Townshend's too ingenious budget of 1767 was cut down and emasculated to temper the wind to the shorn lamb. "The proposition is peace," said Burke, the voice of reason, on March 22, 1775. "It is simple peace, sought in its natural course and in its ordinary haunts. It is peace sought in the spirit of peace, and laid in principles purely pacific. . . . My hold of the colonies is in the close affection which grows from common names, from kindred blood, from similar privileges and equal protection. These are ties which, though light as air, are as strong as links of iron. Magnanimity in politics is not seldom the truest wisdom; and a great empire and little minds go ill together. . . . We ought to elevate our minds to the greatness of that task to which the order of Providence has called us."

It was one of the greatest speeches ever made in the British Parliament: it pointed to the future and to the Commonwealth to come. But in its own day it counted for little. It was too late for magnanimity where America was concerned. Britain had no hold of any kind on her thirteen rebellious offspring, and already, in one of his incomparably pungent letters Horace Walpole had written:

The war in America is determined on . . .
What that will beget,
The child that is unborn will rue!

And then again on June 1, 1775, on hearing of the first skirmish at Lexington:

So here is this fatal war commenced!

Walpole was an original. What other Englishman of his time would have forecast that the next Augustan age would dawn in the New World; that there would perhaps be a Thucydides at Boston, a Xenophon at New York, and in time a Virgil in Mexico and a Newton in Peru? More pertinently, after Lexington, he wished success to the Americans. Clearly no typical John Bull, for the war at first was popular with all classes. But through his eyes, under that sharp, cantankerous, rather bilious gaze, we can watch doubt deepening into a pessismism which was gradually to infect the majority of his fellow countrymen.

A war on our trade is popular! Both Houses are as eager for it as if they were conquering the Indies.

What politicians are those who have preferred the empty name of *sovereignty* to that of *alliance,* and forced subsidies to the golden ocean of commerce!

I cannot expect to see England revive. I shall leave it at best an insignificant island. Its genius is vanished like its glories.

This last letter was written in July 1778, and not long afterwards the war with the rebellious colonies, which had already dragged on for three years, was hideously enlarged by the advent of France and Spain into the ring of Britain's enemies. The shock was traumatic and was to have lasting effects on British policy and self-confidence —it seemed a denial of natural reason and justice that colonists of our own blood should have allied themselves with the traditional enemies of our race. Walpole, of course, was in despair about it:

I see no way by which we can escape happily out of this crisis. . . . We shall now suffer a great deal, submit at last to a humiliating peace, and the people will be content. *So adieu England!* It will be more or less a province or kind of province to France. . . .

This calamity, far-fetched as it now seems to us, could easily have come to pass. In the summer of 1779 and again in 1781 a Franco-Spanish fleet of sixty sail was cruising impudently off Plymouth, master of the Channel, while grossly inferior defending squadrons took refuge in Torbay. Drake must have turned in his watery grave off Portobello. Not even when the Dutch had come up the Medway in Charles II's time and their guns were heard in London had "a deeper political gloom overspread England than in the autumn of 1779," wrote Sir Nathaniel Wraxall, that true-blue patriot and supporter of the war. In this same year, one of the worst in our history and comparable only with 1918 during the German spring offensive and the weeks in 1940 after Dunkirk, not only was the country open to invasion by overwhelmingly superior forces from the sea, but Ireland was in almost open insurrection, with huge forces of volunteers arming to assert Irish rights. From his belea-

quered island, which in the meantime had nearly witnessed the sack
of London during the Gordon riots at the hands of an enraged anti-
Papist mob, Horace Walpole saluted the desperate year of 1781:

Gibraltar is besieged, Minorca is besieged, New York, I believe,
besieged; and I am sure that Great Britain is besieged—forty-seven
or nine French and Spanish ships of the line at the gates of the
Channel and Admiral Darby with only twenty-two in Torbay is a
blockade to some purpose.

And he added an epigram:

Oh, England, no wonder your troubles begin,
When blockaded without, and blockheaded within.

Was it because of these defeats that public opinion in England
began to veer towards some accommodation with America while
still breathing defiance against France and Spain? Not altogether, for
as early as the victory of Brandywine the Prime Minister, Lord
North, had expressed the wish to "get out of this damned war" if he
could do it with honour. But certainly about this time a whole chorus
of hostile voices began to be heard in Parliament against the war
with the Americans which had landed us in so desperate a pickle. It
was a chorus of star quality. There was Charles James Fox to lead
off with, calling the war "impracticable in its object and ruinous in
its progress." For John Wilkes it was a war "unfounded in principle
and fatal in its consequences . . . a bad and mischievous cause":
for the younger Pitt, just rising into prominence, it was "a most accursed, wicked, barbarous, cruel, unjust and diabolical war . . . conceived in injustices . . . nurtured and brought forth in folly." And
what were the results? In a debate in the House of Commons in May
1780 General Conway declared that we had been rendered objects
of horror in the eyes of Europe. We had been "turned out from
the hunt like the stricken deer, deserted and abandoned by all the
herd." In the Lords, the Earl of Shelburne, the subtlest statesman in
England, perhaps the only statesman in England at that melancholy

time, agreed that we had become "the contempt and standing jest of Europe," and from a great, glorious and happy people "were fallen to a degree of insignificance and humiliation" which ought to earn us the compassion of our bitterest foes.

But then Shelburne, for all his bitter political abuse of Lord North's government, was still of the opinion that the granting of independence to the Americans would mean that "the sun of Britain is set" and we could no longer remain "a powerful or respectable people." And though North himself might be wavering and anxious to end a disastrous civil war on almost any terms, the King at Windsor remained intransigently sure that "giving up the game would be total ruin" and would lead to the annihilation of Britain as a major power.

George III was not only the stoutest hearted Briton of his age, he was also one of the most perceptive; and the fate he envisaged for an ex-imperial power was not less true because its full effects were delayed for two centuries till our own equally troubled times. After Cornwallis' surrender at Yorktown the writing was on the wall. In an engrossing passage of his memoirs, Wraxall describes how the news reached the Prime Minister, Lord North, that "noble lord in the blue ribbon" whom we meet day in, day out, in Hansard's parliamentary reports—not the ogre of American demonology but an affable, able, compassionate, eloquent and witty man whose only crime lay in his advocacy of a policy of repression in which he never believed. North took it "as he would have taken a ball in his breast," the Secretary of State for American affairs, Lord George Germain, told Wraxall at the time. "For he opened his arms, exclaiming wildly as he paced up and down the apartment during a few minutes, 'Oh God, it is all over.'"

By one of those happy chances that befall the best raconteurs, Wraxall was dining at Lord George's house that night when the King's response to the dismal news was brought across by messenger. When the ladies had been coaxed out of the room Lord George opened the royal letter, remarking to his guests that the King had written "just as he always does, except that I observe he has omitted to mark the hour and minute of his writing with his usual precision." "I have received with sentiments of the deepest concern," the letter ran, "the communication which Lord George Germain has made to me of the unfortunate results of the operations in Virginia. . . . But I trust that neither Lord George Germain nor any member of the cabinet will suppose that it makes the smallest alteration in those principles of my conduct which have directed me in past time, and which will always continue to animate me under every event in the prosecution of the present contest." Wraxall says that the very handwriting showed composure of mind. Consols, which had stood at eighty-nine on the eve of the war and had fallen to seventy with Burgoyne's surrender at Saratoga, fell after Yorktown to fifty-four, and in a Lords' debate on the *débâcle* the Duke of Chandos bewailed America lost, and Minorca lost, and the sugar islands of the West Indies likely to go down one by one "like ninepins," but the King still looked to a "good end" to the war, and in opening the autumn session of Parliament roundly reaffirmed his trust in divine providence and in the justice of the cause. Wraxall's fine tribute should not be denied to this stubborn but brave and consistent man:

> In the midst of so universal a dejection the King remained altogether unmoved. Neither Defeat nor difficulties, nor the number of his foreign Enemies, nor Domestic Opposition, unhinged his mind or shook his resolution. . . . He never vacillated. . . . He only desired to abide the issue and to maintain the contest.

His chosen servants, the King's Friends, showed themselves less resolute. After clinging to power for another four months, Lord North's administration, "that puissant administration," as Walpole called it in derision, which for nine years had presided over disaster, fell out of office without even waiting for defeat on a vote of the House, to be succeeded by an uneasy alliance of Rockingham Whigs (who were all for Independence for the Americas at any price) and Shelburne Whigs (who would have liked to keep a bargaining counter or two but were otherwise resigned to the inevitable). "Thank God! Thank God!" wrote Walpole of this desperate change of horses in midstream. "What remains of the country and constitution may be saved. . . . If England is free, and America free, though disunited, the whole earth will not be in vassalage."

Shortly he had other causes for rejoicing, for to this ramshackle coalition of divergent interests that was the government of England there was now granted a remarkable and splendid event to break the long and disastrous sequence of defeats that had marked the war by land and sea—at the battle of The Saints, off St. Lucia in the West Indies, Admiral Rodney routed the French fleet in those waters and captured the French admiral, De Grasse, into the bargain. It was like an echo of the glories of Blenheim, with Marshall Tallard a captive in Marlborough's coach. Wraxall, who had been alive at the time of Lord Hawke's victory of The Glorious First of June and lived to hear the news of Trafalgar, thought that The Saints aroused a still greater delirium of joy, bringing "a sort of Compensation to Great Britain for so many years of disgrace, for so great an expenditure of blood and treasure, and even for the loss of America itself. The country, exhausted and humiliated, seemed to revive in its own estimation and to resume once more its dignity among the nations." Poor Horace Walpole could hardly sleep for the rockets and squibs exploding under his window till three o'clock in the morning, and in the House of Commons the Rockingham spokesman, Charles James Fox, dilated on "the glorious tidings from the West Indies" brought about by "the able and gallant officer"—whom in fact his government had attempted to recall. And by a fortunate chance, about this time, there were other victories against odds which helped to bind up the bitter wounds of defeat—Eliott's heroic defence of Gibraltar against the might of Spain; Eyre Coote's defeat of Hyder Ali at Porto Novo in the Carnatic; the capture of Trincomalee in Ceylon which drew a burst of half-triumphant, half-ironic praise from even so surly an old curmudgeon as Horace Walpole:

> Fortune's weathercock has changed once more in our favour; we were drowning, but now ride again in triumph through the streets of our capital, the ocean . . . We expect to be up to our ears in rubies, elephants, cinnamon and pepper.

These successes were not only useful in themselves in helping to preserve the fabric of a damaged empire, but they saved face and in so doing helped to prepare the nation for the act of abdication in America to which the government was inevitably committed. On the death of Rockingham, there had succeeded to the highest office a realist of enlightened but subtle views, the Earl of Shelburne.

Where Britain's "European" war with her age-old rivals was concerned, Shelburne had few anxieties—he was fairly sure that France would make peace on reasonable terms, provided she recovered certain territories snatched from her by the elder Pitt which had deeply hurt her *amour propre*. He was equally certain that once these territories were restored to her, she would not continue in the fight to help Spain regain Gibraltar which no British government could cede—if she did, he would probably have echoed the bulldog growl of a Mr. Hammett in the House of Commons, who had urged the nation to continue fighting for another ten years at the cost of another £200,000,000 rather than to submit to ignominious terms.

But where America was concerned, Shelburne's position was more delicate. He was on record in parliamentary reports as having shared many of the opinions of Lord North on the inadvisability of granting independence, and few of his enemies—few even of his colleagues—were prepared to let him forget it.

In the House of Lords, soon after taking office as Prime Minister, he boldly put his cards on the table. He had always, he declared, held that independence for America would be "a dreadful blow" to the greatness of Britain, and that if it were granted, "the sun of England might be said to have set." He had always laboured to prevent it. But now "the fatal necessity" appeared "in full view," and to necessity he might be obliged to bow. His aim was now "to improve the twilight and to prepare for the rising of England's sun again."

This was window-dressing—very desirable, even necessary, but of course no one had much choice, and in opening the new session in December 1782 the King (a most reluctant convert to necessity) announced that the preliminaries of peace with the rebel colonies had been agreed on. He prayed that the nation might not feel "the evils that might result from so great a dismemberment of the empire," and to his eternal credit he added another prayer, that there might be a bond of permanent union between the sundered countries. Privately, he thought the grant of independence was "a dreadful price" to pay for peace. "It is certainly very painful to me, who had the honour to ratify the Peace of Paris in 1763," he wrote to Lord Grantham, "to be obliged to consent to such terms as the factions within my kingdom, not the weight of my Enemies, make necessary." Shelburne himself, defending his policy in the House of Lords, called it a bitter pill, the bitterest he had ever had to swallow. So evident was his distress, that his one-time colleague Fox (who had resigned from office soon after Rockingham's death) unkindly twitted him in execrable verse:

You've done a noble turn in nature's spite,
For though you think you're wrong, I'm sure
　　you're right.

To Horace Walpole they were tidings of great joy. "The day that I little expected to live to see is arrived!" he wrote. "Peace came this morning; thank God!" "My wish," he added, "was to have peace, and next to see America secure in its liberty. Whether it will make good use of it is another matter." Even North himself, though he held the grant of independence to be calamitous to the country and something only to be accepted "with deepest sorrow," nevertheless faced up to the inevitable with his usual urbanity.

Not so his humbler supporters up and down the country. As the terms of the proposed peace became known and it was clear that the submerged "Loyalist" element in the population of the Old Thirteen was to be thrown to the Congress wolves without redress, without compensation for its sufferings, without protection from its victorious enemies, the feeling of revulsion in Britain blew up into a storm. Shelburne, who had done his utmost for these unfortunates, explained his dilemma in poignant terms:

I have but one answer to give: it is the answer I gave my own bleeding heart. A part must be wounded, that the whole empire may not perish.

It did not save him from the attacks of the rapidly growing body of his opponents, outraged by his concessions and full of generous indignation at the "bloody sacrifice," as Viscount Stormont put it, of Britain's "most valiant and faithful sons." For every pasquinade and rodomontade that had been mounted against Lord North for continuing a senseless war, there was now as loud an outcry against his sucessor for trying to end it. Viscount Sackville fulminated against "the most unwise, impolitic, ruinous treaty" that Britain had ever made; Richard Brinsley Sheridan said that it was of the most disgraceful nature which relinquished everything that was great and glorious in the country; and a Mr. Lee—odd to find a Lee and a Sheridan in the same camp—was of the opinion that it simply beggared all description: "a disgraceful, weak and treacherous peace."

Parliamentary speeches at this time always followed a set pattern, and most of them, whatever the topic, usually ended with an appeal to what the elder Pitt, Lord Chatham, would have thought or done. Letters to the press are better reflections of the national mood, and as Shelburne's terms leaked out it was a sombre one. Was Great Britain only losing "a set of refractory and disobedient children"? The *Morning Herald* had come up with this consoling thought. In the *Morning Chronicle* a correspondent had descried that God had long since dissevered America from England "by the great Atlantick Ocean" and things were perhaps best left that way. But the opposing squad of letter writers were in no wise prepared to accept it—in the same paper, one signing himself "Sennex" thought that nothing but "the most urgent extreme of distress" should ever induce England to vote America independent. One of the hazards of office in those times was the hot fire of open letters to ministers and other guilty parties that rained down on them from the press. "A Seaman" apostrophised Admiral Keppel with the warning that any Briton who approved of letting the rebel colonies go was an enemy of his country; poor Lord Shelburne was for ever being advised that this policy meant ruin for Britain; and only a week before the peace preliminaries with Congress were signed, a patriot even more rampant than the King or Mr. Hammett was instructing the Prime Minister to let the Tower of London be taken by the Yankees sword in hand before such "disgraceful ruin" as American independence was agreed on.

Through this raucous chorus of deeply felt fears and chauvinistic ambitions the occasional voice of reason sounded now and then in the letters of correspondents who believed that trade was everything, that a free America would trade with Britain much as before, and that an American navy was unlikely (as "A True Briton" had suggested in the *Morning Chronicle*) to gobble up every British possession in the seven seas. Most British politicians of the time were too involved in the disaster to take a reasoned view and were slow to read the lesson of the times.

But there was one exception. Surveying the wreckage of an old imperialism, William Pitt, the younger, rose in the House of Commons to speak on a motion censuring the Earl of Shelburne's peace, and he said:

> Let us examine what is left with a manly and determined courage. Let us strengthen ourselves against inveterate enemies and reconciliate our ancient friends. The misfortunes of individuals and of kingdoms, that are laid open and examined with true wisdom, are more than half redressed: and to this great object should be directed all the virtue and abilities of this House. Let us feel our calamities—let us bear them too like men.

* * *

So the peace was made and the inevitable loss accepted. The finest jewel had been plucked from the royal crown. The poet Cowper said it; Fox said it; and nearly everyone agreed.

How had it happened?

The King, lamenting that the peace had quite completed "the Downfall of the lustre of this Empire," put it all down to vice and dissipation and the collapse of religion and public spirit, and for once Horace Walpole agreed with him. It was a sign of the times that not half as many coaches had attended Chatham's funeral as had attended the actor-manager Garrick's; and there was the growing folly of late hours which brought the fashionable world to Ranelagh at midnight, two hours after the music had stopped. On fornication and cuckoldry Horace Walpole ("I never deal in scandal, Madam") was particularly strong. "After Doctors' Commons had lain fallow for a year or two," he wrote soon after Yorktown, "it is likely to bear a handsome crop of divorces. Gallantry in this country scorns a mask. Maids only intrigue, wives elope. *C'est l'étiquette.*"

Yet Walpole, that modern Cato, did not rely for his sermon only on faithless wives and complaisant husbands; he took a wider view, lamenting the general breakdown of law and order, the huge increase in the number of highwaymen and footpads infesting the roads, and the growing permissiveness of a society mad for scandal:

Nothing will be left of England but the vestiges of its grandeur, and what shakes one already is that the vandalism that overspreads ruined empires has anteceded our last moments. Bad taste, spite, calumny, pert dullness, and blundering affectations of humour have taken place of everything agreeable. I would not quote such records as the newspapers if they were not the oracles of the times . . . Besides Macpherson's daily column of lies, is there a paragraph that is not scandalous or malevolent? . . . Is not a country more savage than Hottentots, where all private distresses are served up the next morning for the breakfast and entertainment of the public?

Commentators at times of defeat and national humiliation often take a high moral line. It may be due to their persistence that revivals often follow, as the age of Marlborough succeeded the cheerful lechery of Charles II's court which good John Evelyn so slated in his diaries.

But clearly there were other reasons than vice and dissipation to account for so calamitous a defeat. What were they? Even those statesmen who seemed most culpably guilty for the loss of the Americas—Grenville, Townshend, North—had tried to show a proper respect for colonial sensibilities. Had they tried hard enough? Was there something missing in the system itself? Could an empire any longer be run along the restrictive lines of monopoly and the Navigation Acts? Was indeed empire a viable commodity at all? Adam Smith had evidently thought not, and in a trenchant passage in his *Wealth of Nations* had ridiculed the system root and branch:

The inconveniences resulting from the possession of its colonies every country has engrossed to itself completely. The advantages resulting from their trade, it has been obliged to share with many other countries.

In his view, the "mean and malignant expedients of the Mercantile System" worked nothing but loss, forcing trade into one vulnerable channel instead of allowing it to course through many.

> In her present condition, Great Britain resembles one of those unwholesome bodies in which some of the vital parts are overgrown, and which upon that account are liable to many dangerous disorders. . . . A small stop in that great blood vessel, which has been artificially swelled beyond its normal dimensions, and through which an unnatural proportion of the industry and the commerce of the country has been forced to circulate, is likely to bring on the most dangerous disorders upon the whole body politic.

Nor had Adam Smith been alone in his opinions; he had not even been first in the field, for before the publication of *The Wealth of Nations* the visionary Josiah Tucker had already prophesied the defection of both America and Canada and had declared colonies to be nuisances which had to be nursed in the cradle, became headstrong as they grew up, and rebellious when they no longer needed the protection of the mother country. As partners rather than as subjects they would be at least of equal value, since trade depended on self-interest alone, a thesis developed by two other visionaries of a still more radical turn of mind—Granville Sharp and John Cartwright—who looked to an association between Britain and her colonies in a free commonwealth under a joint crown and actually anticipated the wording of the Statute of Westminster, which a century and a half later gave exact expression to their views.

When it became evident that the loss of the American colonies had not meant the loss of their trade; when by 1800 the figures showed that that trade had substantially doubled since independence and that the Americans, though politically inclined to France, were commercially much happier with their lost and unregenerate motherland; then these voices that called into question the economic sense of having colonies seemed more and more justified. But for the demands of the life and death struggle with revolutionary France and with Napoleon, which caused a revival of imperialist thinking in beleaguered Britain, the collapse of the old mercantilist system might have been hastened by several decades and free trade might have triumphed long before the age of Cobden and Bright. Even through the desperate days of that struggle with France the lessons of what had happened in America were remembered. The voice of the economists continued to be heard: and just as certainly the humiliations Britain had suffered at the hands of her colonial children remained so green in the national memory that half a century after Yorktown some minor disturbances in Canada were enough to send a nervous administration in hasty search of new panaceas for old ills.

Thus, the American revolution was in a very real sense the foster parent of Lord Durham's famous Report and of "Responsible Government" for colonial territories, from which seeds sprang the future dominions and the Commonwealth which Cartwright and Granville Sharp had glimpsed. It provided a vision of judgment which helped, if only by the awful force of example, to inspire a new colonial system out of the ruins of the old.

But by that same token it had hurt that sublime self-confidence which had marched the redcoats up Breed's Hill and had dictated the King's letter at the news of Yorktown. The loss of the First Empire was one of the ingredients in that long process by which the Second was acquired and lost in its turn. It was one of the causes of that distaste or at best indifference with which colonies were regarded in mid-Victorian England, and remained to haunt the minds of even the Jingoes and the triumphant new imperialists of the palmy days of Queen Victoria's Diamond Jubilee with the nagging thought that perhaps their glittering and gorgeous empire was no more than a magic lantern show, an illusion, as Adam Smith had said.

III

Ireland and India

On the eve of the War of American Independence the British Empire had been an empire of the West, and its focal point had lain at the convergence of the trade routes to the thirteen colonies and the sugar islands of the West Indies. To most Britons, the East was still a land of fable, a world of cinnamon, pearls, elephants and nabobs; Africa as a continent hardly entered the national consciousness at all; and it was only at its western end, around the bases of Gibraltar and Minorca, that British penetration into the Mediterranean had begun.

The loss of the Old Thirteen was radically to alter the whole structure and style of this Empire which had suddenly been shorn of a quarter of its most productive inhabitants. What could be more natural than that a nation so cruelly deprived should straightway have turned to the remaining pillar of support, "that brightest jewel still left in the King's crown," which was evidently India, and to the staging posts along the land and sea routes that led to it—the Cape of Good Hope, St. Helena, Mauritius, Corsica, Sicily, the Aegean islands, and above all Malta. The whole axis of the Empire was to be bent back eastward, leaving Canada and the islands at the mouth of the St. Lawrence and the West Indies temporarily in a kind of limbo.

But this eastward spread was not the immediate first priority of the statesmen in Britain who signed the peace: the broken bits of Empire had first to be picked up and reassembled. They had in common prudence, as well as by natural sympathy and inclination, to be westward-looking for a while. What was to be done about relationships with the lost Thirteen? How could Canada and the West Indies be best protected and their valuable trade preserved?

The peace preliminaries that had led to American independence had been conducted through the chosen agents of the Earl of Shelburne, perhaps as true a friend as Americans had in Britain at the time. From the outset he had shown a realistic and generous desire to let bygones be bygones and to let the victors stay in the club and keep their old share in imperial trade, particularly with the West Indies.

After his fall the way to reconciliation still lay open, but somehow it was not found, even by statesmen as enlightened as Fox and that disciple of Adam Smith, the younger Pitt. A lack of understanding, of generosity, on both sides prevented it. British public opinion was outraged by the harsh treatment meted out to the "Loyalists" who had fought for the motherland, or at least sympathised with her, during the course of the war. Aggressive American designs against Canada had been widely canvassed, and the threat they posed to what was left of our possessions on the mainland was resented, feared and magnified out of all proportions. The victors in the war were no more prepared than other victorious peoples have been to compromise with the defeated. There was too great a legacy of bitterness. And Britain, smarting under the humiliation of what was felt to be an unmerited and unnatural loss, very soon began to question the nature of that loss and to deny, with the logic of the fox in the fable, that it was a real loss at all. Josiah Tucker had said in one of his pamphlets that colonies would trade with even their worst enemies if it suited their interest to do so. Lord Sheffield, a far weightier witness, was soon repeating the dictum in still more vivid and compelling form. The Americans would willy-nilly have to trade with us; they had no real option in the matter—such was his thesis. And trading figures bore this out. If the lost and wayward children were still inclined—indeed obliged—to trade at the back door, why indulge them by giving them the key to the hall and to all the delights of the imperial garden?

Under such mutual discouragements, Shelburne's vision of a reconciled America and of a reunited Anglo-Saxon union of hearts and sympathies died and was buried in Jay's lopsided treaty, resulting in the virtual exclusion of the emergent United States from the old mart of empire for many wasteful years.

It was a lost opportunity, leaving behind it a legacy of resentment and distrust which nearly a century later, in Lincoln's and the Prince Consort's time, was still strong enough to bring the nations to the brink of war, and as late as the 1920s led a mayor of Chicago to express a wish to punch King George V on the nose in retaliation for George III of infamous memory. But at least the main issue had been settled, and thirteen colonies, predominantly Anglo-Saxon in blood, had been allowed to go their own way and find their own destiny. It was to be Britain's misfortune that this solution was denied another rebellious colony, alien by race and tradition, and that the same imperial power that had allowed Americans to be American became dedicated to the proposition that Irishmen were English.

*　*　*

The Irish problem had had its origin centuries earlier when in Plantaganet times English troops had crossed into Ulster, gradually extending their sway over the years into the wilds of Munster and Connaught. There had followed the usual cycle of oppression, rebellion, re-conquest, re-settlement, new rebellions, civil war, and fresh refinements of oppression. After much hard fighting Ireland had been dragooned into subservience, and as a reward, as one throws a dog a bone, she had been given a parliament which could debate Irish affairs, always provided that the agenda had previously been cleared with the King's ministers in London.

But though in the Empire, Ireland was not really *of* it. She shared the burdens but not the rights of partnership. The advantages deriving from the Navigation Acts, which had at first been conferred on her, had been withdrawn, so that she had fallen into complete commercial as well as political subjection and could trade only through English ports in English ships. As though this were not bad enough, tariffs were levied on her industrial goods, particularly linens. She was there to be governed and milked.

In 1779, in the black summer that saw the French and Spanish fleets masters of the Channel, Ireland rose against this tyranny. A large body of Protestant Irish volunteers stood armed and ready to defend the island against any French invasion. In fact, they served another purpose: they were the spearhead of a revolution. Scottish by blood and Presbyterian by religion, they felt the call to assert the independence of an Irish nation of which they formed only a small and alien *élite*. It was a very Irish manifestation. What passed for a parliament in Dublin was only the shadow of a shadow, for the "Ascendancy" was Anglican, with small love for dissenting Protestants, never mind the vast unleavened, unlettered mass of Catholic peasants. Nevertheless, even this rump of unrepresentative placemen, supposedly dependent on English patronage and English money, had begun to feel the flush of Irish nationalism rising in its veins, and its leader, Henry Grattan, was demanding that Britain "go back to freedom" and allow the Lords and Commons of Ireland to govern themselves.

This was in the year before Yorktown, and when in the spring that followed that disaster Grattan moved his third declaration of Irish independence, no one in the Irish parliament could be found to vote against it. It was cause and effect. The movements for Irish and American freedom were very closely entwined; they reacted one upon the other and upon the mutual enemy. But it was the Irish at this stage who were a step or two ahead. They had a greater nuisance value, a greater capacity for trouble-making. America was far away, but Ireland was on Britain's doorstep and her volunteers, if provoked too far, could let in the French with incalculable consequences.

Even the myopic government of Lord North had glimpsed this danger and had made some tentative concessions to avert it. With the arrival of Shelburne the problem was faced for the first and, with one exception, last time till the days of Gladstone. Shelburne was a perfect product of the Age of Reason, fond of repeating a quip of Sir Richard Wilmot's that no one went to Ireland who did not lose his wits within six months. But he was also a statesman and a realist. That "God never intended one country to govern another but that each country should govern itself" was a maxim he held to throughout his brief time in power. It was also his opinion that Irish independence would be more likely than not to ensure her dependence on England—a piece of inspired cynicism which it was to take a century and a half of "troubles" to justify for the truism it was.

Under his enlightened guidance the necessary surrenders were made and all claims to English authority over Ireland effectively given up. In the months after his fall the coalition of Fox and

North was driven to go a little further still, and an act was passed at Westminster to remove all doubts concerning the exclusive rights of the Irish parliament and the Irish courts to legislate and litigate for themselves. With the younger Pitt's accession to power at the age of twenty-four, this political solution seemed likely to be extended into the commercial zone, for Pitt was a disciple of Adam Smith and it was his hope to apply his mentor's free-trade principles and sweep away all the old evils of discrimination and monopoly which had brought Irish commerce to the verge of ruin. One small concession was asked for—the Irish must contribute their share towards the costs of imperial defence. Was this not just? Grattan thought so. He believed in English goodwill and hoped to find an answering echo even among his own extremists.

But then the fates—as has happened so often in the history of Anglo-Irish relations—turned sour. There seems something in the very air and soil of Ireland that thrives on argument and resists solutions, particularly when they are imposed from across the St. George's Channel. And on the "Saxon" side there has always been a corresponding lack of understanding which afflicts even those who most devotedly wish Ireland well. Certainly all those on either side who have striven hardest for conciliation and amity between the two nations have fared extremely badly in the end—Mr. Gladstone, wrecked in his old age on the rocks of his second Home Rule Bill; Lloyd George, driven from office after the treaty of 1921; Michael Collins, dead of an assassin's bullet.

Pitt was more fortunate. He did not press the logic of the thing too far. But his hopes also were overturned by too much intransigence in the Ireland of his time and by the ungenerous refusal of his own merchant class to concede a share in prosperity. In a welter of parochialism, greed, violence, political claptrap and the strident cries of Jacobin idealism, the independence of Ireland was still-born, submerged under the rising tide of revolutionary war with France; and in 1800 the worst of all solutions was imposed in an Act of Union which tied Ireland to her uncongenial partner, so that in due course there was brought to the Parliament at Westminster a crop of irreconcilable Irishmen far worse than any dragons' teeth sown in Aegean fields.

*   *   *

All this had come about through the shortcomings of a society that was at heart a society of merchants intent on making an empire pay. When Napoleon said that the English were a nation of shopkeepers he was not being original; Adam Smith had said it in *The Wealth of Nations* many years before; and great advantages stemmed from it in an age that was about to feel the thrust of the Industrial Revolution. But it was a mixed blessing, both for Britain and for her subject peoples. "To concentrate on commerce only," as Professor Coupland has said, and "to neglect the political and moral issues, was folly in America and worse than folly in Ireland; in India it was a crime."

This was particularly true because in India the government of vast territories had been undertaken by a trading company which had by no means outgrown its merchant venturing origins. It had come about by accident. If the Mogul empire had remained as it had been in Jehangir's time, the East India Company would still have been confined to its trading posts around the rim of the sub-continent. With the crumbling of that empire and the coming of the French, the Company had had to bestir itself to keep its trade routes open, and in the process, largely through the genius of Robert Clive, it had suddenly found itself an imperial power, lording it over millions of Bengali peasants and dealing in thrones as it had once dealt with rolls of cloth. Small wonder that the experience went to its collective head and that there had developed among the one-time clerks, now turned governors of provinces, a scramble for riches and a corruption as notable as anything seen since the last days of Rome.

Clive himself took bribes. He was right to say on reflection that he marvelled at his own moderation, for Ali Baba's cave was nothing compared to the opportunities that had come his way, but no one ever marvelled at the moderation of his subordinates and successors until the strong hand of Warren Hastings took control. Indeed the three decades that followed the battle of Plassey were terrible years for India, ravaged by war and famine and the rapacity of governors. In 1760, during one of Clive's absences in England, the throne of Bengal was sold by auction. Between 1769 and 1770 a third of the population of this huge and teeming province died of starvation. "India," said Chatham, "teems with iniquities so rank as to smell to heaven and earth." Reading the parliamentary debates of the time we catch constant echoes of these horrors. In the spring of 1783, Burke, in harrowing terms, described the famine in Madras, where two hundred were dying daily and hundreds of vultures hovered over the city to share "with the wolves and the dogs" in devouring the carcasses lying in the streets, while the unfortunate survivors had also "wolves and vultures in human shape eager to devour."

One has to make some allowances for Burke, who knew a good atrocity story when he heard one and whose natural eloquence hovered sometimes on the verge of farce. "Colourful overstatements" was how one opponent charitably described these outbursts. But there can be no doubt that Burke was right when he referred to acts "of cruelty, barbarity and rapine" that would shock any man of sensibility, and that Charles James Fox was speaking no more than the sober truth when he described the Company's rule in India as a "government of anarchy and confusion." Five years earlier Lord North's attorney general of the time had himself agreed that the natives were oppressed beyond measure and that there had been "shameful abuse" of the peasants by Company servants who had copied the barbarous policy of the princes they had supplanted. We hear little of the sufferings of the poor, but a rajah's harem forcibly entered, his temple polluted, his idols thrown into a basket with other rubbish, a ranee driven from her palace and forced to watch the hanging of her servants, the execution of an Indian prince for a crime not capital by Indian law and committed before the sentencing court was even formed—were these not indeed "malpractices," to use one of Burke's less impassioned words for them? And was not Wraxall right when he wrote that under the "flattering and dazzling exterior" of British rule there lurked so many "hidden seeds of political disease and death" that he marvelled at our presumption and folly in holding down "in the insolence of conquest" a land so vast, so far away, and so utterly dissimilar to our own?

To this widespread and generous indignation on behalf of the oppressed there was added the social irritant caused by the sight of the Company's ex-servants returning home with the brassiness of *nouveaux riches* to buy themselves properties in the country and even—horror of horrors—seats in Parliament! The nabobs had become objects of envy and derision long before Thackeray immortalised the breed in *Vanity Fair* in the person of Josh Sedley. The letters of Horace Walpole are full of it. So bitter was his dislike that he was even prepared to crow over a disaster to British arms and influence provided it put paid to the pretensions of these upstarts. On hearing of Hyder Ali's victories in the spring of 1781 the vials of his wrath poured out:

Adieu the golden sands of the Ganges (all the waters of which
would not wash away our corruptions)! adieu the diamonds of
Bengal! Rumbold is the last waiter at White's whose babe will be
rocked in a cradle of gems; and Sykes the last footman who will be
created a baronet for being worth some lacs of rupees! The Nabob
of Arcot will have no more members of Parliament for retainers.
. . . Hyder Ali has dispersed all our visions of endless wealth.

Then to another correspondent:

The East Indian fleet of great value is safely arrived in Ireland.
Sir Thomas Rumbold is on board it and *his* value is estimated at a
million. I do not wonder that a nabob can afford to buy a gang of
members of Parliament.

Two years later he was still at it with the same target in his sights.
"This Rumbold was a waiter at White's: there are two or three of
like origin who have returned from Bengal incrusted with gold and
diamonds. This trial has disclosed a scene of tyranny in the East
India Company itself as royally iniquitous as could issue from the
council chamber of Petersburg. We talk and write of liberty, and
plunder the property of the Indies." The social venom is unmistakable, and it expressed itself more happily in verse, not apparently his
own:

When Macreth served in Arthur's crew
He said to Rumbold, "Black my shoe,"
To which he answered, "Ay, Bob."
But when returned from India's land,
And grown too proud to brook command,
He sternly answer'd, "Nay, Bob."

This feeling of envious resentment played its part in the general
sense of outrage against the Company's misgovernment in India
which was driving all the parliamentary factions towards a search for
a solution which would both clear Britain's good name and assert

British authority over territories whose importance had suddenly, with the loss of America, been recognised as the main pillar and prop of the nation's position in the world. The King himself was in sympathy with the national mood, and his speech at the end of the summer session in 1782 praised the diligence and ardour with which Parliament had debated Indian affairs. "To protect the persons and fortunes of millions in these distant regions," it read, "and to combine our prosperity with their happiness, are objects which repay the utmost labour and exertion." The problem and the aim could hardly have been better put, and in opening the autumn session the King, now speaking for the Earl of Shelburne's government, returned to the charge, hoping that it would be possible to frame laws which would make her connection with Great Britain "a blessing to India." "The regulation of a vast territory in Asia opens a large field for your wisdom, prudence and foresight," the speech went on; and in the autumn of the following year, with the first reading of Fox's India Bill, the good sense and justice of these sentiments began to bear fruit. There were still people, however, who required to be shocked into a realisation of what was at stake, and Burke provided the spadework in a marathon speech which opened with a catalogue of Britain's failings and worse than failings towards those who had trusted her. The East India Company, he said, had never made a treaty it had not broken; all who had confided in it had been brought to utter ruin. But these were only the sighting shots for a far hotter cannonade:

England has erected no churches, no hospitals, no palaces, no schools; England has built no bridges, made no high roads, cut no navigations, dug no reservoirs. . . . If we were to be driven out of India this day, nothing would remain to tell that it had been possessed, during the inglorious period of our dominion, by anything better than the orang outang and the tiger.

These things were to be remedied, but at the time they were true. It was an indictment of formidable power. Now and again the speaker's over-ripe periods lost the attention of the House as he castigated some outrage to a ranee. "It was the pious hand of a son that was selected to tear from his mother and grandmother the provision of their age, the maintenance of his brethren, and of all the ancient household of his father." ("Here a laugh from some young members," Hansard censoriously reports.) Then again: "This ancient matron, born to better things . . ." ("A laugh from certain young gentlemen.") "I see no cause for this mirth," Burke tartly replied. It is easy to understand why the House tended to empty during his interminable orations.

But on the position of the Company in relation to India he had the root of the matter in him. "I therefore conclude," he said, "what you all conclude, that this body, being totally perverted from the purpose of its institution, is utterly incorrigible; and because they are incorrigible both in conduct and constitution, power ought to be taken out of their hands; just on the same principles on which have been made all the just changes and revolutions of government that have taken place since the beginning of the world." And his peroration, when he eventually reached it, was noble and played its part in bringing about the better government of India:

> For my own part, I am happy that I have lived to see this day; I feel myself overpaid for the labours of eighteen years, when, at this late period, I am able to take my share, by one humble vote, in destroying a tyranny that exists to the disgrace of this nation and the destruction of so large a part of the human species.

The last word was left to Mr. Secretary Fox, winding up the debate. It was a greater speech than Burke's, for all that it fell into some of his excesses and was cast in the same overblown mould—greater if only because of its closing lines:

> What is the end of all government? Certainly the happiness of the governed. Others may hold other opinions; but this is mine and I proclaim it.

Fox's India Bill did not reach the statute book. He was driven from office, and Pitt's India Act, which took its place, was to prove a clumsier solution to the problem than the one he had proposed. But it was inspired by the same principles, and never again was a British government to forget them for long.

IV

The Rights of Man

The parliamentary debates during the years immediately following the loss of the American colonies were marked by some of the noblest oratory and some of the longest speeches ever made until the invention of the filibuster. Burke's performance for the managers at the impeachment of Warren Hastings lasted for days, and he had competitors. But underneath the passion and the prosiness lay a steady and a workmanlike aim—it was to put what was left of the imperial house in order and to keep the dependents happy by a judicious mixture of firmness, fairness and bribes.

This policy was marked also by caution. Neither Adam Smith nor Josiah Tucker had expected that empires would ever voluntarily give up what they had won, and it was unlikely that busy statesmen would be more liberal than professors. Thus in 1791, when it was felt that Canada would have to be given representative institutions, these were by no means an advance on what the Old Thirteen had rejected fifteen years earlier. Perhaps this was only to be expected, since Canada in the last years of the eighteenth century was still a thin veneer of settlements strung out along the St. Lawrence River, lapped about on all sides by the wilderness, and her fantastic growth and expansion to the Pacific never to be dreamed of

by statesmen who had been brought up to think of the American far
north in terms of the fur trade around Hudson's Bay and the disput-
ing claims of French and English fishermen to dry their catch on the
shores of Nova Scotia and Newfoundland.

Given an interval of peace, the speed of this advance would no
doubt have quickened. Pitt certainly intended it. His commercial
treaty with France and his proposals for an Irish settlement were inspired by the need for a new approach to international problems,
and it was hardly his fault that both foundered under the weight of
old antagonisms, in the extreme Irish nationalism of Wolfe Tone and
twenty years of war with France. The result was to slow down the
thaw in British political thinking for three decades and to turn the
earnest free trader into the prisoner of Napoleon's continental system, the great peace minister into a war minister of limited abilities.

In the process some very odd results occurred. Britain, whose
Mediterranean interests had been confined to the seas between the
Balearics and Gibraltar, suddenly began to project herself hundreds
of miles to the eastward among the Aegean islands of Homer's "wine
dark sea." She cajoled Corsica into declaring George III its king. Attempts to introduce trial by jury to the islanders proved even more bi-
zarre, when it became obvious that any verdict of "Guilty" by twelve
good men and true would start twelve simultaneous blood feuds with
the family of the condemned. As a last gift to the Corsicans, it was
proposed to hand them over to the Russian Tsarina, the most arbitrary rule in Europe, but this plan fortunately miscarried along with
the rest.

It was a situation full of paradox, and Napoleon, lingering fretfully
on St. Helena and wondering every day how he had come to lose
Waterloo, might have pondered instead on the question whether he
had not been one of the agents of a new British Empire. His ambitions in the Orient had drawn Britain inexorably the same way. If he
had not gone to the Pyramids and Acre, would his enemies have
gone to Malta or the Cape of Good Hope? If he had not threatened to become a new Alexander on the banks of the Indus, would
Britain have taken on the role of the Great Mogul which earlier
British governments had declined? Perhaps the lure of Walpole's "elephants and rubies" would have drawn her that way in any case, but
it is a remarkable fact that each French intrusion into India ended

with Britain one stage nearer the domination of the whole sub-continent—Dupleix's genius had been answered by Robert Clive; the pro-French activities of Hyder Ali and Tippu Sultan gave us the Carnatic; the Napoleonic threat brought the *Raj* to Lucknow and Delhi, much against its better judgment.

These aggressive moves had not been planned; they were responses to other people's aggressions. Pitt's India Act had been passed with the express aim of *controlling,* not extending, the activities of the Company's servants who had been rampaging with their armies all over southern and central India, deposing rulers and setting up puppets without any reference to nominal superiors in London. If Fox had had his way, he would have regulated the Company's trading activities also. But Pitt was warier. He knew there was a price to pay for the support of the East India lobby at Westminster which had helped to wreck his predecessor's bill, and he was prepared to meet it by leaving the Company's trade alone provided he could bring its political dominance in India to an end. And this he achieved. There were to be backslidings, and there were to be Governor-Generals who slipped their leashes more than once and acted on the high-handed model of Clive and Warren Hastings, but from now on—at least in theory—Indian affairs were no longer to be settled by nabobs in Calcutta under the lax supervision of shareholders in the City. Authority was to lie with a board of control with real teeth to it, under a minister responsible to Parliament.

Here then in embryo was the means by which India could be governed in some sort of accord with the principles of the Rights of Man. The aim was limited, but at least it brought about the rule of law and gave protection to those millions for whose welfare George III had prayed and Burke had spoken. There *were* to be roads, hospitals, schools, canals, great irrigation works, even "palaces," though hardly of the style and elegance that Burke would have approved. For better or worse, the British were going to leave their mark on India, and no one would ever ask again for proof that they had passed that way. The moral factor had appeared in British imperial thinking, and Burke's conception of government as a Trust by the governors on behalf of the governed had been accepted as both a philosophic, legal and practical truth. But how did this principle apply to people still further down the social scale than Indian villagers—to those indeed who were not even people in the law's eyes but simply chattels, property, goods, to be exploited?

*   *   *

The British Empire, like other empires of the time, included a large body of slaves. When Pitt's India Bill was passed there were 300,000 of them in Jamaica alone and their numbers had for centuries been increasing all the time. Every British "sugar" island had its slave population, and the influx into the mainland colonies of Georgia and the Carolinas had been so large that most of the states of the Old Thirteen—though not Georgia and the Carolinas—had tried to write this grievance into the Declaration of Independence as yet another of King George's crimes. In 1713, by her victorious peace treaty at Utrecht, Britain had won for herself the coveted *Asiento,* the right to provide an annual quota of negroes to meet the demands of the Spanish colonies also. By far and away the greatest naval power, even after her reverses in the War of Independence, she was by the same token the greatest slaving power. No nation had a greater stake in human suffering and no nation exploited it more efficiently and with less care for the human cargoes, stuffed like broiler fowls in the holds of vessels making the "Middle Passage" between Gambia and the Caribbean. Spain was a paragon of virtue compared to her; France was by a small margin more humane.

Slavery as a status was almost as old as mankind, but it was only slowly in the course of the eighteenth century that its nature came to be studied and understood in Britain. Realisation might have been even longer delayed if it had not come to the public attention that a sizeable number of house servants of planters who had returned home from the "sugar" islands were actually living in slavery in Britain itself. Could such a status exist in the very cradle of the Common Law? Step by reluctant step the legal authorities were driven by the activities of a few maverick laymen from the certainty that it could, to the despairing admission that it could not. Lord Mansfield's famous judgment in the case of the runaway slave Somersett was no high-flying declaration of the Rights of Man; it was as narrow, grudging and legalistic a decision as was ever handed down from an English bench, but it contained the one revolutionary declaration that slavery was a condition so repugnant to nature that it could only be justified by some positive law proclaiming its legality, and since in England there was no such law, "the black must be released."

Few can have imagined at the time that this was a milestone on the road to wider freedoms. Lord Mansfield was an upright judge but a poor humanitarian—he had tried to dodge the issue by every trick known to him. But however hedged-about, however grudgingly, a doctrine of immense force had been proclaimed, and its effects, like those of a stone thrown into a stagnant pool, spread outwards from the consideration of the fate of one poor negro slave till, three quarters of a century later, its ripples swept away the status of slavery itself from British soil.

The slowness of the flood and the difficulties and obstacles it had to cross seem incredible to-day. Almost two hundred years ago William Wilberforce said that we would find it so. The climate of opinion of the times was not inhumane. When the Quaker anti-slavery petition to Parliament was set before Lord North, who never lacked compassion, he agreed at once that this was a worthy cause; he merely feared it was chimerical. Too many vested interests were involved in every major European country. When the campaign for abolition of the trade was launched under Wilberforce's leadership, with such paladins as Fox and Pitt in close support, the rationalisations of the system made both comical and gruesome reading. A Mr. Grosvenor acknowledged that the trade was not an "amiable" trade, but neither was the trade of a butcher an amiable trade, "yet a mutton chop was nevertheless a good thing." Mr. John Stanley, a searcher after revealed truths, could find no conflict between slavery and Christian principles: St. Paul had never said a word against it.

This was after most of the facts of the trade had been established by a committee of enquiry and some of the grimmest statistics ever recorded had been laid on the table of the House of Commons.

To take the year 1791, on the government's own figures, 74,000 slaves had been imported into the Caribbean in British ships, 34,000 of whom had then been re-exported to foreign dealers. Over the century since the glorious revolution of 1688 a total of some two million had been transported to America and the Caribbean; over 700,000 of them since 1751. These commodities had been bartered between the masters of British ships, their agents at the ports and African tribal sellers; had been seized, marched in manacles to ports along the Senegal; the survivors had been loaded aboard the slavers into shelves in the hold with hardly room to turn; had been chained in pairs, and had then been subjected to a sea journey which could last for several weeks.

From figures taken over a twenty-year period it was generally conceded that one in ten Africans died under this treatment. Sometimes the ratio was much higher when disease broke out among the cargo. It could hardly have been otherwise with ships of 130 to 150 tons that carried twice, sometimes four times, their own tonnage in slaves. A case was quoted where of 650 negroes, 155 died. Half of another cargo of 405 perished. The captain had put these losses down to "a fixed melancholy and dejection" that made them lose the will to live. On some ships nets had to be placed around the rails to prevent suicides during the slaves' brief periods of exercise above-decks; the negroes called these plunges to their destruction in the waves "escapes." Fox's figures were still more horrifying—counting losses on the slave roads to the ports, in the ports themselves and on the sea crossing, he estimated 14,000 deaths a year in the British trade alone, and no one rose to refute these figures to his face.

How could such things have happened in an age in which Burke's theory of trusteeship had been defined? Much was simply due to ignorance and lack of understanding—the House of Commons was a long way from Senegal and very few in Britain had seen a slave ship, except perhaps as just another sail in the crowded harbours of Bristol and Liverpool. After the Nazi death camps it is easier to know how a brutal trade brutalises its practitioners by mere repetition, to the point when all humanity is lost. And slaves were hardly reckoned human by the practice of the times. Though a negro in prime condition could fetch up to £50 in the West Indies in the 1790s and show a profit of perhaps 30 per cent, he was still property, much on a par with codfish netted off the Newfoundland Banks. When the captain of the trader *Zong* bethought himself in the middle of a storm at sea that an indemnity might be obtained by jettisoning some of the less valuable cargo and threw a batch of elderly slaves overboard, no one except a lunatic fringe of abolitionists demanded that he be tried for murder. In the law's eyes, as Lord Mansfield pointed out, the master of the *Zong* had done no better and no worse than if he had consigned a number of horses to the waves. It was a civil matter, not a criminal one. Lord Mansfield's strictures (*obiter*) on the inhuman nature of the act are sometimes forgotten, but the fact is that though he rebuked it, he did nothing about it, could do nothing about it, for he too was trapped within a system hallowed by long commercial usage. Reading the Hansard reports of the great debates on the trade which followed in the years between 1788 and 1793, the most striking thing is the virtual unanimity of speaker after speaker rising in the House to declare that the infamous thing must stop. "There is no excuse," said Pitt, "for us seeing this infernal traffic as we do. It is the very death of Justice to utter a syllable in support of it." And hardly anyone did. They simply voted for its retention. Inertia, tradition, respect for property, fear of the "spirit of innovation" against which one member begged gentlemen to be on their guard, and the deep resentment of men faced with arguments they could not answer, all these kept the silent majority on the side of slavery. Now and then a speaker, fit to cross swords with the abolitionist leaders, rose to give voice to this reaction. Lord Sheffield expressed it perfectly when he moved in April 1792 for an end not so much to the slave trade as to "a mischievous discussion." Or take Lord Carhampton, complaining in a brilliantly caustic speech that the inhumanities of slavery against which the "negro-philanthropists" were protesting were as nothing to the inhumanity of those who inflicted four-hour-long speeches on their suffering fellow men.

What bores the abolitionists must have seemed. And what bores most of them remain in the cold print of Hansard—page after sanctimonious and self-righteous page. As one reads, one almost feels a sneaking sympathy for Lord Sheffield and for Lord Carhampton's claim that but for a merciful escape door behind the Speaker's chair the more infirm members of the Commons would have perished on the spot; and indeed the effect of this blanket oratory may have been more to conceal than to reveal the horrible truths involved in the greatest moral issue ever debated at Westminster.

Yet it was right that small men as well as great ones, boring men as well as wits, should have stood up to be counted. Some of these minor figures said some of the best things, perhaps because they said them less often. "Show me a crime of any sort," said a Mr. Beaufoy, "and in the slave trade I will show you that crime in a state of tenfold aggravation. . . . All other injustices, all other modes of desolating nature, of blasting the happiness of man and defeating the purposes of God, lose in comparison with this their very name and character of evil." In his view even the Inquisition had nothing worse to show than this "cool, reflecting, deliberate, remorseless commerce."

Wilberforce, the parliamentary leader and soul of the Abolitionist campaign, said nothing better. He was concerned—perhaps too much concerned—to dress up a revolutionary aim in terms of cool reason and in step with the ideas of Adam Smith, who had quarrelled with slavery as being economically wasteful and inefficient. To lower the temperature of debate and accept his opponents as wrong-headed rather than wrong-hearted made good political sense, and with a rougher approach even the gradual abolition of the trade might not have been won in his lifetime, but there was a price to be paid for so much self-restraint and it is only on very rare occasions that Wilberforce in print—as compared with Wilberforce in action— touches the heart, as in the aside where he remarks that funerals, which in Africa were always occasions for ritual weeping and lamentations, were greeted in the slave huts of the West Indies where journeys ended "with every mark of exultation and joy."

Here is eloquence at its most poignant. In a sentence which perhaps takes a few liberties with truth, truth itself is revealed and slavery is seen in its real terms of human hope and despair. "I know of no evil," said Pitt almost exactly a year later, "I know of no evil that ever has existed worse than the tearing of seventy or eighty thousand persons annually from their native land. . . . Thus, Sir, has the perversion of British commerce carried misery instead of happiness to a whole quarter of the globe. False to the very principles of trade, misguided in our policy and unmindful of our duty, what astonishing mischief have we brought upon that continent. . . . Shall we deny rendering this justice to Africa?"

Pitt's own position throughout these debates on Wilberforce's campaign for abolition was equivocal to say the least. A Prime Minister speaking to a friend's motion, recommending it, urging it, wet-nursing it but never using his full powers of patronage to enforce it, is hardly a sympathetic figure, and his later near-desertion of the cause at the century's end has puzzled and distressed a host of admiring biographers.

Almost certainly Pitt detested slavery and was prevented from bringing his full weight to bear against it only because of the overriding need not to divide the nation at a time of acute danger. If this view of him is too generous and he used abolition for just so long and only for so long as it provided him (as some have alleged) with a weapon of commercial war, it still remains true that his was the most influential voice that was ever raised against the trade and that in the course of a single speech—rated by his contemporaries as the greatest ever made in their time—he virtually destroyed the case for the slave trade and for the status of slavery itself.

He did more. For in his peroration he soared far beyond the squalid arguments and practical demands of the debate and even past that still visionary point in time when all the citizens of Africa would be free. A century and a half are overtaken in a burst of inspired insight, and here—in the cadences of a vanished Augustan age—are the unfulfilled promises and the deferred hopes of to-day:

> If we listen to the voice of reason and duty, and pursue this night the line of conduct which they prescribe, some of us may live to see a reverse of that picture from which we now turn our eyes with shame and regret. We may live to behold the natives of Africa engaged in the calm occupations of industry, in the pursuits of a just and legitimate commerce. We may behold the beams of science and philosophy breaking in upon their land, which at some happy period in still later times may blaze with full lustre. . . . Then may we hope that even Africa, though last of all the quarters of the globe, shall enjoy at length in the evening of her days those blessings which have descended so plentifully upon us in a much easier period of the world.

It was the last speech of the night, a very long one, but 315 members were still sufficiently awake to vote a majority of 145 for "gradual abolition" of the trade. "The House adjourned at half an hour after six in the morning," Hansard records impassively.

V

Lord Durham and the First Dominion

"Gradual abolition" is a surprisingly inexact phrase to find in a parliamentary motion of such importance, but in its context it was unavoidable—it had to be all things to all men. For the West Indian planters it meant postponing things till the Greek Kalends; the Abolitionists wanted action on the spot and by 1796 at the latest; the government had 1800 in mind, which would have meant eight years' delay. Fate settled for 1807, when Parliament finally brought itself to decide that "all manner of dealing and trading in slaves" should be "utterly abolished, prohibited, and declared to be unlawful" and that all ships participating in such traffic should be forfeited to the Crown.

The end of the slave trade did not mean of course the end of slavery. It continued, as in places it may still continue to this day. But since the British were far and away the greatest suppliers of slaves, the decisions they made on the illegality of the traffic were bound, in the end, to settle the fate of slavery as an institution over most of the globe.

For its decisions in 1792, 1807, and 1833, when the whole infamous status was declared illegal on British soil,* the Westminster

---

* The 1833 Act was also to prove less effective than had been intended. Attempts to destroy slavery root and branch in India and elsewhere had

Parliament had a right to claim credit. And though it was an *ad hoc* body, bothering about day-to-day and month-to-month but seldom about year-to-year affairs, it had within the comparatively short span of half a century since its *débâcle* over the American taxes thrashed out in detail certain principles which might otherwise have languished within the covers of humanitarian tracts. The feelings of a colony had to be considered; in a white colony they were paramount. Corruption was unacceptable as a system of government. Human rights existed and were coming to have the force of laws.

Much of this had run ahead of public opinion; indeed the doctrine that the Empire was not a free for all for entrepreneurs was a very revolting one for the commercial community to swallow. The East India Company had been founded under the most august royal auspices to uphold just such a philosophy that trade was everything, and on the other side of the world the West Indian plantations had been turned into going concerns on the assumption that cheap sugar was one of the pillars of British prosperity. And it was a well-founded assumption, for without the produce and profits of those highly exploited islands Britain could hardly have kept afloat during the years of French economic and military pressure which reached its height during the Napoleonic blockade. Even in peacetime the City of London and the great slaving ports of Liverpool and Bristol would hardly have looked with pleasure on these liberalising trends, but this was wartime, and the really astonishing thing is that in the course of it the voice of conscience was never stilled and the abolition of the slave trade, Britain's greatest humanitarian act, preceded Waterloo by nearly a decade.

Had this come about as a result of philanthropy, enlightened self-interest or, as foreigners preferred to call it, sheer hypocrisy? The British, for all their apparent simplicity, do have their inscrutable side, and though the crusade against slavery cost Britain many million sterling and the decline of her West Indian islands, there have always been voices to proclaim that the triumph, when it came, was less due to "negro-philanthropy," to borrow Lord Carhampton's useful term, than to commercial sleight of hand. Yet if a great deal of

---

so disruptive an effect on primitive societies, which from time immemorial had depended on the system, that it became necessary to slow the pace of progress; and it was only piecemeal over a period of decades that the status was whittled down and gradually eliminated in British territories.

realism underlay the Abolitionists' most Utopian thinking, one would have to be a cynic indeed to feel that the end they pursued was a wholly selfish one. It was, in fact, like so many things in British life, a compromise, a fusion of two attitudes of mind, one of which looked to heaven and the other to the main chance, and was perfectly reflected in the actions of a government which after twenty years of mortal struggle with its main continental rival, picked up, dusted down and restored that rival with one hand to its old position in Europe, and with the other beat the commercial hell out of it by taking on huge new accessions of territory in the East.

All this was highly contradictory, but not to the English. The victors of Waterloo ardently desired peace, and to restore Bourbon France to her old authority in Europe seemed the most likely way to achieve it. The conquests in India and the seizure of the strategic keys to it through the Mediterranean and at the Cape had simply happened, much as the capture of Jamaica and Quebec had happened in the course of earlier wars, and the sensible thing seemed to be to hang on to them.

Thus, here in embryo at the beginning of the new century is that baffling dualism at work which was soon to display Britain as both the world's most liberal power and its most imperialistic one. It was partly the result of accident and partly the habit of swapping ideologies and clothes that went on to a fantastic degree among the political parties and their allied pressure groups. Only if we make proper allowances for it can we begin to understand a system in which it was the Duke of Wellington, the prototype of reaction in the popular eye, who brought in Catholic emancipation, which no progressive had been able to do; that it was the conservative Disraeli, not the liberal Gladstone, who carried out the great measure of franchise reform establishing household suffrage and made the first attempt to abolish the slums; and that it was Gladstone, not the imperialist Disraeli, who was to invade and seize Egypt.

If this has a perverse sound, it was at least an age when perversity was rich. The three decades that followed Waterloo are bewildering in the complexity of their thought on every level, political, social and religious. There is no need to label them or to distinguish between High Tories and followers of Huskisson, Tories and Whigs, Whigs and Liberals, Liberals and Benthamites, Benthamites and Radicals, Chartists and Free Traders, the warring factions within the Church of England and the nonconformist sects, themselves bitterly at odds with one another—it was one huge intellectual ferment in which colonial policy, though often swamped by the weight of party argument over disestablishment, the Reform Bill, the condition of the factories and the administration of the Poor Law, remained one of the central issues. In the words of Elie Halévy, the historian of Britain's great century, "England was beginning to awaken to the fact that she was a colonial power and her colonies nothing less than a new world in process of birth . . ."

No doubt this was so. Yet approach a little closer to this problem and the same dualism, the same divorce at once appears, not only between the commercial community and the philosopher-economists but also between the philosophers themselves, who might have been expected to agree, since they were all in one way or another disciples of Adam Smith and Josiah Tucker, no longer voices crying in the wilderness but a school of weight and prestige whose members had infiltrated many of the organs of government.

"Emancipate your colonies" was the advice which their chief elder, Jeremy Bentham, had given the French long before the advent of Bonaparte, though it had not been published till many years later when that advice would have been better addressed to London; and Charles James Fox, a Benthamite sympathiser in Bentham's prime, had expressed much the same idea when he had suggested that the only way of retaining distant colonies "with advantage" was to help them to govern themselves.

But what sort of colonies had they been talking about? Certainly not about India, which Fox had seen in Burke's terms as a European trust for backward peoples and which some of the Benthamites had frankly excluded from their thinking. "Certain colonies absolutely require a despotic authority," said Sir William Molesworth. ". . . our government of a hundred million people in India . . . is anything but democratic. Yet I know not if a better could be devised for the people who are subject to it." Was this racialist doctrine? Up to a point, though we should beware of applying the standards of modern thinking to old problems. It was natural that the best minds in one of the most advanced of European nations should have felt their distance from Bengali peasants and negro workers in the West Indian plantations who were so evidently unable to look after themselves and so much in need of firm and paternal government. Practically everyone was agreed on this, just as they agreed on the whole that recent conquests like Malta, Mauritius and Aden (though not the Greek Ionian islands which troubled everyone) should remain in British hands. Where they differed, and differed fundamentally, was in what should be done with colonies settled by people of European stock such as existed in Canada, at the Cape of Good Hope and in the newly discovered territories in Australia and New Zealand.

One wing of Benthamite thought was blossoming out as advocates of an enlightened and controlled imperialism which would settle such virgin lands with groups of respectable white farmers—a far cry from the convicts the government had brutally dumped there and the London prostitutes who had been shipped out to join them in the brave new world. But among the older generation of philosophic-radicals there existed a deep-rooted distaste for colonies of this "European" kind which they saw as burdens rather than advantages. The debate divided generations, even families. John Stuart Mill leaned towards the new imperialism: his father, James Mill, had imbibed the milk of pure Benthamism. Both worked for the East India Company. Could dualism of thought go further?

No wonder the public was confused. Was empire justifiable morally? Was it even viable commercially? Some said one thing and some the other, but there would have been few to agree with that acute French observer the Abbé de Prat who had forecast as early as the 1820s that by her world position and the attraction of her "perfect institutions" Great Britain was destined "without force of arms to impart a new aspect to the world." The national mood was far more pessimistic, far less influenced by what people imagined might happen than by the evidence of their own eyes—the recent humiliating loss of the thirteen colonies; the serious unrest in the West Indies among the recently emancipated slaves; and the unhappy example of Spain and Portugal whose colonial power was crumbling into ruin. At the very moment when their own empire had outstripped all rivals and had become a vital factor on the world stage, the British had begun to show towards it an attitude that would have been appropriate at the time of Yorktown and the ignominious peace that had followed it. Perhaps it would be truer to say that it was less pessimism than indifference that had gripped the nation: the sense of *déjà vu*. For on the same continent where one empire had been lost an almost exact repetition seemed in the making.

*   *   *

In the 1830s Canada was more a historical accident than a country: the result of fall-out from explosions elsewhere which had scattered groups of British seafaring folk in the Maritime Provinces around the mouth of the St. Lawrence, fur trappers in the wilderness of Hudson's Bay, French peasants in Quebec, and a displaced "Loyalist" population which had fled from the Old Thirteen after independence to settle on either side of their Gallic neighbours in a part of Nova Scotia renamed New Brunswick and in Upper Canada to the west of Montreal. There were over a million of them in all, of whom between a third and a half remained as French by speech and blood as on the day, more than seventy years earlier, when Wolfe's victory over Montcalm on the Plains of Abraham had cut them off from their cultural motherland. Yet it was not loyalty to France they felt so much as to their French image of themselves. They were *les canadiens, les habitants,* the original settlers of the land, and nearly half a million strong they stood in the valley of the St. Lawrence, a community entrenched in its own grievances.

The English, with their long experience of minority troubles with Welsh and Scots, had reacted with a good deal of forebearance and even sophistication. If they had failed to pacify Ireland, they had a much better grasp—or at least they thought they had—of this problem which they hoped to solve by letting the *habitants* enjoy their own culture and code of laws. Religion was recognised as the key issue, and here no disabilities or strings of any kind were attached. What in 1791 was still denied to British Catholics had been freely granted to French Catholics in Quebec. The defeated—and this is almost unique in history—had been allowed a province of their own (lower Canada) where, being in a majority of three to one over settlers of British stock, they held most of the seats in the Legislative Assembly under the executive rule of a British governor and his nominated (not elected) council. They were thus in almost exactly the same position as the British Canadians in their own

provinces of upper Canada and the Maritimes: they enjoyed much
the same rights that the American colonists had enjoyed before
the Boston Tea Party, and was this not enough? The vision of one
unified Canada stretching from the Atlantic to the Pacific had not
yet been dreamed of. But in the background of many statemen's
minds lay the hope that by this tender concern for French culture,
combined with a little persuasion and the force of British example,
the *enfant terrible* that was lower Canada or Quebec might be
weaned from its parent and turned into the semblance of a good
Anglo-Saxon. Failing that, it would have to be outbred by the more
numerous British on either flank, until, in the words of Lord Durham's report, "by the working of natural causes" this perpetual
minor would "abandon its vain hope of nationality."

Whose was the vain hope, the future was to show. And even at
the time, by no means all British statesmen expected much of these
farouche and difficult peoples of either stock except that they would
all sooner or later go the way of their republican neighbours to the
south. "If ever the Canadas separate from this country," Lord Stanley had declared in the 1820s, *"as they must some day or other* in
the ordinary course of things, it is in our power to retain their friendship."

It was a modest enough expectation. But in lower Canada the
elective Legislative Assembly with its French majority, incensed by
the government's confiscation of certain Jesuit properties, refused
year after year to pass the budget and demanded that the governor's crown-appointed council should be elected by the people.
Even in the province of upper Canada, which included hardly one
Frenchman, the Assembly was insisting on financial control of revenue and on a cabinet responsible to the people of the province, not to
its London-appointed rulers. In the 1780s no more passionately
loyal or pro-British groups had existed anywhere. But the veterans
who had found a home and a refuge under the British flag after the
War of Independence were dying off and a new generation had
sprung up, less grateful for old favours and far more responsive to
the magnetic pull of the great republic to the south. This was only
natural. Every traveller between British North America and the
United States noticed the difference—stagnation and lethargy in the
one, the immense dynamism of the other. Few made allowances for
the disparity in wealth and population between Canadian backwoods

and the state of Massachusetts. The blame was laid on the dead
hand of British colonial rule, and in 1837—only a few months after
Queen Victoria's accession—the simmering discontent in both provinces came to the boil.

The ingredients of the brew were various—in upper Canada they
were political or constitutional; in Quebec, racial. This was a rebellion of the French. Both uprisings were put down with ease—they
were the work of two sets of extremists who had no joint plan, no
common aim, no sympathy whatsoever with one another. Far more
interesting was the reaction in government circles in London, which
had for some time been watching Canadian affairs with a jaundiced
and wary eye. In the summer before the outbreaks the Prime Minister, Lord Melbourne, had been trying to coax the most radical
Whig grandee of his acquaintance—Lord Durham—into going to
Canada as the Queen's emissary to sort out the growing mess, and
incidentally into removing himself from Westminster where his radicalism and his popularity as the people's friend were equally embarrassing.

Lord Melbourne's letter to his nominee is a perfect reflection of the
colonial feelings of the age, particularly towards Canada, which was
being a nuisance. "The final separation of these colonies," he wrote
to Durham, "might possibly not be of material detriment to the
interests of the mother country, but it is clear that it would be a
serious blow to the honour of Great Britain, and certainly would be
fatal to the character and existence of the Administration under
which it took place." Quite. It would bring down the government,
and just at a time when Lord Melbourne had begun to enjoy himself—and astonish everyone else—by turning from a Regency man
of fashion into the friend and mentor of a young and charming
queen. What happened to Canada, what was good for Canada, was
not the point, and even the honour of Great Britain has a remarkably hollow sound. Actually Lord Durham refused—he was a sick
man. Only after rebellion had broken out in both provinces did he
accept the mission (which in the meantime Melbourne had upgraded
into an "essential service for the country") and go out as the
Queen's commissioner and Governor-General for all the territories
of British North America, armed with his chief's promise of "the
firmest and most unflinching support," which at the first hint of
parliamentary trouble was promptly withdrawn.

Lord Durham—"Radical Jack" to the northern pitmen—was one of the great family of the Lambtons, from whose Crusading days a grisly tale is still sung towards closing time in the myriad public houses of the area—the tale of The Lambton Worm:

> Whisht, lads, haad yer gobs,
> An' aal tell ye arl an aaful story,
> Whisht, lads, haad yer gobs,
> An' aal tell ye aboot the Warm.

Readers' feelings must not be unduly harried, but it was a worm of gigantic size milking the local cows that "young Lambton" found on his return from Jerusalem to his ancestral castle on the hill. Brave lad, he slew it. A St. George and the Dragon story. And it was symbolically mounted on a white horse that his descendant appeared before the people of Canada to rescue them from what? From the twin dragons of rebellion and tyrannical British rule? More probably from the *habitants* with their Frenchified culture for whom Lord Durham was soon to conceive a deep antipathy.

This comes out clearly in the famous Report written two years later on his return to England after a mission which in worldly terms had failed. Canadians as a body he approved, seeing them as "a great and peaceful people, possessing the means of securing good and responsible government for itself." But French Canadians were bad—a community exhibiting in North America "the characteristics of the peasantry of Europe": "an old and stationary society in a new and progressive world." "It is to elevate them from that inferiority," Lord Durham continued, "that I desire to give to the Canadians our English character." In an ineffably smug passage he developed this vision: "I entertain no doubts as to the national character which must be given to Lower Canada; it must be that of the British Empire . . . that of the great race which must, in the lapse of no long period of time, be predominant over the whole North American continent." To give effect to which illusion he proposed—and the home government implemented the proposal—that pending the creation of one super-state embracing the whole of British North America, from the Great Lakes to Newfoundland, the two major provinces of Upper and Lower Canada should at once be merged, thus converting the three-to-one majority the French enjoyed over the Anglo-Saxons in Quebec into a minority by some fifty thousand in the reconstructed province.

It has to be said that this political gerrymandering greatly mars a report which has been traditionally regarded (though not in France) as a great state paper and even the Magna Carta of the Second British Empire. But the report was never intended as an idealistic declaration of human rights, for that was not why its author had been sent to Canada. He was a Whig nobleman investigating a crisis in a backward part of the world and trying to find a remedy. Naturally he looked for guide-lines along the way, which he found in the English-speaking majority, whose affection for the mother country should, in his words, ensure "a safe, honourable and enduring connexion." There was a danger that many at home might be sceptical about Canadian loyalties and think his policy of trust misplaced, but he urged it in a passage of sweet reason, calculated to appeal not only to the merchants who were favourably disposed to the imperial idea but also the hard-line disciples of Adam Smith. "The experiment of keeping colonies and governing them well," he wrote, "ought at least to have a trial, ere we abandon for ever the vast dominion which might supply the wants of our surplus population and raise up millions of fresh consumers of our manufactures . . ." Only a very rash or unthinking man could have denied such a thesis which accorded with almost everything which the philosophic-radicals expected of international relations between industrial states and their overseas customers. Where Durham differed with them was in his belief that Canada could be kept within the imperial family to everyone's mutual profit if only the natural affection which he was sure the majority of Canadians felt for Britain was returned and guided along the right channels. If it was not—if that affection was ignored or rebuffed—then instead of an asset, Britain would find herself in Canada with a people politically rebellious and economically stagnant—with nothing more in fact than "a barren and injurious sovereignty."

Disease and cure. In the brilliant closing passage of his report Lord Durham appears to posterity like a surgeon, scalpel in hand, over the recumbent body of Canada. Was the disease malignant? It certainly had malignant properties. What was its nature? He diagnosed a political ailment which the British had got out of their system during the "Glorious Revolution" of 1688 but which took the form of a disharmony between the legislative and executive powers of the body politic. In Britain the Crown no longer had the power to impose its will on the elected representatives of the nation. Sometimes it tried, by using sections of Parliament as its personal agents. George III had attempted this ploy through his system of the "King's Friends," but it had not outlived Lord North, and no one any longer pretended that Crown prerogatives could be revived, let alone extended. As a result of a constitutional revolution there was no longer any divorce in Britain between the executive and legislative powers which worked on the whole in harmony with one another. Ministers came from Parliament and were responsible through Parliament to public opinion. Even the House of Lords dared not press its obstructionism too far. But when one applied this system to Canada the divergencies at once appeared. There the governor and his nominated council in each province were "responsible," but not to the electorate; they took their orders from London and imposed them—or tried to impose them—with only the barest show of consultation with the representatives of the Canadian people.

The remedy therefore was simple. The patient, that had been brought low by this clotting of the flow of blood which should nourish a free and vital spirit, should be given a massive dose of plasma to bring it to that state of health existing in the motherland. It should be given responsible government in the fullest sense—well, perhaps not quite in the fullest, for Lord Durham intended to reserve to the imperial government control of the Canadian constitution, foreign relations, trade and the disposal of public lands in the still unexplored territories. But in all domestic matters it was his aim that the new Canada should decide what it wanted without reference to Westminster or interference from Westminster, and that no manoeuvres of the British-appointed governor should receive support from London if they conflicted with the Canadian peoples' will. Like William IV faced with the massive demand for the Reform Bill, the governor could argue and cajole but would have to bow in the end.

It was "Radical Jack" speaking, not the man on the horse. And with a full knowledge of what he was proposing he spelt it out. "I admit," he wrote, "that the system which I propose would in fact place the internal government of the colony in the hands of the colonists themselves." The only consolation was that if they elected corrupt officials and passed bad laws the burden would fall on their own backs. And perhaps they would then learn to do better.

It was an act of faith—not fully implemented for some years and for which the author in the short lifetime left to him received little except abuse. But the Report was to prove its own justification in Britain and Canada. "I believe that the connexion," he wrote, "would only become more durable and advantageous by having men of equality, of freedom and of local independence." The doctrine supplied the wherewithal by which the Second British Empire flourished for nearly a century and also the whitewash used on its tomb.

VI

The Policy of Imperial Disintegration

For all its fame as a progressive document, the Durham Report was not without its imperialist side; London had exported to a colonial territory something more valuable to itself than goods or immigrants —the working model of a constitution made in Britain and designed to serve British ends. Its pedigree was unmistakably Whig: by necessity out of Fox's principle of "assimilation," which aimed to raise up the white-settlement colonies in our image. How fast the pace would be, how adaptable the system would prove and how far it would carry everyone, including India and the other non-white dependencies of the Crown, had not of course been glimpsed even by Durham himself. Eight years of shilly-shallying had to pass before, in the governor-generalship of his son-in-law, Lord Elgin, the principle of Responsible Government was applied and Canadian ministers were called to office—one of them a French-speaking *habitant* —whose sympathies in the past had been irredentist if not actively disloyal. Almost their first act was to pass a bill compensating rebels who had suffered losses in the late disturbances: a deliberate provocation which resulted in the burning of the provincial parliament by the Loyalist mob, outraged by Elgin's support of what seemed like treason to the good old cause.

Back in Britain the young Mr. Gladstone, that rising sprig of

Toryism, gravely rebuked the Whig government of Lord John Russell for permitting acts "essentially dishonourable to Imperial rights." How Dizzy must have laughed if he remembered those words twenty years later. At the time few cared, for neither imperialism nor Responsible Government was a popular cause, and the majority would probably have agreed with Lord Brougham that the amicable separation of Canada would be a positive gain to Britain, if not with the *Edinburgh Review* which a few years earlier had wished Canada and Nova Scotia still in the hands of the American Indians. Even the government was divided about its own policy, for as Lord Grey, the Colonial Secretary, confessed to Lord Elgin in 1849, "There begins to prevail in the House of Commons, and I am sorry to say in the highest quarters, an opinion (which I believe to be utterly erroneous) that we have no interest in preserving our colonies and ought to make no sacrifices for that purpose." He found such opinions existing within the cabinet itself, and Elgin agreed that even Secretaries of State had got into the habit of talking of the link between Canada and the mother country with so much indifference as to suggest "a disposition to prepare the way for separation," a policy which would certainly be acceptable to sections of Canadian opinion desiring annexation to the United States.

How then did it happen that in face of so much pessimism and rancour on both sides of the Atlantic "Responsible Government" had by 1854 become the rule throughout British North America, including even the offshore island of Newfoundland, setting the stage for similar experiments in the Pacific and South Africa which were in turn to lead to the growth of great self-governing dominions?

Probably it was the sheer force of inertia which made almost any settlement of a tiresome problem welcome both to pioneers struggling to build a new nation out of the wilderness and to statesmen in London grappling with what seemed more vital matters nearer home—for this was the time of the Chartist agitation, of O'Connell in Ireland, and the debate about the Corn Laws which led to the fall of protection and the triumph of free trade. Very few people had much faith in the solution which Lord Durham had proposed and Lord Elgin was imposing on an apparently ungrateful colony, but as the years passed and the threatened secessions did not occur, it began to dawn on thinking minds that the political machinery had been

invented that would keep the imperial train on the rails and obe-
dient to at least some of the signals sent to it from London.

It was a useful if surprising discovery. Yet political ties and levers
were only of secondary importance. Economics was what empires
were about—certainly the British Empire as it had developed by
mid-Victorian times—and here the picture was far less promising.
In a brilliant and bitter speech in 1849 Disraeli had laid the system
bare:

> I know very well that it is utterly vain for me to tell you that
> there are other considerations connected with this subject than the
> price of a pound of sugar. That is all past and the commercial
> principle now rules this country. We had an imperial principle in
> the time of those who preceded us, but you may rest assured
> that if you convert the Senate into a counting house, it will not be
> long before the nation degenerates into a factory.

He was the last person who had any right to preach political or
commercial idealism, for throughout his career he took up and
abandoned causes as they suited him and the interests of his party.
And if the cap fits, and we have here in two sentences the supreme
indictment of the Age of Cobden and of *laissez faire,* we must not
forget that the golden time to which Disraeli claimed to be looking
back (when principle and not sordid self-interest was the rule) had
existed more in his imagination than in fact. True, the select committee on aborigines in British settlements had proclaimed that the
main mission of the empire was to carry good government, civilisation and Christianity to the ends of the earth, but this was the creed
of visionaries, and when the Empire had really been founded on a
principle, that principle had been monopoly and its aim the enrichment of Britain and the supremacy of her fleets and commerce. When
first under Huskisson in the 1820s and then under Peel between
1841 and 1845 the shackles of monopoly were loosened, trade
liberalised and a system of moderate protection erected around the
Empire, there was still no single coherent imperial policy. The 1500
Acts affecting trade that had existed at the time of Waterloo had
been severely slashed—six hundred of them had been thrown over-

board by Huskisson in 1825—but even under Peel the system remained an incorrigible jumble of preferences at varying rates, with vestiges of monopoly still adhering in the diluted but still potent Navigation Acts. Inconsistencies were rife; no attempt was made to erect a true customs union of the empire on the lines of the recently created German *Zollverein;* and bewilderment was among the dominant feelings of those entrapped within the system. Listen for a moment to a Mr. William (later Sir William) Hutt presenting a petition to Parliament on behalf of certain Australian interests:

> You remove the duties from European wool and tell the Australian farmer that the proceeding is required by the principle of Free Trade, and then you insist on charging a duty on his corn and justify your conduct on the principle of protection and monopoly.

What was a poor colonial to do? And there was worse to come. From practising a system which was illogical but at least took notice of colonies and their commercial needs, the British government in the 1840s suddenly went over to a trading policy that was all logic but had no real reference to colonies at all.

*   *   *

If any one man was reponsible for breaking up the old fabric of monopoly, which had governed British commercial thinking since the time of Cromwell, that man was Huskisson during his tenure of the Board of Trade in the 1820s, when he set himself to achieve a general reduction of duty rates, a modification of the Navigation Acts and reciprocal trade agreements with foreign powers.

But this policy, though destructive of the old shibboleths of empire, had not been anti-imperialist in aim. On the contrary, it was an attempt to breathe fresh commercial life into an organism which had begun to atrophy through tariffs that were self-defeatingly high. It was under Huskisson—however imperfectly—that the unity of the Empire as one commercial entity devoted to the well-being at least of its white members was developed for the first and last time, and here if anywhere was the golden age to which Disraeli was referring.

Yet even in Huskisson's short lifetime his policy had been attacked, not by those who thought it too radical, but by those who thought it not radical enough. The doctrine of free trade had been making converts among the manufacturers and merchants, and with the founding of the Anti-Corn Law League the intellectual conversion of the nation began rapidly to be achieved, till in 1840 a committee of the House of Commons recommended that the whole system of protection be reviewed.

Cheap food, low production costs, the abolition of tariff barriers, free access to markets were all attractive notions to a country ideally placed by nature (as Lord Shelburne had pointed out half a century earlier) to dominate the sea routes. It was the opinion of Cobden, one of the religion's twin high priests, that this was the road not only to profits but to peace. Instead of commercial rivalries between nations, there would be amity and disarmament in a kind of Eden where the fruitful wealth of the world could be exchanged. Such men were untroubled by doubts whether trade rivals would follow England's example and throw their own markets open to British goods: as Manchester traders they found the merits of free trade unanswerable. And between them and political triumph, on ground already mined by their propaganda, stood only one bastion —the entrenched agricultural interest of the English squirearchy which depended on protection of its wheat and on a narrow protectionist majority in Parliament.

In 1845, after a series of good harvests, came the rains that rained away the Corn Laws. The Prime Minister, Sir Robert Peel, though pledged to protection, was already at heart a free trader waiting to be publicly converted by some sign. In 1844 he had abolished the duties on foreign wool. Now the poor harvest in England, the ruined potato crop and the imminence of famine in Ireland convinced him of the urgent need for the import of cheap foreign grain—and not for the duration of the emergency only, but for the future. Protection of British wheat must be swept away, foreign and colonial grains admitted at nominal duty; the people must be fed.

By these measures Peel did not save the Irish, two million of whom either died of famine or emigrated during the crisis. Nor did he bring down the price of wheat. As a practical measure the repeal of the corn laws achieved little, except an acute agricultural depression two decades later when the full tide of American prairie grain came tumbling in.

But as a symbol the repeal was of prime importance. At the blast of the trumpet the main citadel had crumbled, and what hope could there be for the sugar and timber and other interests which enjoyed no such massive parliamentary support as did the gentlemen of England? Protection had become a lost cause, and in 1853 even Disraeli and the Tories abandoned it as a thing "of rags and tatters." By 1860 the last vestiges had gone.

*   *   *

Now in this great reversal of the nation's trading policy, which set the tone for three quarters of a century and marked out the Victorian era from all others in our history, the colonies were not consulted. "Destroy this principle of Protection," the Tory statesman Lord Stanley had said, "and I tell you in this place that you destroy the whole basis on which your colonial system rests." It was his view that political independence would follow very closely on commercial independence, and who shall say in the light of the future that in the wider scale of things he was wrong?

Yet few believed this at the time and fewer cared. The outraged cries from colonies robbed of their preferences in British markets were not ignored—for they were used by the government as ammunition to destroy the Navigation laws—but the complainants were treated in a very governessy manner and sternly lectured on the vices of tariffs and the virtue of free trade. No doubt it was felt that with a little prodding and coaxing the colonies could be brought out from behind the protective fences they had been erecting, just as by the force of example foreign nations would hurry to justify the Manchester School's faith in them. That neither of these things happened was greatly distressing to Liberal minds. "If the imperial government," wrote the Colonial Secretary, the third Earl Grey, "is not to exercise its authority to prevent the general commercial policy we have adopted as best for the Empire at large from being thwarted by the measures of a particular colony, I should agree with Mr. Cobden in saying that the sooner we parted from our colonies the better."

Here, in the words of a man who genuinely believed in empire and thought that free trade would cement the bonds between colonies and the mother country, there is no inkling to be found of any sense of lost opportunity or any understanding of the viewpoint of young struggling agricultural nations compared with rich industrial ones like Britain which could ride the currents of free trade. But though doctrinaires like Grey insisted that colonies must accept decisions taken in their best interests in London, it was felt in return that some kind of relief should be given them for the loss of their preferences in English markets, and this pointed to unshackling them from the Navigation Acts which still tied the Empire's trade to British ships.

There is a good deal of irony to be found in the way a free-trade government proceeded to knock down the last pillar of monopoly by appeals to the sufferings of colonies which it had itself inflicted. Yet it would be wrong to imagine that cynicism played any part, for in the great debate over the fate of a system which for two hundred years had presided over the growth and glory of Britain there can be sensed, even on the reformers' side, among all but the high apostles of free trade, a kind of regret, an aura of genuine doubt over what was being done. Had not Adam Smith himself approved of the Navigation Acts, taking his stand on the priority which national defence must have over mere "opulence"? This support from the father of free trade took some explaining away. Even Gladstone, who spoke several times in the debates, was uncertain whether by repealing the laws without some kind of return from other nations which had their own versions of the Navigation Acts too much was not being given away on mere promises of reciprocity. For once he and Disraeli were more or less on the same side and went into the same division lobbies. And, of course, among the traditionalists there was only outrage against any tampering with the age-old system. Petitions against repeal came flooding in from almost every seaport in the country—24,700 signatures from Liverpool, the second commercial city of the Empire; 27,000 from London, from "persons of the most respectable classes," as their spokesman in the Commons was able to assure the House. What the unrespectable thought was not stated, but public opinion as a whole was probably against repeal. The thought of foreign ships in the ports of the colonies and mother country put the Marquess of Granby in mind of the Trojan Horse. And through the mouth of this same speaker we catch a fascinating glimpse of the old unregenerate England that had lost America and won Trafalgar and the Nile. Let Hansard tell the tale:

> Oh! (said the noble Marquess in conclusion) that I had the power to dispel the delusions with which we are now assailed! Oh that I had the power to stir up that patriotism and that love of country which should animate every breast! For if I had such power . . . I think I should see the gallant vessel that is now struggling with the storm sail triumphantly above the waves that threatened to overwhelm her. Sir, I have no fear for the result of this great question. Despite of all disadvantages, if Englishmen are but true to themselves and their country, we shall be able to weather through the storm that impends over us, we shall be able to retain the command over that glorious element that is our natural protector, and which is the connecting link between this country and the countries dependent on us abroad; and for years to come . . . the flag of England will float triumphant through every sea.

And so it did—so it continued to do for nearly a century. The Navigation Acts were repealed in substance if not in every detail, the Empire's trade was thrown open to all-comers, and though a recession followed in the immediate wake of repeal, by the 1880s the Empire's tonnage in merchant ships was more than 50 per cent of the world's total tonnage and in steam was more than double all the rest.

So had the "noble Marquess" been wrong? Had the Navigation laws become redundant?

They had probably become irrelevant to Britain's future on the seas, because a new factor had appeared most providentially on the scene—the advent of the iron ship which could be built more economically in Britain's yards than in those of her competitors. Even politically the old laws had outlived their usefulness and had become the cause of deep resentments in the colonies. But at least they had been a symbol, the outward and visible sign of an imperial unity which had been real enough; and with their passing and the conversion of Britain to free trade there went not only the lumber of restrictive laws but the underlying *reasons* for empire. If colonies received no advantages in trading with the motherland, much of the attraction of the motherland was gone. If trade was to be free, if colonies were to send and receive their goods in foreign ships, what was the use of colonies? In a world devoted to what Disraeli had called "the commercial principle," what repaid Britain for the expense of defending and garrisoning dependent territories?

These questions were crude but they were basic. There was to be a time in the heyday of a new imperialism, towards the century's end, when they ceased to be asked. But empire in any meaningful sense of unity had received a mortal blow with the repeal of protection and the Navigation Acts. The economic bond was severed and, despite later attempts, was never fully restored. What took its place was only "the projection of an empire," in Adam Smith's famous words of an earlier dominion. And for a while—for a period of twenty years—the British people tired even of that.

* * *

"If you look through the history of this country since the advent of Liberalism forty years ago," said Disraeli in his Crystal Palace speech in the summer of 1872, "you will find there has been no effort so continuous, so subtle, supported by so much energy and carried out with so much ability and acumen, as the attempts of liberalism to effect the disintegration of the Empire of England."

Of some Liberals this was grossly and manifestly untrue: the third Earl Grey and his henchman in Canada, Lord Elgin, had been true Liberal imperialists, far stauncher friends of the colonies than Disraeli, who as late as 1866 had been prepared to lose Canada and Africa in order to get "a good budget." "What is the use of these colonial deadweights which we do not govern?" The questioner was not Grey, not Cobden or Bright or even Mr. Gladstone, at whom the Crystal Palace speech had really been aimed—it was Disraeli himself, only six years before he set about branding his opponent with the mark of the beast.

Yet in a sense the indictment was not unjust. With two short interludes of Tory rule the Whigs were in power from the fall of Peel in 1846 to the fall of the Gladstone government in 1874, and this was precisely the period during which the anti-imperialist tide rose to its height and threatened to submerge all the old landmarks. There were ministers like Grey who stood out against it, and theorists who tried to reverse it with nostrums of their own—men like Edward Gibbon Wakefield and Charles Buller who had been with Durham in Canada and were offering new concepts of planned emigration to the virgin lands of North America and the Antipodes—but the influence of such men was limited, and in Professor Creighton's words: "There was scarcely a front rank statesman in early Victorian England who was not prepared to view the departure of the colonies with cheerfulness decorously mingled with resignation."

This was true of Russell, Granville, Gladstone, even Palmerston, on the Liberal side, and of all the cleverer Tories until Disraeli grabbed hold of the Empire as a vote winner in '72. Once the storm over the Navigation Acts was over, there was very little to interest anyone in colonial affairs; debates were poorly attended, and there was a general ignorance about these distant and costly possessions —if Mr. Micawber thought Australia "The Land, the Only Land" for himself and his family, he was only guessing.

And this carelessness about colonies, which amounted at times to active dislike of them, was not confined to politicians and the public but also animated the civil service, where Sir James Stephen, the virtual ruler of the Colonial Office, regarded at least the smaller of them as "wretched burdens to this country which in an evil hour we assumed." That they would soon be detached from the mother country was his heartfelt conviction—we have his son's word for it —and most of the permanent officials shared this view. So did the bulk of the press. *The Times* almost throughout the period was deeply hostile to the imperial idea, and even sympathisers like the *Quarterly Review* felt bound to recognise the inevitability of the day when "rich, prosperous and self-dependent colonies, grown into nations" would demand the ending of the partnership. As for the Manchester School, it never ceased uttering anathemas against ties which bound Britain to her colonies "by a mistaken notion of self-interest." The words were Cobden's, and even at dinner parties in the company of lively women he kept at it remorselessly, informing Lady Dorothy Nevill "time after time" (as she records in her *Reminiscences*) that we should be ruined by our foreign possessions.

So pervasive and universal was this climate of opinion that visiting statesmen from the colonies could hardly fail to notice it—"They want to get rid of us" was the view of the Canadian, Alexander

Galt, in 1867, just a year before the high-water mark of separatism was reached with the formation of a Gladstone ministry that had Bright at the Board of Trade and the strongly anti-imperialist Lord Granville in the colonial secretary's chair. "Gladstone and Co. deliberately intend to shake off the colonies," wrote the historian Froude, reading the same signs, and more in sorrow than in anger the *Saturday Review* summed up the melancholy lesson:

> Men who have accustomed themselves to appreciate nothing which they cannot weigh or count have added up the sum total of the expenditure which we incur on behalf of the colonies and have been wholly unable to discover a money equivalent which springs out of the once cherished relation. So much outlay for a mere sentiment is an extravagance which they cannot endure. The dream of a united nationality with its grasp on every quarter of the globe counts for nothing with these philosophers. The strength of traditional and hereditary bonds making one brotherhood of many kindred peoples is to them an idle fancy. Their eyes can see in colonial attachment to this country nothing but a desire to grasp practical independence and at the same time to evade its responsibilities. So, resolutely setting all sentiment on one side, they are ready to draw at once the logical inference from their narrow premises and to let the colonies depart in peace.

This was unjust, and it was almost certainly true that the government as a whole was not separatist in intention. They had only themselves to blame, however, if suspicions of their motives were widespread throughout the country. Mr. Gladstone's own explanations of his policy were hardly reassuring:

> There ought to be nothing to preclude the hope, when the growth of a colonial possession is such as to make separation from the mother country a natural and beneficial result, that that separation, so far from being effected by violence and bloodshed, might be the result of a peaceable and friendly transaction. Surely it is a great object to place, if possible, our colonial policy on such a footing, not for the purpose of bringing about a separation but

of providing a guarantee that, if such a separation should occur, it should be in a friendly way. That is the sense, the principle and the secret of our policy.

What did this mean? The Prime Minister's extraordinary powers of rhetoric were capable of infinite refinements of meaning, but his colonial secretary, Lord Granville, had certainly been feeding Canadian opinion with hints that separation would not be unwelcome in London, and the foreign secretary, Lord Clarendon, had privately expressed himself as favouring the outright annexation of Canada to the United States. "We can't throw them off" was the limit of this statesman's commitment to the imperial idea, and in the public actions of the government there was more than a suggestion that, this being so, a little leverage here and there, a little financial pressure and the gradual tightening of screws, might work the trick and get these troublesome colonial incubi to remove themselves of their own free will.

To make them pay their share of the costs of garrison troops was only common sense. Too much insistence on this principle had been one of the causes of the loss of the Old Thirteen, but times had changed, and in an age that took a more realistic view of values and obligations such burdens could not be borne for ever. Even in Grey's time the colonies had been faced with demands for contribution, and these continued to rise as the "commercial principle" became accepted as the yardstick by which such things were judged. Canada always got special treatment and an actual increase in garrison troops during the American Civil War, when hostilities between Britain and the North had loomed dangerously close, but in the East Asian colonies, in Australia, New Zealand and at the Cape, peremptory demands were made for subsidies towards imperial defence and garrisons were thinned out without apparent reference to colonial needs.

This process reached its height in 1869 in relation to New Zealand, where a Maori uprising caused the colonial government to request the postponement of troop withdrawals and the backing of a loan. Both were refused by Lord Granville in terms so sharp as to raise an outcry in the colonial press. "The despatches of Earl Granville," wrote the *New Zealand Herald*, "have caused no small

amount of indignation in this colony. . . . Contempt and haughti-
ness are to be found in almost every line, and studied insult in
every sentence." Such treatment, the paper feared, would make
people feel that connection with Britain was neither "beneficial nor
pleasing," and a month later, bitterly complaining that the colony
had been left to bear the brunt of attacks by savages whom British
"pseudo-philanthropists" had incited into rebellion while British
soldiers were kept in their barracks, "idle spectators" of the struggle,
its leader-writer burst out into impassioned and scathing protest:
"This is that assistance which Great Britain affords us! This is what
a nation once the proudest and noblest in the world has fallen
to! . . . We could almost wish it a pity that the English ship out-
sailed the Frenchman's little more than a quarter of a century ago,
and was the first to plant its flag in these islands."

That men of British stock should express even half a wish to live
under the tricolour! No wonder that at home the *Standard* thought
the "policy of Imperial disintegration" was proceeding merrily and
that Lord Granville's skill in the art of goading a colony was being
rewarded with a success which was calculated to make the shade of
Lord North "turn pale with envy."

And not with regard to New Zealand alone, for there was trouble
also with Tasmania over Britain's responsibility for the convicts she
had dumped there: which obligation was being dishonoured by a
government seized with "a perfect gush of repudiation," with a
"kind of confiscating, disestablishing and dilapidating mania." "A
few more such despatches as that of Lord Granville," the *Standard*
ended, "and the new Liberal scheme of Empire will become perfect. There will be no colonies."

VII

The Brightest Jewel in the Crown

"Well! When we break in Europe," wrote Horace Walpole in the troubled year before Yorktown, "we may pack up and move to India and be emperors again."

There was to be no break in Europe, but in other respects he was a good prophet, and the same half century after Waterloo that saw Britain increasingly defensive and separatist where all her white colonies except Ireland were concerned saw also a burst of imperialism in the East, which by the 1850s had brought almost the whole of India, Ceylon and parts of Burma into British control. Alike under Pitt, Wellington's High Tories, the more liberal Canningites, Lord John Russell's Whigs, the pragmatical Peel and the Whigs again after his fall, the advance had continued. Where its pace varied it was often in direct contradiction to political trends at home. Thus, the enlightened period of the Durham Report coincided with the shameless invasion of Afghanistan, a sovereign state outside India's historic borders; and the granting of Responsible Government to Canada in 1849 was coupled in the East with the second Sikh war and the annexation of the Punjab.

It may seem on the face of it odd that a nation should behave like Doctor Jekyll at its front door and Mr. Hyde at the back, but there were sound historical reasons for it, and few Englishmen believed that the methods had been greedy or tyrannical. The intentions—certainly of the home government—were of the best. The too bellicose governor generals were recalled. Their annexations were not handed back. How could they be? It would have meant returning states and human souls to anarchy in breach of Burke's "trusteeship" principle which had replaced the trading principle as the British *raison d'être* in India—another clear reversal of trends at home.

For since the break-up of the Mogul empire in the middle of the eighteenth century India had fallen into a chaos of warring states, of brigandage, bloodshed and corruption, in which the East India Company's three presidencies of Calcutta, Madras and Bombay stood out like oases of order and comparative plenty. The inevitable happened. Efficient organisms swallowed inefficient ones. Acting defensively at first to shield Madras and its buffer state of the Carnatic against attacks from Mysore, the Company had overrun and pacified most of southern India, incorporating some of its territory and leaving the rest under the rule of princes bound to it by treaty. From Bengal it had simultaneously been moving westward across the plain of the Ganges into the central states, where it was faced with Oudh, a weak and misgoverned puppet kingdom, the friendly Rajput princes south of Delhi, the Mahratta confederacy occupying a huge arc of land in the centre of the peninsula between Bombay and Gwalior, and in the west the equally warlike Sikhs in Kashmir and the Punjab.

All these were eaten up or "protected" in turn—in fairness it should be said that the Company was by no means always the aggressor. In 1817 the last of the Mahratta wars ended with the pacification of central India; in 1849 the Sikhs were tamed and the Punjab annexed. Some years earlier Lord Ellenborough had taken Sind at the mouth of the Indus to round off control of the western coasts and is said to have announced his coup in the shortest, most cynical and possibly apocryphal diplomatic despatch ever sent: *"Peccavi"* ("I have sinned")—a confession which a later governor general, Lord Dalhousie, might have echoed in 1856 when with a fine show of outraged morality at native misgovernment he annexed the state of Oudh.

If this had happened anywhere else, the outcry in Parliament would have been enormous: where India was concerned, it scarcely raised a murmur from the humanitarians. And this was traditional, for as early as 1780 Horace Walpole had complained that the seizure of a "trifling district in India" with four million sterling in revenue had hardly been thought worth mentioning in the London press.

Then it had been indifference—there had been a war to be thought of much nearer home. But even in Walpole's time the germ of Britain's special relationship with India could be distinguished, and with the loss of the American colonies, its true nature had emerged as a dual principle of responsibility and dependence—responsibility, because backward peoples were a charge on advanced ones; dependence, because India had succeeded the Old Thirteen as the indispensable makeweight without which Britain would sink to the status of a second-class power.

It was this replacement of one reliance by another, this clutching at the substitute "jewel" in the nation's crown, that accounted for much of the emotional involvement of Britain with India and for the easy conscience with which each increase in control was greeted by public opinion. India meant opportunity and obligation. What she needed was firm guidance from the centre, protection against foreign states, just laws, an equitable tax system, internal peace, a common language, better communications, irrigation, a police force, schools—all things which only Britain could supply. That the British had not originally come to India to supply them had long since been forgotten. The old trading company with its scattered factories around the coasts and its modest diplomatic contacts with suzerains in Delhi had graduated over the years into one centralised all-powerful bureaucracy whose business was no longer business but the government of India from Cape Comorin to the Himalayas. The nabobs had been succeeded by a new kind of man. Where India was concerned even most free traders were Imperialists.

*   *   *

That this was a prodigious achievement was recognised by those who were most opposed to it, like Cobden, who found this ruling of one hundred and forty million people by "a Committee of Stockholders in Leadenhall Street" a "perilous adventure." Thomas Babington Macaulay agreed that it was strange that a Joint Stock Company should run an empire, "But what constitution," he added, "can we give to our Indian Empire which shall not be strange?"

He was speaking in 1833 in a Parliamentary debate and in a famous passage went on:

> That a handful of adventurers from an island in the Atlantic should have subjugated a vast country divided from the place of their birth by half the globe . . . a country which Trajan never entered—a country lying beyond the point where the phalanx of Alexander refused to proceed—that we should govern a territory ten thousand miles from us—a territory larger than France, Spain, Italy and Germany put together . . . a territory inhabited by men differing from us in race, colour, language, morals, religion—these are prodigies. . . . Reason is confounded. We interrogate the past in vain.

Others nearer the scene felt this sense of wonder, not only for the achievement of empire over such a country but for India herself. "It gave me inexpressible pleasure," wrote Sir William Jones, who in 1784 had founded the Royal Asiatic Society of Bengal, "to find myself in the midst of so noble an amphitheatre . . . the scene of glorious actions, fertile in the productions of human genius," and this thread of admiration for an ancient culture runs through the thought of many of the best minds, from Burke to Warren Hastings and Thomas Munro, who found Indian society finer in grain than that of the conquerors in many of its aspects, particularly in the practice of charity and hospitality.

These were men of intellect and sensibility. Not all the Company's servants were of this kind; but in the early days by the very nature of things even the coarsest of them found themselves thrown into close contact with the native population, and if they did not love India, at least they did not despise its people for the colour of their skins; their snobbery was social, not racial, and as G. O. Trevelyan wrote many years later, few officers of that time would have been "ashamed to call a native by the name of 'friend' and would have been very much ashamed to talk of him by the appellation of 'nigger.' " Nor would they have been ashamed of having native mistresses and introducing them into society—in the 1790s William Hickey, that prolific recorder of the Anglo-Indian scene, had delighted in his spirited and lovely Jemdanee, who lived with him, respected and admired as a general favourite by all his friends. It was for Jemdanee that he set up in his country home, his "little *château*" on the river at Chinsurah, thirty miles from Calcutta, and when she died in childbirth he mourned her with tender sincerity— "Thus did I lose as gentle and affectionately attached a girl as ever man was blessed with."

He might almost have been speaking of a wife from home, but this state of racial harmony which we glimpse sometimes in the writings of the time did not last, could not perhaps have lasted, once the British ceased to be petitioners of native princes and took over the government of vast territories. Even Trevelyan, who was thoroughly sympathetic towards India, thought there was something about the country that made the amalgamation of conquerors and conquered "an impracticable idea": a notion which one finds echoed in our own century in the closing words of E. M. Forster's *A Passage to India*. Not long after the departure of Warren Hastings this perhaps inevitable trend had become evident to those with eyes to see, for we find his friend General Palmer writing to him in terms all too prophetic of what was to come:

> But little or no attention is paid to the Vakils of the native courts by Lord Wellesley. They are not permitted to pay their respects to him oftener than two or three times a year, which I think is as impolitic as it is ungracious. The above mentioned gentlemen all retain the strongest attachment to you. And indeed the sentiment is general among the natives. . . . I observe with great concern the system of depressing them adopted by the present government and imitated in the manners of almost every European. They are excluded from almost all posts of great respectability or emolument, and are treated in society with mortifying hauteur and reserve. In fact, they have hardly any social intercourse with us.

Macaulay too foresaw the danger that members of the ruling nation might consider themselves a superior class—an easy enough assumption in an already caste-ridden society. By the time he had spoken, it was already too late: the thing had happened. With the rapid increase in the number of Englishmen and of their *Mem-*

sahibs—that *escadrille volante* of eager brides who made the lot of their menfolk bearable and helped them to lose the country in the end—the system became set, for as T. S. Spear tells us in *The Nabobs,* it became no longer customary for the Company's agents on arriving at a station to call on the local notables, and indeed certificates of respectability were soon being required of natives before they could receive the courtesy of a chair to sit on during visits to British officials. That the general officer commanding should demean himself by standing in the presence of a "dirty miserable old dog" (who was, in fact, the Mogul Emperor) was a cause of outraged comment among these parvenu invaders. Gone were the days when it had been by no means unusual for Englishmen to wear native clothes, chew betel, take Persian wives, study Indian literature and art: now, noted a sharp-eyed observer, Maria Graham, as early as 1811, it was their boast to be "outrageously a John Bull." She was speaking of English society in the towns, and of course among the senior administrators on the councils and among the district officers in the villages there was often much affection— even love—for those under their charge. But taken at their best these feelings were paternalistic, and if foreign conquerors, as Thomas Munro observed, had in the past treated the natives with violence and great cruelty, few had regarded them with so much scorn as the English or had stigmatised a whole people as unworthy of their trust.

Munro, one of the most experienced of the Company's servants, was not alone in his views. Bishop Heber from another standpoint castigated our "foolish surly national pride" in shutting out the natives from our society and for the "bullying insolent manner" so often used towards them. No doubt much of this came from ignorance, from an attitude of mind which Maria Graham had observed among the brash young newcomers to the country who were so taken up with their own imaginary importance that they disdained to learn and had nothing to teach. "They esteem themselves too highly," wrote a French observer, Victor Jacquemont; "they despise the coloured races too much even to be flattered by their homage." As for the English women, their contemptuous attitude of mind which E. M. Forster deplored in the 1920s is presaged in Meadows Taylor's most interesting novel, *Seeta,* set in the period just before the Mutiny of 1857 though published a generation later. Where Hickey's "favourite" Jemdanee was admired and accepted in society, poor Seeta, an Englishman's lawful wife by Hindu rites, suffers sadly at the hands of the *Mem-sahibs* of "Noorpoor." "The woman is here, actually among us!" is their outraged cry. They find it horrible, "positively a shocking public indecency"; and though it is agreed that Seeta is in colour as fair as any of them, it makes no difference—"she's a native and they are all niggers."

From this novel the white menfolk of "Noorpoor" emerge with slightly more credit than their ladies, particularly Seeta's husband, Cyril Brandon, whom we are told had "many native friends of all classes" and had studied native manners and customs deeply. But our author goes on straightway to lament the other kind of Englishman, impliedly very much in the majority, to whom India was "an infernal hole," who spoke and thought arrogantly of its people, holding them to be "black fellows" unworthy of sympathy and friendship.

For such attitudes, always more prevalent among the less educated of the conquerors, there were some explanations if not excuses, for it was a hard life the Company's servants lived, far from home, in a vile climate, before in the middle of the century the retreat to hill stations became the norm during the worst of the weather. "Died unmarried in Calcutta" reads a line in my grandmother's handwriting on a photograph of a portrait of one of her great-uncles who made the one-way journey to the Hooghly. He has an engagingly cynical air, and I can understand why my grandmother, an Army chaplain's widow in the '80s, gave him so curt an epitaph. His was no unusual fate. On an evening's drive out of town Maria Graham passed the English burial ground and was appalled by its size and the youth of those who lay there under their monumental tombstones. A soldier might go through three battles of Waterloo with no greater risk to his life than he incurred during a year's residence in Fort William (Calcutta), wrote G. O. Trevelyan in *The Competition Wallah,* and this was much later in the century when the medical services were presumably more efficient than in my great-great-great-uncle's time. On Trevelyan's count, made just after the Sepoy Mutiny of 1857, sixty-four of every thousand soldiers quartered in Bengal and forty-four of their wives died annually, the mortality rate among the officers being nearly three times higher than in London. After his first year in Calcutta, Trevelyan wrote, an Englishman could no longer sleep as he once slept, could no longer eat as he once ate, and would be lucky if he drank no more than he once drank. Mental faculties deteriorated. The mind like the body became languid and flabby; men lived on the capital of their energy and intellect stored up during the cooler days:

> The hot weather has set in. These words may convey to you no very definite idea beyond the general one of punkahs and iced champagne; but to us they are the earnest of miseries which are unutterable. The amenities of life are over for the year. The last waltz has been danced in the assembly rooms; the last wicket has been pitched on the cricket ground; the the last tiffin eaten in the Botanical gardens; the last couple married in the cathedral at the very sensible and uncanonical hour of half past five in the afternoon. People have settled themselves down to be clammy, and gloomy and hepatic for six grilling months.

If Plato's "Guardians" had been in charge of such a country, what would they have made of it? Would there not have been injustices? And resentments among the governed? Perhaps the miracle is that for three quarters of a century after Pitt's India Bill the British met with so few setbacks and there was so wide a tolerance on both sides.

The watershed was, of course, the Mutiny of 1857. It was not a rising of India or of all the sepoy armies, for only that of Bengal was affected, but in the course of it enough was done to sharpen a racial cleavage that was never wholly healed. G. O. Trevelyan, who was on the scene soon afterwards, describes the defeat of a British column in the first days of the revolt when it seemed that the *Raj* would be swept away for ever:

> Some of the fugitives were shot down as they ran. Others, disabled by wounds or fatigue, were overtaken and slain. Others again, who sought preservation by leaving the line of flight, were mobbed and knocked on the head by the peasants of the neighbouring villages. More than one unfortunate European, who, after being pursued for miles, took to the water like a tired stag, was beaten to death

with bludgeons from the brink of the pond in which he had taken refuge. All who remained on the ground in the vicinity of the temple, whether dead or alive, were hung on the trees which fringed the road.

The shock of such events was all the sharper because to the vast majority they were so totally unexpected. Even many of those in closest contact with the sepoys refused to see the signs of coming trouble which to wiser minds had been evident for months, and that this blindness was not confined to the military, whose trust in their men was as poignant as it was disastrous, is shown by the fact that *The Times* correspondent in Bombay was reporting the "perfect tranquility pervading the whole of India" at the actual moment when the first news of the outbreak came in from Meerut.

Trust had been betrayed. For a while it seemed that the whole huge investment in India was at risk. And as the atrocity stories gathered strength and the papers were filled with tales of savage murders, rapes and the butchery of children, a kind of racial hysteria burst out among all but the sanest, "a rabid and indiscriminate vindictiveness" in the Governor-General's words, a spirit that looked only to revenge.

Eighty years earlier the Black Hole of Calcutta had outraged the nation, but it had been kept in perspective as an isolated act. Now the brutalities and treachery of the Nana Sahib at Cawnpore were repaid in kind wherever a mutinous sepoy could be hunted down. In a speech at Westminster, Fowell Buxton, deploring the "tempest of rage" which filled his countrymen, quoted a magistrate as reported in the Anglo-Indian press who boasted he had "hanged ninety-five human beings and hoped to complete the round hundred on the morrow"; of another who expressed delight at "the shrieks of the writhing victims beneath the blood-stained lash." Buxton went on to read from an officer's letter after a battle:

We champagned it that night and drank confusion to the Pandies. . . . The stragglers that are brought into camp by the Natives (for the dear villagers are beginning to sell the Pandies to us—unarmed 30 rupees, armed 50 rupees) are hanged, shot or blown away from guns. We polished off a risaldar yesterday.

The tone is unmistakable. It is one from which all pity, all humanity has been banished, and one can understand the compassionate Trevelyan's wonder when all was over that "English Christians could talk to other English Christians of 'fine bags,' not of hares and pheasants but of human beings." In the same debate in which Buxton had spoken a Mr. Rich quoted from another letter in the Anglo-Indian press: "We are hanging them by dozens: every Sepoy without a certificate is hanged at once; the Zamindars are giving them up to us to be hanged right and left—those who harbour them or who do not give instant information of their whereabouts are hung themselves. We are making good work of it." According to Rich, a Calcutta paper had urged that Oudh should be made "one great slaughterhouse" and that those who escaped our bayonets and the knives of the Gurkhas should be driven into the swamps to be devoured by wild beasts. "Hear, hear!" a Captain Scott interjected at this point in the debate, and the next speaker to rise contemptuously dismissed Rich's plea for sanity as "morbid sensibility." "There was only one prayer," wrote a contributor to the *Englishman*, "and that was that everyone should meet death after a fair trial." Gilbert's *Mikado* could hardly have done better, and that this sentiment had reached even that hive of progressive causes, the Oxford Union, is proved by a debate which G. O. Trevelyan attended in which the following words were used:

> When the rebellion has been crushed out from the Himalayas to Comorin; when every gibbet is red with blood; when every bayonet creaks beneath its ghastly burden; when the ground in front of every cannon is strewn with rags and flesh and shattered bone;—then talk of mercy. Then you may find some to listen. This is not the time.

This peroration, Trevelyan remarks, was received with a tumult of applause.

*   *   *

A spirit of revenge so alien to Victorian England's established traditions of tolerance and "fair play" would not have lasted long, even under a Governor-General far less humane than "Clemency" Canning.

When the killing stopped it became the aim to give a new deal to India—a new and more logical power structure that replaced the anomalies of government by Cobden's "Committee of Stokholders in Leadenhall Street" and vested British India (though not, of course, the protected princely states in treaty relationships with it) squarely under the rule of a Viceroy and Council responsible to a Secretary of State in London,* who was responsible, in turn, to Parliament and the British electorate—the first step along the constitutional road that other colonies had been following towards eventual independence.

But the achievement of that goal lay nearly a century ahead, and if the new settlement proved anything at the time, it was British determination to stay in India and govern it resolutely. The traumatic shock of the Mutiny made what had so nearly been lost seem infinitely more desirable. English attitudes towards Indians stiffened noticeably in the years that followed—one has only to compare the world of comradeship whose passing Trevelyan laments in *The Competition Wallah* with the chilling relationships existing in E. M. Forster's Chandrapore.

For the British an investment had been rescued and reclaimed. Faults of management had been committed: they would be rectified. Trust had been abused: it would not be given so wholeheartedly again. As early as 1812 James Mill had been of the opinion that "a simple form of arbitrary government tempered by European honour and European intelligence" was the only possible form of rule for Hindustan, and if the harshness of this prescription was to be tempered in some respects in our actual administration of the country, its spirit lived on in a growing divorce between the rulers and the ruled.

The British, long established as custodians, turned themselves into a caste. It took a man like Trevelyan to remember that the indigenous natives of the place had had a vigorous and elaborate culture when in Britain "wild in woods the noble marquis ran"; that there had been merchants at large in that community between the Indus

---

* The Secretary of State also had a council to advise him, composed of men with wide experience of India.

and Ganges when beside the Thames "Fortnum and Mason were doing a booming trade in acorns, and Swan and Edgar were doing a good thing in woad." Kipling's India, in fact, was on the wing—the world of the British club, the princely tiger shoot, the Simla gossip, the tightly enclosed world of Anglo-India which to the newcomer seemed so alien and irrelevant to the teeming life outside the cantonment walls. Just after the Mutiny, Trevelyan noticed its extraordinary sybaritic side—the "time honoured palanquin" in which he set out on a journey accompanied by a suite of "sixteen bearers, two fellows with torches and four banghy wallahs to carry the luggage," and the Josh Sedleys he met on the way complete with a *"batterie de cuisine"* in a state which would not have displeased the Emperor Jehangir at the height of his power. Such a style had become traditional from the time of the nabobs. When William Hickey left India in 1808 he listed his retainers: 1 butler, 1 steward, 8 kitmudars (table servants), 1 hairdresser, 2 aubdars (wine waiters), 1 comprador, 2 bakers, 2 cooks, 9 bearers, 5 hircarrahs (messengers), 3 mussaulgees (torch-bearers), 4 maullays (gardeners), 1 tailor, 2 durwans (door-keepers), 2 washermen, 1 tinner, 2 maters (under servants), 1 sweeper, 4 grooms, 3 grass cutters, 2 beestees (water carriers) and a coachman—58 hungry mouths to feed.

Those who experienced this luxury, this sense of an infinity of bondservants to work the *punkah,* to hand the *Burra-sahib* his shirt, to cook for him, clean for him, sweep for him, to pitch his tent, to cut the tennis court, to hold the stirrup while he mounted his horse, never forgot it—witness Winston Churchill who to the end of his days remained in some respects the cavalry subaltern he had been in the nineties.

And these were only pale individual reflections of the *Raj,* of the vice-regal court, the uniforms, the elephants, the trunk roads crossing the plains and mountains, the railway lines, the vast and intricate web of finance and trade that tied Britain to India and made of a small Atlantic island one of the chief arbiters of world power across the globe. Not till the late 1870s did the newly coined word "imperialism" cease to mean the machinations of Second Empire France and become associated with what Britain and her European rivals were doing among the coloured races of the world. But certainly in India Britain had become an imperialist power in the modern sense of that term. She had no reservations about it as she had else-where. She was in India to stay.

*   *   *

Nevertheless, even here the anti-Imperialist serum had been in-jected at least as early as 1794, when Parliament had declared that to pursue schemes of conquest and extension of domination in India were measures repugnant to the wish, the honour and the policy of the nation.

A quarter of a century later the Governor-General, Lord Hastings, was envisaging a time not very remote "when England will on sound principles of policy wish to relinquish the domination which she had gradually and unintentionally assumed over this country," and though perhaps this comes rather oddly from a man who, unin-tentionally or not, enlarged that "domination" by several tens of thousands of square miles, it is at least significant that he should have felt impelled to volunteer such words which pointed to a very different India from the one he was administering.

A man can usually be judged by the subordinates he keeps around him, and Lord Hastings, to his credit, had some very good ones—Thomas Munro, for instance, one of the best servants India ever had, who looked to the day when those he had in trust would overcome their "superstitions" and become sufficiently enlightened to "form a regular government for themselves." When such a time came, Munro thought, it would probably be best for both countries if British control were gradually withdrawn. His contemporary, Mountstuart Elphinstone, was also in no doubt that when India came to herself she would expect first a share in her own government and *then the whole*—a sentiment expressed by another of the Company's most distinguished servants, Henry Lawrence, who a full decade be-fore the Mutiny saw that we could not expect to hold India for ever but could hope, perhaps, that the end of the connection between the peoples would be marked by "mutual esteem and affection" and that India would become for Britain "a noble ally, enlightened and brought into the scale of nations under her guidance and fostering care."

"Enlightened" was a fine word, but few of those who were legis-lating and thinking for India would have chosen to use it; they were all too sombrely aware that in relation to the vast problems of India they were men "walking in darkness," in Macaulay's words. But by the token of their own passionately held faith in a democratic system, they rejected the continuance of that darkness and wished to penetrate it and bring light to India and to Britain's relationship with her. "No nation," said Macaulay in his great speech in Parliament in 1833—"No nation can be perfectly well governed till it is competent to govern itself." Indianisation must therefore come. "We are free, we are civilised to little purpose, if we grudge to any portion of the human race an equal measure of freedom and civilisation." And then in the peroration, in perhaps the most celebrated words used of India by a British statesman before the declarations of the Attlee government at independence, Macaulay foresees a time when Indians may demand European institutions for themselves—"Whether such a day will ever come I know not. But never will I attempt to avert or to retard it. Whenever it comes it will be the proudest day in British history."

*   *   *

If these words were sincere—and in spite of a certain air of "Jam to-morrow" about the phrasing there can be no doubt that Macaulay, the spokesman of liberal opinion, *was* sincere—then they implied that India must be groomed and educated by her foreign rulers for her role as an enlightened and independent nation.

In 1813 the Governor-General had been induced by Parliamentary pressure to earmark a lak of rupees, £10,000, annually out of the rents, revenues and profits of the Company's territories for "the revival and improvement of literature," the "encouragement of the learned natives of India," and for the "introduction or promotion of knowledge of the sciences among the inhabitants."

For the next thirty years the company sat rather peevishly on this nest egg, but by 1834, when Macaulay arrived in person on the Indian scene as legal member of the Governor-General's council and president of the Committee of Public Instruction, the kind of education that the Company should provide for its subjects had become a burning issue—a remarkable fact in itself, since in Britain this was the age when Dr. Wackford Squeers's establishment at Dotheboys Hall and Dr. Creakle's Academy for young gentlemen were both flourishing.

As to what should be done for India (where apart from primitive native schools and a few missionary foundations there was no education worthy of the name) the Committee of Public Instruction was deeply divided. On one side stood the "Orientalists," who respected Indian culture and wished to use its languages and methods as the basis for advance: on the other, the "Anglicists" or "Westerners," who were determined to tear up everything indigenous root and branch, to replace it with a system that would educate a small native *élite* in the English language and western thought, in the pious hope that this knowledge would gradually filter down like water through porous rock to irrigate the whole mass of illiterate India.

Into this argument Macaulay, fresh from his Parliamentary triumphs, threw himself with his accustomed energy. He was not a man who suffered greatly from self-doubt—"I wish," remarked one less-confident soul, "that I could be as certain about anything as Tom Macaulay is of *everything*"—and as a man of the enlightenment it was from the first inevitable that this herald of its virtues should react with generous and indignant anger against what native "superstitions" had done to India: the widespread killing of unwanted female children; the abominable practice of *Suttee,* by which unrecorded thousands of Hindu widows had been driven by social pressures to their deaths in the flames of their husbands' funeral pyres; the macabre rituals of *Thuggee* and, even worse, the system of *Meriahs,* by which villagers would fatten a human scarifice as one might a pig before dismembering it in scenes which would have been familiar to the *Bacchae* of Euripides.

From these horrors Macaulay drew certain deductions. All natives cultures were bad. Where they were not cruel, they were obscurantist, ridiculous, altogether unworthy of consideration in any educational policy for the future. For what indeed, as he scornfully demanded in a famous Minute for the council, could be made of "medical doctrines which would disgrace an English farrier, astronomy which would move laughter in girls at an English boarding school, history abounding in kings 30 feet high and reigns 30,000 years long, and geography made up of seas of treacle and seas of butter"?

In fact, Macaulay had only the most rudimentary knowledge of the culture he was deriding. He belonged in spirit to the school of the Governor-General of the time, Lord William Bentinck, a man equally devoted to progressive causes who had the luminous idea of pulling down the Taj Mahal and selling its marble at auction. Nor were beliefs in kings thirty feet high and seas of treacle and butter much more unlikely marvels than Macaulay's own naïve conviction that Western educational methods would ensure that within thirty years there would not be a single idolater among the respectable classes in Bengal! Yet if there was any one man who settled the future course of Indian education under the *Raj,* then Macaulay was that man—his prestige allied to a burning belief in the rightness of his cause settled the great debate in favour of the "Westerners," and though in the century that followed there were many attempts to reverse that decision, the pattern had been set, the intention had been formed not to build up from the grass roots through primary and technical education to raise the peasant masses, but to rely rather on the process of "filtration" down, to work through a small high school and college-trained *élite,* a class of persons who, in another of Macaulay's resounding phrases, would be "Indian in blood and colour, but English in tastes, in opinions, in morals and in intellect."

From this, great events were to flow, if hardly in the direction that Macaulay had envisaged. He was not wholly wrong. Indeed, among the nobility and the warrior caste in the northern and western provinces his prophecy was largely justified—one has only to look at any group photograph taken in late-Victorian times of the officers of a Sikh, Pathan or Punjabi regiment to see that only the turbans and the complexions distinguish British from Indians; the martial attitudes even down to the curl of the moustaches are invariably the same. Yet—and here is the irony—the warrior caste was precisely the one where Macaulay's education was most scorned. What the Sikhs and the Rajputs took from Britain and adopted as their own was not the English syllabus as taught to *babus* in the high schools and colleges of Calcutta and Benares; it was the comradeship of the camp, western military skills, the uniforms, the ceremonial, the bands and pennons, a frontier code. In such circles intellect was of small account; loyalties were everything, and so it remained through years of staunch mutual devotion to the end, when one of the world's greatest fighting forces found itself split into two.

But of course it was not sepoys whom Macaulay had had in mind when in his Minute of 1834 he visualised an India with English tastes, appetites, even soul. He had been thinking of the "mild Bengalee," a biddable and unwarlike race whose natural bent for law and letters he hoped to encourage along English lines as an example for the rest.

And even here Macaulay's naïve vision found at first a kind of justification. Chiefly in Bengal, but spreading outwards till in the end it reached the frontier territories beyond the Indus and the jungles of the Deccan, a rage developed among the new intelligentsia to be trained in English speech and methods—it was the only road to government service and the higher branches of the law, the two prestigious professions in the towns.

From the old "Orientalist" lobby warning voices made themselves heard—was it wise to train generations of high-grade clerks for low-grade jobs, often for no jobs at all? for it was not till very late in the day that Indians were to be admitted on anything like equal terms to the coveted posts in the "covenanted" civil service which their abilities merited. And was the system that had grown out of Macaulay's doctrines providing more than a veneer of western culture? The old jibe about the *babu* boasting of his "Failed B.A." was never as funny as it must have sounded in the British club—it masked real personal tragedies and was a commentary on a system set on self-destructive courses. What should the product of such an educational system do if he failed to qualify, or if he qualified and found no suitable employment? Go back to his village, to the apathetic and desperately poor environment from which he had tried to rise? Engineering, agricultural and technical education were not entirely neglected, for as time went on attempts were made by the authorities to meet this growing need, but they were pitifully inadequate, and far too many of the ambitions which education stimulated in the schools were stifled after graduation.

None of this happened all at once: it was a gradual process. The Indian National Congress was not founded till 1885 and for many years remained a body with modest ambitions, deeply subservient to the *Raj* and to an empire in whose benefits it merely hoped to share. But inherent in the *élite* which British educational policies had fostered lay the seeds of a future nationalism which was bound in the end to use Western theories as justifications for casting out Western rule. Since India in the future was to be the pacemaker, the exemplar of coloured nationalism, this fact was of immense importance. The way was prepared for it in the high noon of British rule.

VIII

The Jingoes

In 1874 Gladstone fell from power to be succeeded by Disraeli, and the most interesting quarter century in Britain's colonial history began.

This was in no sense due to the new Prime Minister, whose many great qualities did not include much feeling for the colonies as such. "Tell me," said Mr. Gladstone to Lady Dorothy Nevill at a dinner party after his rival's death, "Tell me, Lady Dorothy, upon your honour have you ever heard Lord Beaconsfield* express any particular fondness for the primrose? The gorgeous lily, I think, was more to his taste." And indeed it was as an adornment, a piece of exotic decoration, that Dizzy thought of the Empire over which he presided. Still, though he did little for it except elevate its queen into an empress and use his native eye for a bargain to corner the Suez Canal, it remains a fact that his last administration was the signal for a quite astonishing burst of creative thinking and dynamic action in the imperial field.

This period, which lasted well beyond his lifetime, till 1900, is now widely deplored—it was "Jingo," it was brash, it resulted in bloodshed and injustice, and it made Britain's name hated over a large sector of the globe. Let us list some of the things that happened in that extraordinary era—a clamour for war against Russia in defence

* Disraeli was created Earl of Beaconsfield in 1876.

of Turkey, the most backward and barbarous of the great powers; the occupation of Egypt; a confrontation with France over spheres of influence on the Upper Nile, with Germany over South-West Africa, with Russia again over Pandjeh; the repression of Irish nationalism and the defeat of two Home Rule bills; a war of conquest and revenge in the Sudan; the acquisition of Cyprus; the annexation of the Transvaal, Baluchistan, Socotra and Upper Burma; the foundation of protectorates over Bechuanaland, northern and southern Nigeria, Uganda and part of Somaliland; the virtual destruction of the Zulus and the Matabele; the foundation of the Rhodesias; an invasion of Afghanistan; the Jameson Raid; two Boer wars. This added up to nearly five million square miles of territory and nearly a hundred million souls added to the Empire, and surely if ever a people showed its aggressive colours without shame, then the British people showed them during this quarter of a century that wound up the long Victorian Age.

Yet if the period is examined more closely, its aggressive colouring will be seen to be much paler than at first glance. Jingoism was much more transient, more shallowly based, much less aggressive and self-assured than the legend would have us believe. It was also a far more interesting and many-sided phenomenon.

*   *   *

Part of the changed climate of opinion in England in 1874 was due simply to the boredom induced by Mr. Gladstone's government. This great statesman might have laid it down that the multiplication of possessions overseas was "to say the least far from desirable" and that constant care was needed to curb the ambition and cupidity involved in "the dominant passion of England" to extend its empire. He might also have held that it would make the nation not great but morally and materially little to claim more than equality of rights in the political intercourse of the world. Yet this was not how the man in the street liked his affairs to be conducted. Even some of the radical liberals who might have been expected to share Mr. Gladstone's view rebelled against what they deemed its gross commercial-mindedness. "They sell gold, coal and cotton to every nation," complained a Mr. Cowan, Member of Parliament for Newcastle-upon-Tyne. "Trade is everything with them. Production and consumption are the objects and the end of life." For Mr. Cowan this "extreme Epicurean philosophy of barter" took far too low and sordid a view of human nature.

No spirited nation could be expected to live for ever by bread alone, and it was on this basis that Disraeli's government changed the political tempo of Britain in its foreign dealings.

The turning point came with the increasing evidence of the breakup of the Turkish Empire, Britain's protégé in the sensitive areas of the Middle East. When early in 1878 it became evident that Tsarist Russia had the inclination and the power to drive Turkey out of Europe and seize Constantinople with its command of the straits of the Bosphorus and the Dardanelles on the flanks of Britain's route to India by the newly opened Suez Canal, then the fears and ambitions of the nation were stirred to their depths. It was in this context that the word "Jingo" ceased to mean a mediaeval empress of Japan or conjurer's gibberish—"Hey Jingo!" like "Hey Presto!"—and became an international word, as featured in a music hall song sung by The Great McDermott, a clarion call for a nation:

> We don't want to fight but by Jingo if we do,
> We've got the ships, we've got the men, we've
>   got the money too. . . .
> We've fought the Bear before, and while we're
>   Britons true
> The Russians shall not have Constantinople.

And why should the Russians have Constantinople? It was not theirs. Rightly or wrongly, their evident intention to possess it seemed a direct threat to British interests. As the crisis deepened throughout the early months and spring of 1878, and Lord Beaconsfield's government decided to send a fleet through the Dardanelles into the Sea of Marmora as protection for Constantinople, a large body of opinion in England echoed The Great McDermott's call.

On February 2 *The Times* reported that twenty to twenty-eight thousand people had met at Pomona Gardens, Manchester to support the government and burn an effigy inscribed, "Gladstone: England's traitor." This easily outshone a pro-Gladstone meeting of some ten thousand in Stevenson Square in the same city, and bands of men of the majority party roamed the streets singing "Rule Britannia." In London, an unfortunate who pulled down a Beaconsfield poster was roughly handled by bystanders and was then for good measure arrested by the police. On February 24, rival demonstrations—peace partisans on one side, anti-Russians on the other—marched and counter-marched in Hyde Park in the presence of an immense number of persons, to use *The Times'* words: a crowd which extended from Marble Arch to Piccadilly, though most of them were mere spectators who had come along to see the fun. The pro-Beaconsfield demonstrators, who greatly outnumbered their opponents, later marched to the Guards' Club in Pall Mall where they cheered Guards' officers in uniform at the windows, cheered Conservative members of the Carlton Club, then proceeded to the liberal Reform Club where what *The Times* called "the reverse of a pleasant demonstration" was made. The parade ended at Number 10 Downing Street, where a spokesman for the Prime Minister, standing on a chair, announced that Lord Beaconsfield was much gratified at this enthusiastic reception. *Punch,* which at this time was strongly anti-Imperialist and pro-Gladstone, was moved by these disorders to set out certain imaginary Rules and Regulations for Hyde Park, ending with a memorable one—"The Public are requested not to commit manslaughter on the grass."

Here is evidence, certainly, of Jingoism rampant, and that it represented a strong factor in the political thought of the time is shown by the complaint of a contributor to *The Illustrated London News* that unless one happened to be a Jingo, and a very vocal one into the bargain, a great risk was run of having stones, mud, brickbats, ginger-beer bottles and dead cats flung at one and of being reviled as a Russian agent, a sentimental fanatic, a mad humanitarian and a treasonable person. *Punch* read the signs of the times and the foreseeable future in similar terms:

> Bang, bang, bang! oh aint it a jolly lark!
> A-cutting the throats
> Of the Russian bloaks
> And a-wading through blood in the dark.

But if this was really the dominant opinion—which is extremely doubtful in the light of the number of mere bystanders as opposed to the militants in Hyde Park—the notable thing is the solid weight of opposition to such antics and to the braying of *The Standard, The Telegraph, Blackwoods Magazine* and *John Bull,* as mounted in the more responsible press. "Peace and neutrality are the words in all mouths," wrote *The Times,* perhaps too optimistically, on January 17, and in its columns throughout that spring one notes reports of meetings up and down the country in support of Gladstonian reason —the Workmen's Neutrality Committee; the Nonconformist Committee of Vigilance on the Eastern Question: cranky minority groups perhaps but vocal and ubiquitous. On January 31 *The Times* reported anti-war resolutions had been passed at meetings as far afield as Trowbridge, Keighley, Darlington, Greenwich, Finsbury, Liverpool, Leigh, Aberdeen and Rochdale. It was obviously proud of them.

Nor was *The Times* alone in this crusade. Both *Nineteenth Century* and *The Fortnightly Review* remained calm and balanced. *The Illustrated London News* consistently showed a similar spirit— horrified not at the drift to war but at the way England seemed to be approaching it under full sail, squaring up to Russia as she came. Above all, *Punch* in its continuous opposition to Jingo sentiment, played a part remarkably different to the tone it was later to display. On January 12 its cartoon featured "The Ass in the Lion's skin," a brilliant picture of this pantomime beast, accompanied as usual with explanatory verse:

Cease, Neddy! in the name of mercy cease!
Spare us these blasts of self-complacent braying,
While for the coming of the New Year's Peace
All ears are listening and all hearts are praying.
Take the tin trumpet from those foolish lips—
Not, as you dream, the mouthpiece of the nation.
When skies are dark with fears of war's eclipse.
We do not need your music's aggravation.

And as comment on an early exercise in brinkmanship its cartoon of January 19 would be hard to beat: a picture of a nervous Britannia being led towards the abyss of war by her Prime Minister—not for a change a slim mountebank with a coronet pulled down over his ears, but an Alpine guide of the less reliable sort urging his charge, "Just a leetle nearer the edge?" "Not an inch further," replies Britannia stoutly. "I'm a good deal nearer than is pleasant already."

Such conduct, such appalling risks, filled the paper's editorial board with horror, not altogether allayed when fears of a direct confrontation gave way to talk of a European congress to settle the Turkish crisis. England, it insisted, should not rely on force but on nobler things: "wisdom well weighed," "unselfish self-control which scorns to brag," "a just sense of rights and duties—"These let Britannia into Congress take."

Into the assembly when it finally met that summer Lord Beaconsfield took something less noble but infinitely more effective—his genius for negotiation allied to his nose for a profitable deal. *Punch* might sneer at the Prime Minister's method—and very delectably it did it in its Conversational Guidebook for Travelling Statesmen, *At a Congress,* in which the sublime egoist, after opening up, "Good morning, gentlemen, I am an Englishman," blandly goes on to ask for Egypt, parts of Turkey, the Black Sea and Armenia, ending with a Parthian shot, "Have you read my novels?"—yet even *Punch* had to admit in the end that this expertise had earned the world's applause:

> There! Shout away—till your strained throats
> are hoarse,
> He is the hero of the day—of course!

The Times, less carping if equally relieved, greeted the Treaty of Berlin, which saved the straits, as an escape from a great danger, and it gave full coverage to the return of the hero and his attendant Foreign Secretary, Lord Salisbury, as they made their triumphant way through Dover, along the red carpet spread for them, then past the posse of small girls dressed in Tory colours who strewed their path with flowers while the military bands played "Auld Lang Syne."

At London's Charing Cross one notes again the Jingo touch which even the "Thunderer" did not feel inclined on this occasion to rebuke —the station was bedecked with ten thousand blooms and shrubs arranged by the Queen's own florist and by the flags of the nations participating in the Congress, the Union Jack being mounted rather higher than the others and wreathed in bay leaves in token of a bloodless victory. "The noble earl" whose imperturbable demeanour had so impressed the citizens of Berlin, *The Times* reported, was visibly affected by this demonstration of popular favour which filled Trafalgar Square with a sea of waving hands and handkerchiefs and ended in Downing Street itself, where the aged impresario took his final bow, then left it to Lord Salisbury to draw the political moral that this "great assembly" proved there would always be popular support for a government (by inference it had to be a Tory one) which upheld the honour of England.

Jingo—yes, up to a point. Yet it was not victory—not even a diplomatic victory such as he had undoubtedly won—that Lord Beaconsfield chose to boast of, but only "Peace with honour": words to be very fatefully repeated sixty years later by another British Prime Minister returning from Germany after a near collision with superior power. As early as February, Beaconsfield had indignantly denied he wanted war. Unbellicose at heart, he knew the national jubilation at his homecoming had been compounded mostly of relief, and when within a year of his pacific triumph at Berlin he found himself engaged in hostilities on two fronts, he certainly did not escape whipping at the hands of the Liberal press, led by *Punch* in sparkling form. Under the heading AN UNSATISFACTORY TERM—"And are these your only prizes?" headmaster John Bull demands of dunces Dizzy and Lord Salisbury as they display the volumes they have won: Zulu War and Afghan War. "We did our best," the boys reply. Clearly this was not good enough, and when the Prime Minister was so rash as to define his policy in terms of *Imperium et Libertas*, the paper fell upon him with indignant scorn:

Imperium et Libertas! How large
And how sublime the phrase! From marge to marge
Of folly's duck-pond how it seems to rise,
An empyrean—to short-sighted eyes. . . .

Empire and Liberty! For all their pother,
They fear to pay for one or trust the other.
Not strength in self-control for self-defence,

> But a self-seeking swaggerer's impotence
> Is the true meaning of this catchword cry,
> Hostile to Empire as to Liberty.

This was in 1879, and the balance of press opinion was evidently critical of Jingoism. In 1880 Mr. Gladstone came back to power on the wings of his Midlothian campaign, which had been a messianic denunciation of his predecessor's sins, only to find himself saddled with war in South Africa, the fatal killing ground of Empire, as it may prove of Commonwealth also.

Cape Colony, with its command of the deep-water route to India, had since the Napoleonic wars seemed of prime importance to Britain. In the 1830s the disgruntled Boers, the first white settlers at the Cape, a frugal, patriarchal, Bible-reading people, had fled from the abomination of British rule and had made the great trek into the veldt beyond the Vaal river where they set up their own independent state. In 1877 under the spur of the Tory colonial secretary Lord Carnarvon, advocate of a "forward" policy in South Africa, the erring republic was annexed. Four years later the Boers rebelled and at Majuba Hill inflicted a resounding defeat on the British General Colley, who was killed in the encounter.

Here was a crushing and deeply humilating blow to British arms, but the press response was on the whole very balanced, sensible and regretful of bloodshed within the Empire.

> 'Tis scarcely disgrace to such foeman to fall,
> 'Tis pity such foemen are foemen at all,

lamented *Punch*. "The war is not a popular war," *The Times* agreed, and a month and a half later, in *Punch*'s pages again, Britannia is saying (apparently quite in earnest) that she is the last person in the world for annexing *anything*.

What could be more responsible, more sober, or more prophetic of the coming peace, by which the Transvaal was allowed to go its way, subject only to a vague acknowledgement of British "suzerainty"? The war that was to spring from this ambiguous word lay some years ahead. For the time being Jingoism seemed at a discount under the new Gladstonian dispensation. Yet within a year—by the summer of 1882—the apostle of peace was mounting a full-scale invasion of African soil at the other end of the vast continent, in Egypt, and the tone of almost the entire London press had become one of strident imperialism which would greatly have diverted Dizzy if he had not died in the previous year.

Why had this happened? Partly perhaps because from the time of Alexander of Macedon, who first discovered he was a god there, Egypt has always had the power to drive Europeans slightly mad— Antony's infatuation with Cleopatra and Bonaparte's descent on the Nile without assuring himself of command of the sea are simply two examples, by no means the craziest, in a long and deplorable story.

For Rome, Egypt was a granary. For Britain, with the opening of the Suez Canal, it was deemed a key point on the route to India and the centre, therefore, of an obsessional way of thinking. Using the excuse of the mounting debts incurred by Egypt's ruler, the Khedive, and with the consent of Turkey, the nominal suzerain, Britain and France had imposed themselves as controllers of the Egyptian purse. There arose—largely in response to this humiliation—a stirring of Egyptian nationalism under the leadership of Arabi Pasha, who swiftly gained control of the country.

In 1878 the Tory Lord Beaconsfield had sent a fleet to protect Constantinople from the Tsar: in 1882 the Liberal Mr. Gladstone sent a fleet to Alexandria—to protect Egypt from the Egyptians? Or the bondholders' money? Eventually, after a long spell of inactivity and in order to protect its anchorage if nothing else, it bombarded the harbour forts and smashed them into silence. "This is how the blue jackets deal with Obstruction" John Bull is made to remark in *Punch* as he surveys the ruined walls. "If only the redcoats had been handy for the prevention of crime, Mr. Horrible Pasha wouldn't have been in it at all." It was a far cry from the way the same journal had greeted Dizzy's much less provocative acts off Constantinople. There had been no bombardment then. Now a full-scale expedition was brought out from England, and at Tel el Kebir, on the road between Port Said and Cairo, Arabi Pasha's army was routed and his rebellion broken, to the accompaniment of a paean of praise from all but a minute section of the London press.

As to what should happen next, the papers were equally agreed, even the *Daily News,* which to its honour had dubbed the attack on the forts "an irregular and unfortunate campaign." It was *not* a bondholders' war, *The Times* insisted, but rather one to re-establish civilisation and prevent anarchy. "As we are the only force making for law and order in Egypt," it had claimed a fortnight before Tel el Kebir, "so shall we remain, when the present task is done, the only force capable of re-organising the country. They are dreamers of dreams, who imagine we can re-embark our troops and wash our hands of this business when we have put down Arabi." After the battle its tone was naturally still firmer—"The hand that has fought and conquered must be the hand that will give the terms of peace" —and it did not despair of seeing Egypt "under proper management" (no prize was given for guessing whose) attain to prosperity once more.

It was a unanimous verdict. *John Bull* was for a British protectorate: it had no patience with "moral considerations" or "disinterested motives." "We have earned the right to be the Protectors of Egypt," the *Standard* wrote while the *Daily Telegraph,* always the advocate of strong measures, saw the victory as conferring on Britain "rights and prerogatives bought with valiant blood, and not to be frittered away by any sentimental theory." As for *Punch,* THE LION'S JUST SHARE formed the subject of its main cartoon, featuring the king of beasts standing triumphant with its forepaws on its kill, the Egyptian crocodile, while animals representing the other European nations look on from a safe distance. More disarmingly, "Lor' bless you, me dears, you needn't worrit yourselves," says John Bull to the bystanders as he cradles a black baby labelled Suez Canal. "I'll look after 'im as if 'e was me own child." Nothing could be clearer. Ours were the spoils of Egypt. And on December 7, to draw the moral from events, *Punch*'s double-page March Past of the Old Year had banners in its midst proclaiming, "We didn't want to fight but by Jingo when we *did!*" It was less than five years since it had satirised the Ass in the Lion's Skin with the tin trumpet of militarism at its lips.

*   *   *

So much acquisitiveness and vainglory was a fitting prelude to Queen Victoria's Golden Jubilee, which was celebrated in the summer of 1887.

"To-day," wrote *The Times* on June 20, the eve of the parade, "the Queen completes the fiftieth year of a reign prosperous and glorious beyond any recorded in the annals of England. . . . It must be a source of profound satisfaction to Her Majesty, as it is to every right-minded person among her subjects, that no sound of strife intrudes upon her Jubilee. The vast empire over which she reigns is at peace with the rest of the world. . . . A considerable force is indeed reducing Upper Burmah to order, but . . ." It was in the paper's view a mere police operation.

That twin pillar of the Victorian Establishment, *Punch,* had not approached the new year of 1887 in a very optimistic spirit but rather wishing on behalf of the public that it would contain as few society scandals, Parliamentary wrangles, all-night sittings, prize fights, east winds, burglaries and bye-elections as were consistent with the continued existence of the British way of life, but by the summer it had cheered itself up and on June 18 produced a cartoon of sublime vulgarity, showing the British Lion dressing for the party, its rear half encased in a pair of tights made out of Union Jacks. What the Queen thought of it was anyone's guess, unless the earthy Hanoverian side of her nature was in the ascendant that day.

For the British people the Golden Jubilee was a kind of tribal rejoicing. Sheer longevity had turned their Queen (a controversial figure during most of her lifetime and often downright unpopular) into a national totem, and the poets were not going to let anyone forget it. Take Lewis Morris' Jubilee ode:

First lady of our English race
In regal dignity and grace,
Higher than all in old ancestral blood
But higher still in love of good. . . .

"Old ancestral blood" was right, for with some help from the College of Heralds the Queen's title was being traced back through Mary Queen of Scots (avoiding Henry VIII) to the Saxon kings, Alfred and Egbert, both men of whom it could be said with confidence that the Prince Consort would have approved.

For weeks before the great day the press resounded with ecstatic reviews of the treat in store—maps of processional routes, lists of guests, pictures of the decorations which would astound foreign visitors to the capital. Although the word Empire was in every headline, it was not so well represented in *Punch*'s double-spread drawing for the occasion, which shows the representatives of India and the colonies well on the outskirts of the festivities, in the equivalent, in fact, of the servants' hall, where they can applaud but hardly participate; and in the parade itself, as it wound its way through the streets of London, the main supporting figures were not tribal chiefs or colonial statesmen but the crowned heads and princes of Europe, dressed in every plume, uniform and decoration known to man, though most provokingly shut into closed carriages where no one could see them. With a clash of cymbals or strokes on the lyre the imperial theme would make its appearance on the programme. No less a person than the poet laureate, Lord Tennyson, apostrophised it:

You the hardy labourers
Patient children of Albion,
You, Canadian, Indian,
Australasian, African,
All your hearts be in harmony,
All your voices in unison. . . .

and so did Algernon Swinburne:

A Commonwealth, arrayed and crowned
With gold and purple, girt with steel
At need, that foes must fear or feel,
We find her as our fathers found
Earth's lordliest commonweal.

"India and the colonies were not lost sight of," wrote the *Graphic*. But apart from a few token presences and Indian officers, forgotten they almost were.

It was, in fact, unlike its "Diamond" successor ten years later, a European show, a family occasion springing from the Queen's ties

with dynasties from Schleswig-Holstein to Berlin. The echoes were
not global but recalled the "Concert of Europe and Waterloo."

* * *

This was when the great era had begun, and during almost all of
it Victoria had been Queen. Undoubtedly it had been happy and
glorious. On Jubilee Day itself, Tuesday, June 22, *The Times* devoted twelve columns of its leader pages to a celebration of the fifty-
year reign and to the "phenomenon" of the rapid expansion it had
seen. During that time the population of British North America had
quadrupled; that of Australasia had increased twenty-five times;
British territories in South Africa had doubled in extent. But trade
was the thing, and here there was much the same story to report.
The total exports and imports of the colonies, which had been £55
million sterling, had gone up nearly eight times; India's gross revenues had trebled and her external trade had risen from £21 million
to £160 million.

Through eleven and a half columns this parade of triumphant
figures and achievement in every field, cultural, financial, social and
political, runs almost without check. Then, nearly at the end, the
bombast stops, a mood of introspection suddenly appears, and the
leader writer remarks—almost by the way—that there are problems.
Other nations are catching up. Europe is changing. There are rivals
in the field—not only France and Russia, but also Germany, which
at the Queen's accession had been a maze of petty states. What is
more, Britain's industrial supremacy is challenged.

These are more than straws in the wind. They are very significant
admissions and proof at the highest level of trends and attitudes
which for some time had been surfacing in the national press. Thus,
at the time of Mr. Gladstone's Egyptian adventures the *Standard* had
uttered a *cri de coeur* that makes remarkable reading in the light of
British imperialist activities—"We have lived so long under the
shadow of the humiliating impression that nothing would induce the
English government to vindicate our rights single-handed, that this
tardy resolution to adopt a manly and patriotic course will operate
on the national mind with all the effects of a bracing and much
needed tonic." The *Graphic* had wholeheartedly agreed: "England
pursues generally so peaceful, sometimes so tame a policy, that the

world had begun to doubt whether she would ever venture again to
act promptly and vigorously."

Was this the protestation of the Wolf in *Little Red Riding Hood?*
Indeed it was not. Englishmen of Mr. Gladstone's time had some
reason for thinking themselves threatened, not threatening of others.
They had seen their national hero, General Gordon, killed in Khartoum by Moslem fanatics because their government had shrunk
from acting with sufficient promptitude or resolution. What is more,
The Times had found in this one dead man's character reason
for hope that the nation was not degenerate. It sounds indeed a
strange conclusion, but it is very revealing too of an attitude of mind
which has been, and continues to be, widely misinterpreted. Jingoism
was not evidence of the nation's overweening pride and sense of
power; it was a response to a growing suspicion of Britain's weak-
ness. It was largely a defensive reaction.

*   *   *

As much might well have been guessed from The Great McDermott's song which had set the tune. After the traumatic experiences
in the Crimea, no one in his senses would have wished to fight
Russia. And the dangers of the situation facing Lord Beaconsfield's government in 1878 had seemed all the more real because
apart from Turkey—a dependency more than an ally—Britain had
no one to lean on. It was her own fault: the result of deliberate
policy. The old ties with Prussia and the Habsburg Empire had been
allowed to lapse because during the long triumphant years of the *Pax
Britannica* there had seemed no need for them—Britain's navy ruled
the seas; even her army had won victories to set beside Trafalgar
and the Nile; the Industrial Revolution had been her child; and once
her social troubles had been eased by the passing of the Great
Reform Bill she had forged commercially ahead of every rival, the
world's workman, policeman and governess all rolled into one.

By the 1870s all this had changed. Where she had once called
coalitions into being to drag down a tyrant, sixty years later the
French and Prussians had fought a war for supremacy in western
Europe without even consulting her. The unification of Germany
under Bismark, of Cavour's Italy, had spelt the end of small and
fragmented states; in America the bloodiest civil war in history had

been fought to assert the unity of a nation over and against its provinces. Yet what was Britain and her empire but a scattered collection of such states, without central direction or control, adrift in the world of naked power that Bismark and Moltke had unleashed?

Seen in this light even the Jingo song loses a lot of its aggression. It was more the sound of someone whistling in the dark. Indeed the thoughtful element in the nation as Queen Victoria's reign wore on was only too well aware of the gathering dangers—not only the sharp rise of German and Russian armed power in Europe but also German colonial ambitions in Africa and the Pacific, a quite new phenomenon to add to an old rivalry renewed in the shape of French moves in equatorial Africa which threatened our interests along the Niger and the Upper Nile.

These strategic problems were grave enough, but what was happening economically was still more fundamental, and on this front also Britain's long supremacy was ending. Superficially, much of the story appeared a brilliant one. Between the Queen's accession and her Golden Jubilee the population of England, Scotland and Wales had almost exactly doubled. The output of coal had risen from thirty million to 160 million tons; of pig-iron from 700,000 to seven and a half million tons. Railway mileage had increased from little more than three hundred to seventeen thousand; the tonnage of the Merchant Marine had trebled; overseas investment earnings had gone up by ten times. Yet at the beginning of the year 1878, while the crisis over Constantinople was building up, *The Times* referred with alarm to the discovery that imports had for some years been exceeding exports "to a constantly increasing extent." The figures it quoted showed that the trade deficit for 1877 had been £145 million sterling, exceeding by no less than £30 million the deficit for '76. Rightly it called this "a grave question." Still graver—though perhaps this could not have been guessed—was the fact that in steel production Britain would be overtaken within a dozen years by the United States and in eighteen by Germany; that by the end of the century German production in this commodity, the barometer of industrial strength, would be half as large again as Britain's and that United States output would be double.

The situation was about to become critical, and not in terms of production only, for the whole pattern of world trade was changing.

In country after country the tariff barriers were going up. Germany went Protectionist in 1879, Russia in 1881, France and Austria in 1882, Italy in 1888; 1890 was to see the ultimate blow, the savage McKinley Tariff in the United States—and how could free-trading Britain survive against this kind of competition? By erecting tariffs of her own? Unthinkable. Free trade was sacrosanct, the ark of the covenant which no impious hand must be allowed to touch. Yet there were some people who would dare—and in 1879 *Punch* produced a drawing of a corpulent John Bright brandishing the trusty "Old Sword" of free trade which Cobden had blessed:

> But lo, now the malignants lift up their heads
>   again,
> I always said the serpents were only scotched,
>   not slain. . . .

What then should be done? The colonies were busily erecting tariff barriers themselves and could no longer be dragooned into proper behaviour or saved from heresy. American and European tariff walls were not susceptible to sermons or blandishments or even blasts on the free-trade trumpet. German and Russian military power, German colonial aspirations, French colonial adventures, were all ugly new facts to be faced, and so was the overall decline of Britain's industrial lead.

It was in such a climate of doubt, anxiety and bewilderment that Britain after the long summer of self-sufficiency began to think of her own position in the world and of an empire which could perhaps be made larger and more unified. It was more a response to a threat than anything consciously aggressive. That it appeared in rather another light to the Egyptians, Sudanese, Burmese, Afghans, Zulus, Ashanti, Matabele and Boers who were the victims of this new thinking, as indeed to the watching world, accounts for the odium that this period inspired and still inspires; yet to British imperialists it all seemed natural enough. They would have agreed with one of the most eminent of their number, Cecil Rhodes, that the Empire was a bread and butter affair and it was up to them to see that it earned its living. In any case it was all for the good of the governed.

* * *

The decisive turn from apathy about the Empire to sponsorship of it came, as we have seen, with Lord Beaconsfield's government, and four years later Lord Salisbury magisterially rebuked his predecessors on the Liberal side for their mistaken policies. "The commerce of a great nation like this," he remarked, "will only flourish under the shade of empire, and those who give up empire in order to make commerce prosper will end by losing both."

"The shade of empire" is in itself a gorgeously emotive and imperialist phrase, calling up visions of justice under the trees; and the rest of the sentence is prophetic of a new way of looking at the empire as a mixture of trading profits and tradition, from which even Mr. Gladstone's governments, when the Liberals got back to power, did not dissent.

Take the practical face of the picture first. As early as 1862 *The Times* had crossed to the imperialist side of the fence. Six years later a colonial society, soon re-named The Royal Colonial Institute, had been formed in London and had held a series of meetings at the Cannon Street Hotel which had attracted wide publicity. In 1879 a Parliamentary commission was set up to examine problems of defence and overseas trade; in 1881 the Fair Trade League was founded as a riposte to foreign tariffs, in 1884, the Imperial Federation League, a far weightier body, with a practical programme and support from members of both the great political parties. At its first meeting Mr. W. H. Smith moved that political relations between Great Britain and her colonies must lead either to federation or disintegration, and though this proved too steep for acceptance, it was nevertheless agreed that some form of federation was essential. This feeling was not confined to circles traditionally concerned with such problems, for as early as 1871 we find among the "Cobden Club Essays" a paper by John E. Thorold Rogers complaining that no one had yet attempted to give stability to what he called "The loose and uncemented structure" of the empire. Ten years later J. R. Seeley in *The Expansion of England* saw in the Federation which Rogers had proposed Britain's sole chance of keeping her status as a power of the first magnitude.

To this notion of Federation we shall return: it seemed to many the most hopeful expedient. But since we are dealing with Victorian England, no one need be surprised that alongside of the search for practical remedies went a great deal of utopianism.

"There is a destiny now possible to us, the highest ever set before a nation," declared John Ruskin from his Oxford citadel to an audience "still undegenerate in race . . . not yet dissolute in temper. . . . Will you youths of England make your country again a royal throne of kings; a sceptred isle, for all the world a source of light, a centre of peace; mistress of learning and of the arts, faithful guardian of time-tried principles, under temptation from fond experiments and licentious desires; and amidst the cruel and clamorous jealousies of the nations, worshipped in her strange valour, of goodwill towards men? . . . This is what England must either do or perish; she must found colonies as fast and as far as she is able, formed of her most energetic and worthiest men; seizing every piece of fruitful waste ground she can set her foot on, and there teaching these her colonists that their chief virtue is to be fidelity to their country, and that their first aim is to be to advance the power of England by land and sea. . . . If we can get men, for little pay, to cast themselves against cannon-mouths for love of England, we may find men also who will plough and sow for her, who will behave kindly and righteously for her and who will bring up their children to love her, and who will gladden themselves in the brightness of her glory. . . ."

Such impassioned, romantic words ring oddly in our ears to-day, though the peroration is better—"All I ask of you is to have a fixed purpose of some kind for your country and for yourselves, no matter how restricted, so that it be fixed and unselfish." Unfortunately Ruskin, for all his genius, had no very fixed purpose imperially himself; his interest in the topic was fitful and shortlived, and in any case in the sphere of the real, as opposed to the ideal, he was never a great success—as witness his attempt to erect with his own hands one of the pillars in the Oxford Museum which had subsequently to be pulled down and re-erected by a more professional stonemason.

For the young Charles Dilke, at the outset of a career which was to take him very close to the Liberal leadership, the Empire was a more practical matter, because he had seen it himself at first hand on a tour of the world. The title of the very readable book that came out of his travels—*Greater Britain*—was to provide the toast at endless colonial dinners, but alas! he was not much better than Ruskin when it came to remedies. Where some parts of the empire were concerned, notably India, Dilke was quite an old-fashioned Imperialist; others of his notions were fanciful, as where he looked to some kind of Anglo-Saxon union with the Teutons to provide the world's natural leaders. It was a startling vision, but the historian A. J. Froude, echoing Ruskin, saw one almost equally remarkable, of Britain as the centre of "an enormous and coherent empire," reinforced with new migrants planted in the virgin lands where they could thrive and multiply *without ceasing to be Englishmen*—an illusion, as time was to show, at least as great as Macaulay's dream of an Anglicized India.

The great writer on the Empire was, of course, none of these but Rudyard Kipling. Few poets have been more misunderstood. A byword for the glorification of the *Raj*, he was often highly critical of it; he knew how to judge it in the time-scale of history. Take for instance his poem *The Jubilee*.

By the well, where the bullocks go
Silent and blind and slow—
By the field, where the young corn dies
In the face of the sultry skies,
They have heard, as the dull Earth hears,
The voice of the wind of an hour,
The sound of the Great Queen's voice:—
"My God hath given me years,
"Hath granted dominion and power:
"And I bid you, O Land, rejoice."

And the ploughman settled the share
More deep in the sun-dried clod:—
"Mogul, Mahratta, and Mlech from the North,
"And White Queen over the seas—
"God raiseth them up and driveth them forth
"As the dust of the ploughshare flies in the
        breeze;
"But the wheat and the cattle are all my care,
"And the rest is the will of God."

If this is an imperialist poem, then imperialism is a very different thing from the word as defined in dictionaries. Having spent the best and formative years of his life in India, Kipling loved and understood her far better than any of his countrymen, just as he understood the bewilderment of that other faithful and grumbling servant of the *Raj*, the British soldier, asked to account for his doings far from home. "Ask my Col'nel, for I don't know":

> We broke a King and we built a road—
> A court-house stands where the Reg'ment goed.
> And the river's clean where the raw blood flowed,
>   When the Widow give the party.

So it is by practical results that the Empire must be judged—if Kipling had a message for his country it was an uncompromising one. Empire was not a matter of dividends but of the welfare of the governed. There were few gains and no gratitude to be won, but it must be undertaken all the same:

> Take up the White Man's burden—
> Send forth the best ye breed—
> Go bind your sons to exile
> To serve your captives' need. . . .

It was a doctrine crying aloud for parody, and Henry Labouchère's *Truth* joyfully provided it—in verse actually addressed to the American but equally applicable at home:

> Pile on the Brown Man's burden!
> And if ye rouse his hate,
> Meet his old-fashioned reasons
> With Maxims—up to date.
> With shells and Dum-Dum bullets
> A hundred times make plain
> The Brown Man's loss must ever
> Imply the White Man's gain.

But *Truth* was far out on the political left and its barbs did not touch an increasingly patriotic nation. By the late 1880s the membership of the Tory "Primrose League," founded in memory of Lord Beaconsfield, had reached the million mark and *Punch* provided a drawing of Primrose Day crowds at the Beaconsfield statue hanging a large garland of his supposedly favourite flowers round poor Dizzy's neck. Evidently the man of the future was no longer likely to be "the fellow who runs," as one disgruntled pessimist had supposed, but a Jingo Imperialist. For the first and last time in a long history the man in the street was showing an interest in empire. It was not to last long—perhaps no longer than the span between the Golden Jubilee and the end of the Boer War—but during that time imperialism was a genuinely popular movement.

Many things had contributed to this. Uncertainty about Britain's status in the world was certainly one of them. A sudden flood of information was another. Not much sense was made of the theorists or those who were trying to rationalise the system; they were far above the heads of the public. But poets like Kipling and the men who day by day reported the exploits of British soldiers and explorers found a ready audience. The travels of David Livingstone, the campaign against the slave trade in central Africa and the spate of missionary activity that followed in his footsteps had done much to reconcile "Humanitarian" and "Chapel" opinion to the need for British rule among backward tribes. High Churchmen, being Tories, had always approved of it, but now that Methodist and Baptist missions were springing up everywhere in the wake of the flag, the Empire was coming to be seen as a progressive force even by those most temperamentally opposed to it. If trade followed the flag, enlightenment followed the missionaries. And, naturally, the Liberals, who had always drawn strength from nonconformity, had to identify with those trends which would show themselves in the voting pattern of the future; so that a Liberal-Imperialist wing made its appearance under the aegis of Lord Rosebery and came to include the best of the younger brains of the party.

Among the public that read *The Globe* and the *News of the World* opinion was not so well instructed. Love of the black brother was confined to the sort of admiration which Kipling was to express through the mouth of the British soldier in his poem on the battle of Omdurman against the Fuzzy-wuzzies—"a poor benighted 'eathen but a first class fighting man"—and again in the still more famous ballad *Gunga Dinn*. Coloured people were not, unfortunately for themselves, Englishmen. But it appeared that many of the bravest of them were British, which was a matter for congratulation all round. The Indian and Colonial Exhibition of 1886 in the Royal Albert Hall, opened by the Queen and attended by hundreds of thousands of her subjects, was like the glimpse of a treasure house. The *Graphic* in three successive issues devoted pages of plates and drawings to what it called this "splendid show" which no other nation in the world could match. Lord Tennyson wrote an *Inaugural Ode*. The *Graphic* rather hoped against hope that the catering department would rise to the level of the occasion, which it palpably did not.

But the public loved it. It was a bond between the mean streets of provincial towns and the gorgeous East which the Empire held in fee. The citizens of an industrial society needed colour in their lives. And to the Empire—to the white settlements at least—many of them had come to look for something more practical: for homes for themselves and their children in the waves of emigration which had followed the trade depression of the '70s and which the United States (the land of first choice for the majority of migrants) could not wholly satisfy.

All these trends met and coalesced in the supreme Victorian event—the Queen's Diamond Jubilee of June 22, 1897.

IX

Apogee of Empire

To have reigned—as Victoria had reigned in 1887—for fifty years
was a great achievement: of English monarchs, only Henry III,
Edward III and George III had exceeded such a span on the throne,
and as the press did not hesitate to point out, the first of these had
been simple minded, the second grossly under the influence of a
whore, and the third, in his last years, incapably mad.

To have reigned for sixty years surpassed everything, and the
Queen's Diamond Jubilee was therefore a fabulous event. "Oh
King of Kings, whose reign of old hath been from everlasting" was
the anthem sung in St. George's Chapel, Windsor, at the thanksgiving service which the Queen attended on June 21, the anniversary of her accession, on the eve of the official celebrations in
her capital. "The Great Day is at hand," wrote the *Graphic* in its
issue of June 19—"the greatest day in English history. There have
been great days before, but they were days of sowing. The Diamond
Jubilee is the day of greatest reaping—the harvest festival of the
greatest Empire, of the most glorious epoch, of the longest reign."

The event of a lifetime, the show of the century—everyone
wanted to be there. The advertisement pages of the press, particularly *The Times,* did a roaring trade in seats along the six-mile
processional route:

Lady has secured quiet ROOM for PROCESSION. Three windows. Excellent view. Only requires one for own use. Glad to SHARE ROOM. Profits (if any) go to Christian work.

In this same edition of June 16, Messrs. Garland, Smith & Drake were able to offer a large selection of seats from one to sixty guineas, while Giddy & Giddy had on their hands a very large selection of ROOMS, windows and seats, descriptive lists of which were available on demand. Had the English gone collectively mad? Some of the Russian papers evidently thought so, reporting a wave of suicides in London out of sheer excitement. The French, however, always clear-eyed where their British neighbours were concerned, put it all down to the commercial instinct rampant and even found it in their hearts to praise the achievements of the reign, "this marvellous impulse given to trade, to colonisation, to business."

But this was not at all how the British themselves saw it—to them the Jubilee was an emotional reunion of races under one flag, a gathering of the clans from which foreigners were not entirely excluded but were to be kept nevertheless in their place. In 1887 four European crowned heads had been in attendance on the matriarch. In 1897 there were none. A posse of crown princes and grand dukes had been invited, but the real core of the Diamond Jubilee procession, apart from the Queen herself, was the parade of eleven colonial premiers and a galaxy of colonial troops from every corner of the Empire under the command of Lord Roberts, "Bobs" himself, on a white horse.

Nothing is more remarkable in the preparations for the celebration of the Diamond Jubilee (wrote the *Graphic* on June 12th) than the essentially Imperial character which the whole function has assumed. . . . It is not many years ago that the apostles of imperial expansion were scouted as perilous Jingoes, and we need not glance very far into the past to discover a generation of influential politicians who were actually opposed to the retention of any of the colonies. . . . To-day there is no cause so hopeless as the Little England cause. . . . The Imperial idea is now triumphant because it is founded in the economic necessities of the component parts of the Empire and fertilised by Liberal ideas of government.

The Times had magisterially agreed:

> The Colonial procession, which is to precede the Royal procession
> to St. Paul's and to follow it on return to Buckingham Palace,
> will be the most significant, and, to those who can reflect, the
> most impressive element in the whole of the magnificent display.
> No State and no Monarch known to history have ever rejoiced in
> such homage as our colonies will pay to our QUEEN.

Sir Wilfred Laurier for Canada, the senior colony, (it was still
in theory a colony, but only just); G. H. Reid for thrustful New
South Wales; the premiers of the Cape, of Natal, Newfoundland,
Victoria, Queensland, South Australia, Western Australia, Tasmania
and New Zealand; a bevy of Indian Princes with romantic, ringing
names: Maharaja Sir Parteb Singh Bahadur of Jodhpur, uncle of
Prince Ranjitsinhji, hero of English cricket fields; Raja Ajit Singh
Bahadur of Rajputana; the Thakir Sahib of Gondal; Sir Jamsetjee
Jojeebhoy—what an imposing list they make and even better
photographs, particularly the Indians, encrusted with jewels from
head to heel.

And the colonial troops that were to accompany them on the
great march through London were still more varied and indeed astonishing—the New South Wales Lancers; the Rhodesian Horse,
commanded by Maurice Gifford who had lost an arm fighting the
savage Matabele; the British Guiana Police; the Sierra Leone Frontier Force Police; the Cypriot Zaptiehs in their Turkish fezzes; and
the British North Borneo Police, the Dyaks, whom the correspondent
of *The Illustrated London News* found "smart little fellows," well
in control of their homicidal tendencies, though at least one of these
ex-head-hunters was rumored to have collected no fewer than a
dozen trophies before the beneficent coming of the *Raj*.

Letters to the press had suggested that room should be found in
the parade for contingents representing the cultural achievements
of the reign, but these were shot down before they could really get
on the wing. "A contingent of men of science," remarked *The Times*
tartly, "or of actors, or of musicians, would add nothing to the pic-
turesqueness or to the national adequacy of the procession." And
the same went for Members of Parliament, who in any case had a

stand of their own in Parliament Square. It was not their day. All eyes would be on the Queen, on her colonial troops, on the glittering Indian escort and Lifeguards around her carriage: the Queen's men: fifty thousand of them in all in the procession and lining the route.

The arts, in fact, had not been entirely relegated from the show —there was Dr. George Martin's *Te Deum* to be sung from the cathedral steps: there were the *Jubilee Odes* which no one could prevent.

The laureate succeeding Tennyson—Alfred Austin—was perhaps the most minor of poets, but he had done his best:

> And ever when June's musk roses blow
> Our race will celebrate Victoria's reign,
> And ever England's greatness gain a glow
> From her pure fame.

It is doubtful if many did much better. The Professor of Poetry at Oxford had produced a very scholarly work for the occasion, which reminded one unkind critic of "a good translation from a Greek chorus," and Lewis Morris' ode harped perhaps too much on the Queen's more negative virtues:

> Princes and Peoples join alike to pay
> Due reverence to a Woman's blameless sway
> And bless with voice and heart this fair,
>   auspicious day.

In fact, the poets with one exception were a flop. Only Kipling's *Recessional* distinguished the day. But one must reserve *Recessional* for a while, for it was an epilogue, not the strident voice of the age, the echo of the rejoicing in the streets.

*   *   *

Eighteen ninety-seven had been a cold, blustery summer, and hopes that the blissful weather of the Golden Jubilee would be repeated were not high among the crowds that began to line the route in the small hours of June 22.

Sure enough, the day began badly with a pall of cloud hanging over London. Yet miraculously, just as Victoria was preparing to leave the palace for her drive, the sun came out and the proverbial "Queen's weather" dutifully appeared.

Since the death of the Prince Consort the Queen had dressed in black, but for this supreme occasion she compromised with her grief. She wore a black dress and mantle, but they were embroidered with silver, and her black bonnet was trimmed with a wreath of white acacia and crowned with an aigrette of diamonds. What is more, to the delight of her subjects, she carried a white lace parasol which had been presented to her by Mr. Villiers, the "father" of the House of Commons.

Thus arrayed, she set herself to carry out her programme. The hundreds of thousands in the windows lining the route, in the streets and on the stands which the London County Council had insisted should provide eighteen inches of sitting space per person—their strength had been tested by the builders' workmen jumping on them in unison—supposed no doubt that they were there to see the Queen. They were wrong. They were there so that the Queen could see *them*. The official edict from the palace had made this perfectly clear:

> The Queen will leave the Grand Entrance of Buckingham Palace at 11:15 o'clock, in state, and drive through London for the purpose of seeing her people and of receiving their congratulations on having attained the 60th anniversary of her reign.

Just before she got into her carriage in the forecourt a very striking ceremony was performed, the living proof of the triumphs of Victorian technology—her message to her peoples, thanking them and calling for God's blessing on them, was sent on its way by the Queen's own hand, by the pressing of a button on "a telegraphic instrument" which gave the signal to the Central Telegraph office to transmit to forty-three addressees in every quarter of the globe. Five cable companies were engaged on the work, and loyal replies were coming in long before the Queen returned from her drive.

As she left, prompt to the minute, a sixty-gun salute began to boom out from Hyde Park. The processional route—via Piccadilly, St. James's Street, Trafalgar Square, the Strand, Fleet Street to St. Paul's, then on to the Mansion House, across London Bridge to the south bank and back by Westminster Bridge and Whitehall to the Mall—was a vivid kaleidoscope of colour. In Piccadilly, ornamented with a species of "Venetian masts," Lord Rothschild's house attracted particular attention. Further on in the heart of clubland, St. James's Street was adjudged a veritable "floral bower" and that hub of liberalism, the Reform Club, flamed with red, white and blue stripes. Marvellous to say, the clubs had opened their doors, or at least their windows, to the fair sex for the day, and were a blaze of coloured silks. The Athenaeum, home of bishops, wore "modest vestments" and gave *The Times*' reporter the impression of being "suitably attired." "Of the Strand and Fleet Street," says this same observer, obviously a man of delicate refinement, "it is perhaps best to say little"; and there was criticism also of the Treasury building for its typically "severe frugality" and for the arches in Pall Mall (adorned with celluloid globes) which were judged as dangerously inflammable.

Through waves of cheering the procession clattered through Trafalgar Square into the Strand and to its junction with Fleet Street at the Griffin monument on the site of old Temple Bar, where the Lord Mayor of London was waiting to offer the sword which Queen Elizabeth had presented to the City. The Queen ceremonially touched it: the Lord Mayor mounted his horse, which to the delight of the crowd all but ran off with him as he bucketed away towards Ludgate Hill. Even Victoria was for once amused; was seen to smile.

At the Golden Jubilee the religious celebrations had taken place in Westminster Abbey before a glittering throng of princes and potentates. Now—and again one sees the immense difference in tone between the two events—the service was in the presence of the People, on the steps of St. Paul's, where Dr. George Martin's *Te Deum* was sung. The papers next day were critical of this offering, but the crowds filling the arena below the cathedral steps loved it and provided a fitting end to the ceremony by bursting impromptu into the National Anthem.

By 1:45 the Queen was home in Buckingham Palace and the reporters could take stock. It had been a great morning which had passed off with few untoward events, apart from the Lord Mayor's horse. Lord Howe had fainted in St. George's Circus, falling off his mount, and two men had dropped out of a tree in the Mall just as the Queen was passing, but none of the stands had collapsed as many papers had feared.

For the Queen, that was the end of the ceremonial: she merely had a Palace banquet to survive. For the people in the streets there were the illuminations, and here the same brilliant success attended the evening that had attended the day—even the Pall Mall arches did not catch fire. Particularly remarked were the Mansion House, lit with 5000 lamps and 1200 Roman flambeaux (35,000 gas jets were used), the dome of St. Paul's, London Bridge festooned with gas lamps along its parapets, the Junior Constitutional Club with its huge Union Jack picked out in lights, and the Peninsular and Orient Steamship Company's building in Leadenhall Street, featuring a Star of India with pendant and a motto: HEAVEN'S LIGHT OUR GUIDE. At ten o'clock 2500 bonfires were lit throughout the kingdom, blazing on the hillsides and recalling the excitements of Armada year.

In every county and province there had been celebrations of one kind or another. Windsor mounted a Venetian fête on the Thames; Liverpool a monster procession and a garden party for 3000; at Cambridge a thousand homing pigeons were released; at Gloucester 120 choristers had sung the National Anthem from the top of the cathedral tower; Edinburgh, not to be outdone by London, had fired a sixty-gun salute. The Birmingham city council had proposed to restrict the celebrations to "philanthropic works," but the people insisted on their procession and fireworks. Dublin got a parade of troops. They were needed. On the 21st the Jubilee radical firebrand, Miss Maud Gonne, had drawn a crowd of Irish Nationalists to a cul-de-sac off College Green bearing black flags. This turned into a riot, with the loyalist students from Trinity College singing "God Save the Queen" while the Nationalists responded with "The Boys of Wexford"—and on Jubilee Night itself there had followed what English papers called "Disgraceful Scenes," Miss Gonne once more being much in evidence.

Ireland provided one sour note—the Nationalist members at Westminster even went into the Noes lobby to protest against Parliament's congratulatory address to the monarch. India provided another, with an appalling sequence of disasters by plague, earthquake

and famine which had ravaged the country during that year, resulting in the cancellation of all festivities in Calcutta and Assam and
even disturbances all too reminiscent of Dublin. But throughout the
rest of the Empire and among the colonies of British residents
abroad the tone was fervently loyal. Winnipeg reported the greatest
demonstrations ever seen in western Canada; Australia enjoyed a
public holiday, and remission of sentence was granted to all first of-
fenders in the gaols; in Batavia the British donated a new wing to
the Dutch cricket pavilion; and in Moscow a subscription was raised
for indigent British governesses resident in Russia. From the Victoria Mounted Rifles came a gift for the Queen in the shape of a
kangaroo named Daisy Belle. President McKinley sent a message of
congratulation signed "Your good friend." For Mark Twain, the
Jubilee had been "a stunning show."

And as such *The Times* reviewed it in the morning:

A long and splendid panorama of Empire unrolled yesterday in the
chief thoroughfares of London before the Queen and a vast representative gathering of her subjects. . . . The completion of the
60th year of a reign equalled in length by that of no former
Monarch, rich in achievement and fruitful in promise beyond any
other, has stirred emotions rarely allowed to reveal themselves in a
nation that prides itself on its practical and positive spirit. Only a
very cold heart and a very stagnant imagination could resist the
combined impression of the pageant itself, and of the immense
mass of people, orderly, genial, good-humoured, and nevertheless
brimming over with the genuine enthusiasm of patriotic and loyal
pride, which assembled to witness it.

Actually the crowds along the processional route had been thin in
places, and after dark there had not been the expected throngs of
sightseers to see the illuminations—one meets this note of disappointment surprisingly often in the press reports. But on the night of the
23rd they turned out in force. This was the night of the gala performance at the Opera attended by the Prince of Wales and seventy
"royals," besides colonial premiers and Indian princes. Ticket touts
had a field day: two stalls are said to have fetched fifty guineas,

and the wife of an American millionaire offered two hundred guineas for a grand tier box—in vain.

The Queen was not present. She was back at Windsor, having reviewed on the way on Constitution Hill "the least warlike of her subjects," as one reporter put it: "10,000 elementary schoolchildren, all of whom had been given a packet of sweets, a bun, a glass of milk and a medal to remind them of the occasion"—*The Illustrated London News* carried a charming drawing of cheering moppets under the trees. Nor had the poor of the East End been forgotten, for on the suggestion of the Princess of Wales free meals had been provided for three hundred thousand of them, "to bring the Jubilee to the slums," as *The Times* put it in its condescending way. "Think of it!" wrote the *Graphic:* "an army of poverty larger than the army of the British Empire, an assembly greater than that which stood in the streets to see the great Procession go by. . . ."

This exercise in elementary welfare wound up the civilian celebrations, but there was one great event still to come, perhaps the keynote of the whole imperial pageant—the Naval Review held at Spithead on Saturday June 26.

Twenty-one battleships, 44 cruisers, 70 torpedo boats, 165 ships in all, covering thirty miles of water and carrying 38,000 officers and men, were drawn up in phalanx between Gosport and the green shores of the Isle of Wight—and this without withdrawing one single ship from its foreign station. It was a nearly new fleet, far more than half of its most powerful ships having been built since the Golden Jubilee. In four days the Channel Reserve, special and gunboat squadrons, with the destroyer flotilla—a total of 120 ships—could be at Gibraltar; in nine days the Channel Squadron of twenty-nine pennants could be at Halifax, Nova Scotia, in twenty-seven days at Table Bay, in fifty-eight at Hong Kong. It was a very mobile weapon, the symbol of the Empire as the papers remarked, pondering on the happy effect such a display must have on the colonial premiers present. "Lor' love yer, my lads, this is the proudest moment of my life," says *Punch's* British Lion as he rows the cubs out to see the show. "I guess, sir, this makes for peace," an American naval officer remarked, whether ironically or not is not recorded. *The Times* quoted Blackstone's words of a century earlier: "The Royal Navy of England hath ever been its greatest defence and armament; it is its ancient and natural strength"—and clearly these words applied with still more force in a world where the international horizon had once more begun to darken. "We rejoice to believe that, slowly and steadily public opinion has hardened on the necessity for retaining supremacy at sea, as it has done in regard to holding the colonies close to our hearts."

The Queen, who had herself reviewed her fleets in 1857, was not able to be present on this occasion: the honour fell to the Prince of Wales, and as the royal yacht steamed between the lines of warships the scene was recorded by the *Graphic*—"this greatest review of our day, perhaps of all time":

> Between 1 and 2 o'clock . . . the scene presented by the Solent was of an indescribably fine kind. . . . The weather was beautiful, the sea glittered as with a sense of pride never felt before, and heaved with unfamiliar emotion. The strains of stringed and brass music, mingled with service bugle calls, made a peculiar symphony of sound; while the eye was equally delighted with the countless vessels of all kinds flutteringly gay with rainbow-coloured bunting, with the flags of every nation in the world, with high over all the royal standard of England, floating proudly like a battle beacon.

To see the show, to form the audience at this unparalleled display of might, another armada had assembled: ocean liners, fishing smacks, down to the most impracticable "once-around-the-lighthouse" craft from every harbour along the south coast. Prices ranged from ten to twenty guineas, but for a day excursion in a cockle boat you could get a bargain at £3.10s. The Queen's proverbial weather held, but only just, for hardly had the last echoes of ceremonial gunfire died away than there arose a storm so violent, so unexpected, that it is hard not to see in it a portent:

> . . . the waves grew black and surly, the clouds gathered in ever more ominous banks, a pitch-like vapour, rain and even hailstones began to descend with ever-increasing force and fury, the heavens were streaked with the vividest flashes of forked lightning, and presently all the Solent, with its shores blotted out entirely from the

view of the fleet, was convulsed with a thunderstorm which showed that even the mightiest of navies cannot vie with nature in the awe-inspiring roll and rattle of its artillery.

On such a note the Jubilee ended: though not for another two weeks did it cease to be the only topic of conversation in drawing rooms and in the streets. As for the Queen, who had been the centre of it all, "It is indeed gratifying," she wrote to the Home Secretary, "after so many years of labour and anxiety for the good of my beloved country, to find that my exertions have been appreciated throughout my vast Empire."

* * *

The key to everything had lain in the Imperial idea which had sprung from Britain's belated recognition of her dependence on what she had long been pleased to call "dependencies."

British is Beautiful. Even the Jubilee banquet, which was graced with the dishes of the continental *cuisine—Potage Bernaise, Filets de Saumon à la Norvégienne, Timbales à la Monte Carlo, Poulets à la Demidoff*—had as its central offering ROAST BEEF. Everything was in keeping. In their barracks at Chelsea, as in the procession itself, the colonial troops had been the centre of attention, and they did not cease to be fêted and lionised once their ceremonial role was over. Selected contingents of them were reviewed by the Queen at Windsor and fashionable London hastened to do them honour: they were taken here, they were taken there; a special show was put on for them by the Beerbohm Trees at Her Majesty's Theatre, where one of the plays presented for them was *The Red Lamp,* whose title must certainly have recalled, for some of them at any rate, many a happy evening in the brothels of the East. As for the colonial premiers, they hardly had time to breathe between one function and the next. Every *divertisement* that their hosts could dream up was lavished on them. They were taken to the Naval Review, to the Army Review at Aldershot, to Liverpool, to the Manchester Ship Canal, to Crewe; they supped with Henry Irving on the stage of the Lyceum; and for good measure were shipped across to Paris to a banquet given by the British Chamber of Trade.

Of this bevy of canny statesmen the highest hopes were entertained. A role had been cast for them. It was very cogently expressed in a letter to *The Times* signed CUSTOS urging them to get together to form some organisation for joint Imperial defence. This expressed a general hope in official and press circles in London that the premiers should now sing for their supper. *The Times* itself had said that separatism was dead and buried, that greater advantage had been perceived to lie in the direction of united force, and that to strengthen the solidarity which was assured by the naval protection of the greatest sea power in the world had become the natural policy of the colonies, those rich and free commercial states. To give effect to such anticipations a series of meetings were held at the Colonial Office under the chairmanship of the Colonial Secretary, Joseph Chamberlain; and soon the *Graphic,* always an optimistic journal, saw them all hard at work "digging the foundations of the future edifice of Imperial Unity in a really Imperial Parliament."

This illusion was fostered at times by the colonial premiers themselves. They were photographed: a sober, black-suited, deferential body of men standing behind Joseph Chamberlain's chair like a coven of butlers. Occasionally, partly out of sheer gratitude or a desire to please, one of them would volunteer a statement of impeccably imperial cut—like Sir Edward Braddon, Prime Minister of Tasmania, who remarked that he would leave England a bitterly disappointed man if some step had not been taken to bring the mother country and the colonies closer together; or Sir Gordon Sprigg of the Cape, who under the influence of a London banquet was moved to offer the Royal Navy an ironclad (or the promise of one). Typically and prophetically the Prime Ministers of Canada and New South Wales, the two most powerful and able of the eleven, were absent on this occasion: they were paying their respects to the aged Mr. Gladstone at Hawarden.

In fact, these politicians as a whole, remembering their home electorates, while saying neutrally agreeable things at banquet after banquet up and down the country, were very guarded when it came to committing themselves to practical steps on the road to unity. The Empire was no doubt a splendid thing, always provided there were not too many strings attached, too many reminders of an old subordination. There was distrust mixed up with all the goodwill— the feeling that all the wining and dining might have some ulterior purposes which it behoved honest, unsophisticated colonials to resist.

Thus, at a banquet given to the premiers in the citadel of Imperialism, the Imperial Institute, where their health was drunk by the Prince of Wales himself, G. H. Reid, speaking for all the Australian colonies, went out of his way to remind his hosts that the Institute had at the time of its foundation been regarded with much suspicion, as a body all too likely to interfere in Australian affairs.

That this, in Reid's view, had not happened, did not detract from the pointedness of the lesson. It was a warning shot over Imperialism's bows, a more or less polite hint to the captain on the bridge not to put on too much steam. And it was no mere bluff. Mr. Chamberlain, who had invited his colonials to conference and had circularised them with a memorandum of matters he wanted to discuss, had set his sights high—Imperial Unity, Colonial Defence, Colonial Representation at Westminster, a Common Economic Policy. The premiers responded by suggesting a discussion of Canadian tariffs, garrisons at the Cape, and a Pacific cable linking Canada and Australia, which the proposers could ill afford.

We shall return to it in more detail later,* but it was all profoundly disenchanting. The papers, avidly waiting with their ears cocked for some great Imperial scheme to be announced, were soon lamenting that the news coming out of the Colonial Office was very milk-and-water stuff. They took some comfort from Sprigg's offer of a battleship, but not much. And it was on rather a subdued note that Britain, in the person of the Queen, took leave of her guests (now created Privy Councillors) at a farewell audience at Windsor which was also a valediction of the whole vast pageant that had filled these summer months. What had it amounted to, now that the balance could be struck? What was the message of the Jubilee?

This, Kipling supplied, just as he had supplied the corrective to the rejoicings ten years earlier—"the voice of the wind of an hour." But now the lesson was clearer, sharper, even less acceptable:

> God of our fathers, known of old,
> Lord of our far-flung battle-line,
> Beneath whose awful Hand we hold
> Dominion over palm and pine—
> Lord God of Hosts, be with us yet,
> Lest we forget—lest we forget!

* See Chapter XI.

The tumult and the shouting dies;
The Captains and the Kings depart:
Still stands Thine ancient sacrifice,
An humble and a contrite heart.
Lord God of Hosts, be with us yet,
Lest we forget—lest we forget!

Far called, our navies melt away;
On dune and headland sinks the fire:
Lo, all our pomp of yesterday
Is one with Nineveh and Tyre!
Judge of the Nations, spare us yet,
Lest we forget—lest we forget!

If, drunk with sight of power, we loose
Wild tongues that have not Thee in awe,
Such boastings as the Gentiles use,
Or lesser breeds without the Law—
Lord God of Hosts, be with us yet,
Lest we forget—lest we forget!

For heathen heart that puts her trust
In reeking tube and iron shard,
All valiant dust that builds on dust,
And guarding, calls not Thee to guard,
For frantic boast and foolish word—
Thy mercy on Thy People, Lord!

X

"Frantic Boast and Foolish Word" The Boer War

In its issue of July 17 which printed the *Recessional, The Times* agreed that the "most dangerous and demoralising temper" into which a nation could fall was that of boastful pride, and the *Graphic* drew much the same sober lesson from the festivities—that they brought home to people the solid meaning behind "the cheaply used rhetoric of Imperialism" by reminding them not only of the greatness of the Empire but of its responsibilities.

At heart the British probably remained as pacific as they had always been. But they were like children who were constantly being taken to a series of too exciting shows—the Jubilee pageants, and rather bloodier ones in out-of-the-way places over the globe. The actions on the stage were invariably colourful and stirring; the programme notes like the reviews next morning made thrilling reading; the realities in the background beyond the footlights did not for a while intrude on the audience in the pit. So it happened that in a world from which *The Times* believed the Jingo spirit had been banished, the last years of the Queen's reign saw a ferment of Jingo activity—four separate incidents within the space of three years, culminating in a major war.

It was no accident that all these events took place in Africa, for just as North America and India in the days of Wolfe and Montcalm,

Clive and Dupleix, had been the focus of great power rivalry, so now it was in the "dark continent" that European expansionism received its final impetus—Belgians in the Congo; the French in Equatorial Africa, Algeria and Morocco; the British in the Transvaal, the Rhodesias, Nigeria, the Gold Coast, the Nile valley, Kenya and the "Horn"; Portuguese in Angola and Mozambique; Italians in Libya and Somaliland; Germans in the Southwest and in Tanganyika.

To blame Britain alone for her part in this "scramble for Africa" would be unjust. She was the most successful and therefore the most abused. But elsewhere, and particularly in the Far East, where Russia was greedily at work detaching parts of the Chinese Empire, her conduct was a model of decorum, not to say timidity. "I think we'd better move back a bit," says *Punch*'s Prime Minister, Lord Salisbury, in the role of King Canute, when bidden by his advisers to order the Russian waves to advance no further up the China shore—an almost exact repetition of Britannia's refusal to engage in brinkmanship against this same rival in Disraeli's time. But then China had never been in the British historic sphere of influence. All we had ever wanted was to trade there and keep an "open door."

In Africa it was another matter. A FIXTURE IN EGYPT reads the caption to *Punch*'s cartoon of a complacent looking Sphynx with a John Bull head squatting by the banks of the Nile; and even the humanitarians would have agreed that it was high time that the unfortunate fellaheen of the Delta should receive "the blessings of a settled government, of a pure administration and of untainted Justice" after centuries of misrule.

Established in Egypt, with a British general in command of the native levies, what could be a more natural step for Britain than the mounting of a joint military expedition into the Sudan to reassert Egyptian sovereignty in that area which dated back to the Pharaohs, and, incidentally, to clear the junction of the Blue and White Niles of the heretical sect of Moslem fanatics which under the leadership of the Mahdi had murdered General Gordon and interrupted the nascent imperial dream of an all-red Cape to Cairo railway.

At Omdurman, just across the river from Khartoum, in a battle distinguished by the last great cavalry charge in British history, in which rode the young Winston Churchill, the Mahdists under the dead prophet's general, the Khalifa, were routed and destroyed. "Sirdar,* I thank you, I am proud of you," says *Punch's* Britannia, actually bowing to the conquering General Kitchener, the only recorded instance of her ever venturing from the perpendicular. In Trafalgar Square crowds gathered at Gordon's statue to hoist a placard: AT LAST HE IS AVENGED. The police removed it. Another was put up. The police removed that also—faithful guardians of the peace of the metropolis but greatly at odds with the public mood. It was left to the *Daily News* to remark of these rejoicings that they would have been deeply distasteful to Gordon's Christian spirit and that the slaughter at Omdurman was too revolting to be gloated over. The public paid no attention to such reproaches, for a new crisis, a new focus of excitement had loomed on the horizon—the appearance on the Upper Nile of a French expedition under a Captain Marchand which had crossed the continent from the west to hoist the tricolour at Fashoda in territory which the British considered well within their own sphere of interest.

Not since Bonaparte's time had such a rumpus arisen between the nations on either side of the Channel. There had been earlier incidents along the Niger in West Africa, where Britishers had long darkly suspected that the French "M'soos" coveted their "African Lily." This conflict of interest, which had nearly led to local war on several occasions, was in a fair way to being settled by international agreement, but Captain Marchand's appearance at an even more sensitive spot in the east of the continent had put the fat properly in the fire. *"Marchez, Marchand!"* was *Punch's* uncompromising message. "I recommend you to pack up your flags and go home." And a real descent into the gutter is shown in another of this journal's cartoons of a French organ-grinder with a monkey labelled FASHODA playing in a London street. "Go away! Go away!" cries honest householder John Bull. "What will you give me if I go?" demands the organ-grinder. "I'll give yer somethin' if yer don't," says John Bull, squaring up to him.

It seems incredible that such attitudes should have been struck for such a cause. But French activities in West Africa had been widely interpreted in Britain as an attempt to pen our settlements on the Niger to the coastal belt, and this sudden switch of interest

* Kitchener was Sirdar, i.e. Commander in Chief of the Egyptian Army.

to the valley of the Nile seemed to sensitive Imperialists just one more move to drive a wedge of French territory across the axis of our southwards advance towards the great lakes. Those who suffered from such nightmares—as Lord Salisbury always used to say when faced with panic talk of Russian intentions against India—would have done well to consult not small atlases but large-scale maps, which might have put Captain Marchand's expedition into perspective against the vastness of central Africa. But everyone's blood was up: the national honour was at stake. "We have dignity to be considered as well as other people," wrote *The Times* in the autumn of 1898, "and we have interests to protect. We mean to see effectually to both. We have not shed British and Egyptian blood in smashing the Khalifa only to be robbed of the fruits by a promenade of eight or nine Frenchmen over soil to which Egypt has an indefeasible right, and over which we and the Egyptians have the added right of conquest." And lest this be thought a merely Tory view, it was shared by some Liberals, by Lord Rosebery—incredibly enough at the dinner of the Surrey Agricultural Association on the occasion of its annual ploughing match:

> If the nations of the world are under the impression that the ancient spirit of Great Britain is dead or her resources weakened, or that her population are less determined . . . to maintain the rights and honour of its flag, they make a mistake which can only end in a disastrous conflagration. (Loud cheers.) The strength of ministers in this country with regard to foreign affairs does not lie in the votes they can command in either House of Parliament. It lies in the intrepid spirit of a united people. (Cheers.)

Who remembers Fashoda to-day? Certainly not the ploughmen of Surrey who are mostly commuters on the London suburban trains. That in the end, after decent civilities had been exchanged with General Kitchener's advancing troops, Captain Marchand took down his flag as advised and removed himself from the White Nile is a matter of indifference to the French, to the British, and above all to the Sudanese. It is part of a pattern of European intrusion into the northern half of Africa which has quite vanished from the scene. But it was at the other end of the continent, in South Africa, that the real test for Imperialism was to come, and the problems it raised are with us still.

* * *

The first white settlers in South Africa had been Dutch: the Afri-kanders, the Boers, as they came to be called. The British had not appeared for another century and a half, until the Napoleonic wars.

As in Canada, so at the Cape: the two races found it hard to agree. They were of the same basic stock and practised variants of the same Protestant religion; yet from the start there was friction, a mutual antipathy that exists to-day though obscured by the wider cleavage between whites and blacks. Towards the middle of the nineteenth century, Boer resentment of alien and what they re-garded as godless British rule drove the more adventurous spirits among them to shake the dust of the coastal settlements off their feet and trek northwards across the drift of the Orange and Vaal rivers into the veldt, much as in America the covered wagons were moving over the great plains and the Rockies to open up the West.

The British reaction to this move which set up two independent Boer republics in the Orange Free State and the Transvaal was confused and slow. Cape Colony, though firmly under London's control, held a large population of Boers who had remained behind in the delectable country south of the Karroo desert yet felt a national solidarity with their brothers in the north. It was a situation requir-ing careful handling. In the 1850s the British governor dreamed of a federation of the white states, but nothing came of it, and it was not till 1877, in the first flush of Disraelian imperialism, that a solu-tion of the problem was applied and the Transvaal (though not the Orange Free State) was annexed to the crown.

For four years the Boers accepted the situation. They were a small people of scattered farms and settlements needing protection from the Zulu tribes which had begun to move into the grasslands from the north. But at Ulundi in 1879 the Zulu *impis* were destroyed, and two years later the Boers of the Transvaal rose against their saviours, following a pattern which had been set a cen-tury earlier at Trenton in New Jersey in the aftermath of the elder Pitt's triumphs in the Seven Years War. Saratoga, Yorktown, the Boer victory over the British at Majuba, are all very similar battles: part of an almost identical progression. But Mr. Gladstone, who had replaced Disraeli as Prime Minister in the elections of 1880, did not wait for as long as Lord North and the Earl of Shelburne before submitting to the inevitable; and by the Pretoria Convention, as later varied by the Convention of London of 1884, the independence of the Transvaal was recognised, subject to certain vague reservations about British "suzerainty."

And there the matter might have rested but for the discovery of a goldfield on the Witwatersrand and near the site of what is now the great city of Johannesburg, in the heart of the Transvaal Republic.

In rushed the diggers and the speculators, among them (by proxy) a young man called Cecil Rhodes who had already rationalised, if not cornered, the infant diamond mining industry at Kimberley just outside the borders of the Orange Free State.

Gentleman immigrant, salesman, miner, entrepreneur, diamond broker, stock jobber, multi-millionaire, colonial politician, soon to be Prime Minister of Cape Colony and one of the two most powerful men in southern Africa, Rhodes has always been a rare puzzle to biographers. They called him the "Colossus," after the statue which in antiquity is said to have straddled the harbour mouth at Rhodes, one of the Seven Wonders of the World—and indeed from his photographs he does have a monumental look, as though carved out of the rock of Table Mountain. Everything else about him is contradictory. To the British public he seemed the living embodiment of Imperialism, but it was of a very personal brand of his own and he spent much of his middle years trying to keep what he called "the imperial factor" out of South African affairs. Born in an English parsonage, no one ever looked more of a colonial. In speech he was often rambling and incoherent, but some of his phrases are not easily forgotten. "Philanthropy plus five percent"—what apter motto for a liberal empire? "Equal rights for civilized men south of the Zambesi"—as a programme for South Africa it is more visionary to-day than when the words were spoken because Rhodes had not excluded the black man from his dream. For all his great imperial plans, his financial ties with London and his hankering for the intellectual world of Oxford which found expression in his famous scholarships, he was at heart a local patriot, a Cape politician, adept at working with the Boer party of the "Bond" which alone could underwrite his premiership. But as a man of acute insight he saw the need also for a wider unity in a greater South Africa which must include the whole country from Table Bay to the Victoria Falls; and as an expatriate who carried the Union Jack in his knapsack he knew that that union must be British. "The government of South Africa by the people of South Africa with the Imperial flag for defence" was his formula. It was to embroil him with another local patriot as strong and single-hearted as himself who believed with equal fervour that South Africa must be Afrikanse—President Kruger of the Transvaal.

* * *

As a boy, Kruger had been on the great trek into the veldt, and even when an old and, as his enemies said, shifty and unscrupulous politician, a pastoralist he remained with virtues and vices to match. Rhodes also had a taste for the great outdoors, for "a chop on the veldt," but with him it was a picnic. With Kruger it was basic, a way of life: he was a voortrekker in a president's chair. "Does he ever wash? is the first thought as one enters the presence," wrote an English journalist after a morning with the patriarch on the stoep. "Does he ever do anything but smoke and drink coffee and spit?" This unfriendly observer did not mention the Bible readings which cynics remarked added usefully to the image of the man of God intent on holy writ even in the press of public engagements. But if there was an air of window-dressing about it, no one could doubt that essentially he was all of one piece—an Old Testament figure, a prophet of the Lord defying the hosts of Midian.

To such a man the discovery of gold on the Rand was a mixed blessing, for if it brought prosperity to his people, it brought also speculators and riff-raff from all over Africa and even further afield —the "Uitlanders," the "Outsiders"—in such numbers that soon the Boers found themselves being outnumbered in parts of their own country by men whom they heartily despised. At the same time a new threat to the republic was rapidly developing, for from his base in Cape Colony Rhodes had been thrusting his way past Kimberley, through the corridor of Bechuanaland on the Transvaal's western border, to open up land in what was then the tribal territory of the Matabele and the Mashona around the site of the present city of Bulawayo. In 1890, the year in which he became Premier of the

Cape, Rhodes obtained a royal charter for his British South Africa Company, the agent of his advance to the Zambesi, and by that autumn his pioneers had founded Salisbury. In 1894 his railway line, which it was hoped would one day link up with the Nile valley via the great lakes, had reached Mafeking, due west of Johannesburg; next year the southern quarter of Bechuanaland, his "Suez Canal" to his "north," was annexed to Cape Colony, a strip of the much larger Bechuanaland Protectorate was handed over to his company, and its territories won from the Matabele after a sharp and bloody war blossomed by royal proclamation into "Rhodesia."

It was a new style of creeping aggression by which the Transvaal was to be caught in the noose of Rhodes's railway which would link the British-dominated south and east in Cape Colony and Natal with the Chartered Company's acquisitions to the north. Nor was the centre forgotten, for in 1892, under personal pressure from Rhodes himself, the Uitlanders formed themselves into the Transvaal National Union. They had grievances to be exploited. In fact, they had no votes. The most active and productive section of the community, the Uitlanders, were denied in Kruger's republic the franchise which in Britain Disraeli had extended to manual workers. Had the children of Belial votes in the days of Elijah? Or the Philistines in the kingdom of David?

Without intervention from outside from powerful interests hostile to the Boers, this denial of elementary rights would have led to little, for the Uitlanders were to show a quite astonishing incompetence and timidity in the face of their oppressors. But their presence, unenfranchised, in the heart of Kruger's citadel made them important elements in the schemes being hatched elsewhere.

The technique to be applied to the Transvaal has since become painfully familiar. An aggressive power suddenly discovers that its racial brothers in the country next door are a shamelessly exploited minority in need of immediate rescue. In the perfected ploy, as shown in Hitler's dismemberment of Czechoslovakia in 1938 with the aid of Hennlein's Sudeten Germans, an iron efficiency rules, force is everything, the pretence is a mere cynical façade. In Queen Victoria's time, when these techniques were in their infancy, the agreement between the conspirators was minimal, the force was lacking, and all that remained was the hypocrisy.

Under the Liberals in 1894 the High Commissioner at the Cape,

Sir Henry Loch, had worked out a plan whereby the long-awaited rising of Uitlanders against their masters would be followed by the arrival of the High Commissioner in Pretoria with a sufficient body of troops to ensure an orderly transfer of power and free elections. This proved too steep for the Liberals at home, and Loch was replaced by a less militant proconsul, Sir Hercules Robinson. The Liberals fell; the Tories came in; the plan was for the moment shelved.

In the meanwhile, the initiative in this undeclared duel had passed to President Kruger. Approaches were made towards the Germans whose territories in South-West Africa lay on the far side of the Bechuanaland corridor; a railway was laid between the Transvaal and the Indian Ocean across Portuguese territory to Delagoa Bay; and to attract traffic to this new Boer outlet and window on the world, prohibitive freights were placed on goods travelling by the British rail link between Cape Town and the Republic. When enterprising traders tried to get round this by off-loading at the border and taking their goods on by ox-wagon over the fords or "drifts" of the river Vaal, Kruger closed them to traffic.

It was a perilous game—how perilous, even the President himself seems to have been only half aware. Faced with a direct threat of force by the British government in answer to this jobbery, he climbed down. No doubt he felt it was all in the fortunes of cold war: one could always draw back, as a farmer might draw back from an unsuccessful attempt to remove a neighbour's landmark. But in the course of it he had inspired in the London government a deep distrust, and among his enemies in Africa, in the circle around Rhodes, a determination to bring him down before he could cause more trouble.

That these two wings of thought hostile to his regime should have agreed about objectives and means seems only common prudence. Any two organisms with a common object in mind might have been expected at least to work together. In Cape Town, in the person of Rhodes, the Empire had at last produced a leader with both vision and practical ability. In London, there sat in the Colonial Secretary's chair the most brilliant, resourceful and determined statesman who had given his attention to imperial affairs since the days of Chatham. Between them they contrived a calamity deeply hurtful to the organism and ideals in which they believed.

How had this happened? How had the extraordinary dichotomy occurred?

When Joseph Chamberlain, the radical from Birmingham who had broken with Gladstone over Irish Home Rule to form an alliance with Lord Salisbury's Tories, took office as Colonial Secretary in the summer of 1895, a perceptive lady who was *The Times'* correspondent on colonial affairs greeted the appointment with rapture—"The change . . . was marvellous; it was a total transformation; the sleeping city awakened by a touch." And in the "drifts" crisis over Kruger's railway freights Chamberlain had acted with a firmness and promptitude which delighted his supporters. The Transvaal was brought sharply to heel.

So why should not progress be made from there? The complaints of the Uitlanders echoed to high heaven. Could their grievances not be used to bring down the republic altogether and reverse the verdict of Majuba?

This was Rhodes's intention. A Uitlander rising was to be fomented in Johannesburg. Simultaneously, a force of his Bechuanaland police and irregulars in the employment of the Chartered Company was to be assembled just outside the borders of the Transvaal, within three days' march of the Rand, to move in when the revolution came.

It was a new version of Loch's plan, and in it the new High Commissioner, Sir Hercules Robinson, would have a part to play by arriving like a *deus ex machina* to confer the legal blessings of British rule.

How far Sir Hercules, a very experienced, elderly and *souffrant* diplomat and valetudinarian, had allowed himself to become aware of the details of this conspiracy may be doubted. He was certainly told a great deal: whether he listened is another matter. But that he had weighed the chances of a Uitlander rebellion and the use that could be made of it was clear from his memorandum briefing London on the crisis which everyone felt was imminent:

Immediately on news being received of a rising at Johannesburg and the establishment there of a provisional Government—for that, I take it, is the form a revolt would take—the High Commissioner as the representative of the paramount Power in South Africa should issue a Proclamation directing both parties to desist from hostilities and to submit to his arbitration. H.M. Government should notify their intention of supporting this attitude, and it might be announced in the Home press that a large force had been ordered to hold itself in readiness to proceed to South Africa.

The High Commissioner should at once proceed to Pretoria and after hearing the complaints on both sides order the election of a Constituent Assembly—such Assembly to be elected by every adult white male in the country.

In London this programme was approved not only by Chamberlain, but by Lord Salisbury and the full cabinet. It was balm both to their imperialist instincts and their liberal souls, for what could be more deserving than the peaceful introduction of democratic rights into a country which was still theoretically a British colony? The thought that this promised rebellion might not be spontaneous but *sponsored* never seems to have occurred to the majority of these busy men. The conspiratorial messages flashing between the Uitlander committee in Johannesburg and Rhodes at the Cape were not brought to their attention. And certainly they had no idea at all that the police forces in Bechuanaland which they were about to hand over to Rhodes's Chartered Company were to be employed in anything other than a peace-keeping role to prevent bloodshed in the event of civil war in the Transvaal.

Did Chamberlain have more intimate and detailed knowledge?

The Parliamentary Committee of Enquiry drawn from both political parties, which was later to sit and report on the fiasco known to history as the Jameson Raid, returned a firm Not Guilty verdict to this charge:

Neither the Secretary of State for the Colonies nor any of the officers of the Colonial Office received any information which should have made them, or any of them, aware of the plot during its development.

The Committee were either great boobies or very intent on closing the ranks in a dangerous situation, for there was ample evidence, if they had looked for it, to suggest quite another conclusion. But to say this is not to imply that Chamberlain knew everything that was to happen. He believed that the Uitlanders were about to rise. He was mistaken, and so was Rhodes who had plotted it. Chamberlain undoubtedly knew that a Chartered Company force under the command of Dr. Leander Starr Jameson lay at Pitsani just outside the western frontiers of the Transvaal, ready to march in to support Sir Hercules on his arrival as arbiter. What he did not know—what Rhodes himself did not guess till it was too late —was that this trusted subordinate, the winning, amiable and able "Dr. Jim," would give way at the crisis to a spasm of sheer paranoia and go to war, unasked, like some modern Cortez, with 470 men.

That almost everyone concerned had become in some way affected by the over-stimulating air of the veldt or dreams of El Dorado seems the most charitable explanation of what followed. Chamberlain was later to wonder what it was about South Africa that made blackguards of everyone who got involved in its politics. It was something in the air: a kind of madness. Only the Uitlanders kept their heads. Their leaders had thoroughly enjoyed the cloak-and-dagger work of conspiracy, the cablegrams flashing along the wires between Joahnnesburg, Cape Town and Pitsani in a code that would have delighted every schoolboy heart—

Tell Dr. Jameson the polo tournament postponed for one week or it will clash with race week.

Of such metal were the Uitlander leaders made. In cable after cable they urged that the "flotation" had better be postponed. For when it came to the point, like the sensible capitalists they were, the Uitlanders much preferred the devil they knew—even Kruger— to the devil they did not know under the Union Jack. At heart they were Separatists—they might have risen for a reformed Transvaal in which they and not the Boers would have the leading voice, but it would have to be an independent Transvaal, not the imperial package they were being asked to risk their necks for.

With increasing incredulity, rage and despair the sponsors of the plot at the Cape and at Pitsani watched this craven abdication which spelt the ruin of their hopes. Rhodes himself kept a stoic front—it may have been his Oxford training, or more probably relief at being quit of an adventure whose dangers he had begun to glimpse. "Is there no one in Johannesburg," he asked, "who will risk being shot and will lead the malcontents?" And on being assured that there was no one—"If they won't, they won't. I shall wire Jameson to keep quiet."

Everyone, in fact, was wiring Jameson. During those crucial days at the end of December 1896 a stream of messages reached the camp at Pitsani, alternately elating and depressing the mercurial personality of Dr. Jim. At one moment he was assured that the revolution was about to start and was even given a firm date. But thereafter every word from the Rand was discouraging to a deepening degree—

Absolutely necessary to postpone flotation. . . . We will endeavour to meet your wishes as regards December but you must not move until you have received instructions to.

Experts' reports decidedly adverse. I absolutely condemn further developments at present.

And finally, from Rhodes's other nomadic doctor and general factotum, Rutherfoord Harris, cabling from Johannesburg after a final meeting with the committee:

All our foreign friends are now dead against it and say public will not subscribe one penny towards it even with you as a director. Ichabod.

The glory had departed; the bubble had burst; the wind had gone out of the plot. The Uitlanders settled down to make a more modest constitutional revolution of their own and their Reform Committee became for a few brief days the provisional government of Johannesburg. Kruger was quite prepared to play with them till the external danger had passed. And then—incredibly—fateful words came in from Pitsani:

The Veterinary Surgeon has left for Johannesburg with some very good horseflesh and backs himself for seven hundred.

Jameson and his force had crossed the rubicon. This was on the evening of Sunday, December 29.

* * *

In London on the 27th Chamberlain heard from the High Commissioner that the looked-for rising would not now take place. On the 29th, troubled by rumours that in spite of this Jameson might take the bit between his teeth, he cabled to Sir Hercules that any such move would be a breach of the British South Africa Company's charter, the seriousness of which must at once be brought to Rhodes's attention. By the time this message was received in Cape Town, Jameson was across the frontier. The Reform Committee in Johannesburg had sent a last-minute messenger to Pitsani to head off the imminent calamity—the messenger joined Dr. Jameson's forces. When they were half way to the Rand a horseman despatched by Sir Hercules overtook the column with imperative orders in the Queen's name for an immediate withdrawal. Dr. Jim and his troops rode on. A second and still more imperative order was treated with the same contempt; perhaps it was the champagne speaking, thirty-six cases of which had been delivered to the camp at Pitsani. It is this mixture of tragedy and low comedy, persisting from beginning to end, which gives the Jameson Raid its unique flavour. According to one story, a vital telegraph line to Pretoria was not cut because the drunken trooper engaged to do it cut a length of wire fence instead.* Certainly a cable from Pitsani to Cape Town explaining Jameson's intentions was delayed en route because the Chartered Company's office was closed for the week-end. It could only have happened to the British.

The general air of fantasy did not even spare the august mon-

* This story may be apocryphal. See Elizabeth Pakenham's delightful treatment of the topic in her *Jameson's Raid*.

ocled Colonial Secretary himself, for when the news of the raid reached him Chamberlain was at his residence of Highbury near Birmingham dressing for the annual servants' ball. Very creditably he did not snatch his coachman from the festivities but proceeded by hired cab and midnight train to London, determined to "crush" a conspiracy which threatened his political life. Cynics might see a ruthless insincerity in this, for Chamberlain had certainly not bothered to enquire too deeply into an insurrectionary situation in the Transvaal which might, if properly handled by Sir Hercules, pay handsome imperial dividends. He had turned the Nelsonic blind eye on the Uitlanders, on Rhodes, on the force at Pitsani.

But what Jameson had done was indefensible. No one in any position of authority could be expected to stomach it—not Lord Salisbury, or the cabinet, or the Liberal opposition, and certainly not the watchful and jealous European powers led by Germany with her own special interests in South Africa. The British people and press in their Jingo mood might stomach it, might even applaud it—and in resisting that thought Chamberlain showed himself a statesman and a man of honour, however devious his later explanations were to prove. He had never really trusted Rhodes or the "Randlords," whom he regarded as jobbers and commercial freebooters whose interests were not those of the Empire. "I have never at any time concealed my opinion," he wrote some months after the Raid, "that whatever defects may exist in the present form of government in the Transvaal, the substitution of an entirely independent Republic governed by, or for, the capitalists of the Rand would be very much worse. . . ." If this was to some degree a later rationalisation and a piece of special pleading to deny his complicity at the time, the essential truth of the words can be seen in the reluctance with which he had handed over the Bechuanaland police to Rhodes's Chartered Company and to his sharp reactions when the rumours spread that some piratical action might be attempted. He had been prepared for a revolution under the auspices of the High Commissioner, not for the kind of uncontrolled and perhaps uncontrollable regime that partisan forces might set up. So from the Colonial Office the ukase went out that the illegal expedition must be turned back.

It was a courageous decision, for as Chamberlain himself well knew, if the Raid succeeded no voice of reason would survive against the wave of Jingo hysteria which would sweep him away into oblivion. On New Year's morning, while the issue on the veldt still hung in the balance, *The Times* printed a letter purporting to have been dated December 28, the day before the Raid, in which the hapless Uitlanders of Johannesburg, fearing for the effects of their threatened rising, implored Dr. Jim to march in at once to save them from the licentious Boer soldiery:

> Thousands of unarmed men, women and children of our race will be at the mercy of well-armed Boers, while property of enormous value will be in the greatest peril. . . .
> The circumstances are so extreme that we cannot but believe that you and the men under you will not fail to come to the rescue of people who will be so situated.

This letter, the text of which had been cabled to London by Rutherfoord Harris, was perfectly genuine in the sense that the Uitlander Committee had signed it—but they had signed it in mid-November, weeks before the Raid, reluctantly, at Jameson's urgent request, at a time when they were menaced by no one but himself. It was, therefore, in fact a forgery: the doctor had postdated it to suit his own convenience when he decided to march in to the rescue of his most reluctant allies. The British press and public, however, swallowed it whole. *The Times* hedged its bets a little, but not much. There was no overt proof of these perils, it said in its leader column, but if Jameson had acted in response to this message, then his action, though "technically incorrect" would meet with general approbation. For Alfred Austin, who had been created poet laureate less than a year before the Raid, it was balm from Gilead, and he forthwith produced a poem which preserves as though in amber the very spirit of Jingoism, so soon to fade from the scene:

> Wrong! Is it wrong? Well, may be:
> But I'm going all the same.
> Do they think me a Burgher's baby,
> To be scared by a scolding name?
> They may argue and prate and order;
> Go, tell them to save their breath:

Then over the Transvaal border,
And gallop for life or death!

There are girls in the gold-reef city,
There are mothers and children too!
And they cry, "Hurry up! for pity!"
So what can a brave man do?
If even we win they'll blame us:
If we fail, they will howl and hiss.
But there's many a man lives famous
For daring a wrong like this.

When these words appeared in *The Times* of January 11, 1896, the Raid itself was over. Kruger's Boers, if not Rhodes and the British government, had been forewarned and forearmed—their mounted commandos had shadowed the invading column almost from the moment it had crossed the frontier, gradually closing in as it advanced, till near Krugersdorp, a few miles out of Johannesburg, they faced the raiders on a hill-crest dominating the road into the city.

Jameson* and his force commander, Sir John Willoughby, still expected help from the Uitlanders inside the town. They received a number of promises that a mounted Uitlander column would come out, but of course nothing happened—the High Commissioner's stern denunciation of the Raid was already circulating in Johannesburg and combined with fear of Kruger's vengeance had hamstrung the Reform Committee. That Jameson and his friends should have *expected* anything to happen is just one more proof of their naïveté and capacity to delude themselves. An attempted flank march round the Krugersdorp position—guided by a man who was probably a Boer spy—brought them up against a still more impregnable line at Doornkop, where a last drive to break through the ring of Boer commandos cost them over a hundred killed, wounded and missing. Outmanoeuvred, outgunned, short of sleep, food and ammunition, Jameson and Willoughby had no choice but to surrender. What they had not omitted to bring with them was a list of their associates in Johannesburg for the convenience of Kruger's

* Jameson was not a military man. His official position was Administrator for Mashonaland.

police. It was another Majuba, as the triumphant Boers proclaimed. The British flag, said one of them, was not red, white and blue; for he had seen it twice in his lifetime and it was a dirty white rag.

*   *   *

What had been achieved was almost total disaster, from which Chamberlain alone survived intact, to be acquitted of all complicity by the famous "Committee of No Enquiry" as the wags called it which later sat in judgment in Westminster Hall. The Raid cost the raiders and the Uitlander leaders their liberty for varying terms in gaol. It cost Rhodes his premiership: he had no alternative but to resign since he had lost the support of moderate Boer opinion, and within three years a Boer government was to be in power in Cape Town. British influence in South Africa had suffered a most damaging reverse, and what is more, even the varying interests and personalities involved had shown an inability to think alike or work together, which augured unhappily for the future. Was the Empire really separatist at heart?*

That in Africa at least its course had been marked by muddled policies and irresolute leadership was all too evident to Chamberlain as he prepared to face a triumphant Kruger and a world whose press had erupted into paeans of malicious joy over Britain's humiliation. This outburst of hatred came as a painful surprise. Worst of all was the wound to national morale which he felt could only be staunched by some "act of vigour," say by a stiff note to Germany, whose Kaiser had wired congratulations to Kruger on the re-establishment of Transvaal's "independence" and the suppression of "armed bands." "It does not matter which of our numerous foes we defy," he wrote to Lord Salisbury, "but we ought to defy someone." There spoke the people's tribune, the guardian of national honour and the colonial empire. He had no intention of allowing the setback of the Raid to deflect him from his long-term aims of British paramountcy in South Africa and justice for the Uitlanders. If Jameson had failed to find a way round the Boer entrenchments at Krugersdorp, that was no reason why a subtler and cooler man should not run rings round Krugerism.

One of the priorities was to find a younger High Commissioner to

* The accession of a French *habitant* to the premiership of Canada was soon to underline this question.

replace Sir Hercules, whose labours in the aftermath of the Raid had been singularly unheroic in surrendering British interests without even a show of fight. And here Chamberlain made no mistake. From the unlikely precincts of the Board of Inland Revenue he snatched a hitherto unknown official, Sir Alfred Milner, who was to prove the very pattern of the proconsul, the founder of a school of Imperialists who in the years to come became known as "Milner's Young Men" or "Milner's Circus."

Unlike Jameson, Chamberlain knew the importance of "the time and the place" in Drake's famous phrase. He had judged to a hairsbreadth the mood of his countrymen, who after two *débâcles* at Majuba and Doornkop had no urge to try further conclusions with the Boers, yet burned in some way to assert themselves and bring the Boers to reason. With Milner's assistance he hoped as a first step to urge Kruger towards an accommodation which would include the granting of a proper franchise to all white citizens in the Transvaal. "I wish it were possible to persuade President Kruger to give us something in the way of moderate reforms for the Uitlanders," he wrote to the new High Commissioner in the summer of 1897, a year and a half after the Raid. It was his hope, if hardly his expectation, that the Boers might be brought to recognise that the British paramountcy on which he insisted meant no invasion of their legitimate rights and that his policy was defensive, not aggressive.

The old President, who had shied away from the lure of a visit to London, remained adamant—having won a battle, he fancied he had won a war. Milner nearer the scene than his chief, recognised this Boer intransigence and felt the need for stronger measures. Always by temperament an out-and-outer, he was soon suggesting that British policy should be aimed at *working up to a crisis* by steady and inflexible pressure on the franchise issue.

Chamberlain's response was discouraging—he knew the pacific mood of Britain which underlay the Jingo gloss. "A war with the Transvaal, unless upon the clearest provocation," he replied to Milner in the spring of 1898, "would be extremely unpopular in this country. . . . We must endure a great deal rather than provoke a conflict . . . Accordingly I wish to emphasise the fact that, for the present at any rate, our greatest interest in South Africa is peace, and that all our policy must be devoted to this object." He repeated this in a cable three days later: "The principle object of HMG in

South Africa at present is peace. Nothing but a most flagrant offence would justify the use of force." In Lord Salisbury's words, expressing the opinion of the cabinet as a whole, Kruger would have to be very "outrageous" before anything could be done about it.

The pacifism in this thinking is to be noted, but so are the qualifications. The time was not ripe for a forward policy, but times might change. "A most flagrant offence" might change them. And at the end of December 1898, almost exactly three years after the Raid, the Boers duly provided one by the killing in Johannesburg of a British workman called Tom Edgar who had become involved in a night brawl with some Boers and was shot at point-blank range, on his own doorstep and in the presence of his family, by one of Kruger's police.

This time the Uitlanders did not protest to the Administrator of Mashonaland but to the Queen. Their protest was rejected by the British deputy High Commissioner acting in Milner's absence, an Irishman whose sympathies were wholly pro-Boer. Uitlander open-air meetings were broken up by Kruger's police, whose gunman was of course acquitted of Edgar's murder; an indoor meeting was similarly treated and lent power to yet another Uitlander protest to the Queen, which reached the Colonial Office in the spring of 1899.

Examining the changed situation, Chamberlain now asked the High Commissioner to put his reactions on paper. Such a move from so cool and provident a statesman shows how far he felt relationships with the Transvaal had deteriorated, or improved, according to one's point of view. Certainly if he was fishing for an argument, he had hooked a whopper, for Milner at once responded with an official despatch couched in the strongest and most impassioned terms, in which he referred to the Uitlanders as being no better off than "Helots" in Kruger's republic and urged that the case for British intervention was "overwhelming."

Observe now the expert angler. Not for him the crudities of Jameson or for that matter of Milner, whose tone had been pitched too high for comfort. To the Uitlanders, who had to be kept in play and in good protesting voice, the Colonial Secretary replied with sympathy yet with a certain coolness that the "exceptional and arbitrary treatment" to which they had been subjected had been noted by the British Government and must of course be rectified. But to Kruger he still held out the hope of conciliation and the suggestion of a conference between President and High Commissioner to deliberate on the urgent and dangerous problems which threatened the peace of South Africa.

Between May 31 and June 5 these two champions came together on neutral ground in the Orange Free State capital of Bloemfontein. As early as April a *Punch* artist had seen John Bull, as Inspector of Transvaal schools, telling headmaster Kruger that complaints had been received from the boys: and now, suddenly inspired, it presented Sir Alfred Milner face to face with a fine piece of livestock with a horned Kruger head to it:

> There was a High Comm who said, "How
> Shall I tackle this wily old cow?
> I will sit on this stile
> And continue to smile,
> Which may soften the heart of this cow."

A fortnight later *Punch* returned to the charge by repeating its own cartoon down to the last particular, except for the figure of Sir Alfred walking disgustedly away. An appropriate verse went with it:

> There was a High Comm who said, "Now
> I have conferred with this wily old cow!
> I *have* sat on this stile
> And continued to smile,
> But it's had no effect on the cow."

In fact, Kruger had remained in Bloemfontein exactly the same man who had outfaced Rhodes and poor Sir Hercules. He saw the situation in basic terms. "It is my country you want," he exclaimed to Milner with tears in his eyes. Much sympathy can be felt for him: much sympathy was felt for him at the time, and Chamberlain was uneasily aware of it. On receiving the first news that the conference was collapsing, he minuted, "This is a serious matter"; and went on to suggest further lines for negotiation by which promises of a fair franchise for the Uitlanders might be exchanged for some formal guarantee of Transvaal independence. He had constantly to keep before him what Milner apparently ignored: that

British opinion had still not been screwed up to war—even *Punch,* now the most Jingo of organs, was advising that what was wanted was an exchange of notes with Kruger, not an exchange of shots.

In face of such reluctance even the most popular of statesmen had to walk warily. But that Chamberlain was in the last resort as prepared as Milner to force the pace is a fact borne out by all the evidence. In his speeches he was careful to disclaim bellicose attitudes, but there is a note of menace all the same:

> Those who say there is a party within the government that desires war are guilty of a mischievous untruth. On the other hand, those fall into grievous error who think that there is a party within the government who, having put their hands to the plough, will now draw back. . . . We will not be hurried on the one hand; we will not be held back on the other.

Three days earlier, in a confidential note to his Under-secretary, Lord Selborne, he had given a little more of the game away in his comments on the tactics required to get Parliament to rise to his line:

> I want to get the water into good condition and do everything *selon les règles.*

He was a diplomat to his fingertips and would do nothing crude. But later to Milner the Machiavellian touch comes nearer to the surface:

> . . . we ought to exhaust the franchise proposals and get a clear refusal . . . before we ask for more. If and when we ask for more it means war, and therefore, before we do this, we must have a sufficient force in South Africa to defend ourselves during the time that will be required to get a full fighting force into the country.

Yet it remains hard to see in him a warmonger. His whole temperament was civilian: he distrusted soldiers. What he wanted was "to win without a fight," as he himself had put it at the time of the Bloemfontein conference. There would be no war if Kruger could be pushed into granting franchise reform and would remedy the other social grievances of the Uitlanders.

And under this pressure it almost seemed for a while that Kruger might be brought some way towards him. In August 1899, at a meeting between the British agent in Pretoria and the Transvaal State Attorney (another eminent Imperialist in the making: Jan Christian Smuts), the Boers seemed to be offering everything that Chamberlain had asked for—a five-year retrospective franchise for the Uitlanders and a quarter of the seats in the Transvaal parliament, the Volksraad.

Then the difficulties re-appeared, the gulf between the negotiators widened, as was bound to happen, since the argument was not really about voting rights but about which of two races should dominate South Africa. "The sands are running down in the glass" was Chamberlain's warning, given to the world from his own lawn at Highbury, his inner citadel. The Boers withdrew the Smuts proposals. From this point the two antagonists were concerned only with keeping up a pretence of negotiation while they got their military forces into position and looked around for diplomatic support. On September 29 the Orange Free State, at Kruger's urging, called up its burghers; on October 2 the Volksraad voted for war; on the 7th, Army reservists were called up in Britain; on the 8th, Imperial troops from India landed at Durban; and next day President Kruger issued an ultimatum to Britain demanding that troops on his border should be removed, that recently landed forces should leave South Africa, and that reinforcements on their way there should be turned back.

Amusingly enough, the British had already drawn up an ultimatum of their own, but had arranged to send it to Kruger by the slowest boat available to give time for more reinforcements to arrive at Durban. It was, of course, never delivered because in the meantime Kruger had obliged with an almost ideal *casus belli* in demands which no Imperial government could possibly accept. The London press exploded in indignant scorn. "The die," declared *The Standard,* "has been cast by our deluded foes"—"presumptuous little foes," it added. For the *Daily Mail* the coming war—for no one doubted any longer that it must be war—was in a just cause against "an almost barbaric system of government," and it cheered its readers with the reflection that the vast expansion of the British Empire and the decline of the Dutch throughout the world had already proved that "brain for brain, body for body," the British were more than a match for their enemies despite superior Boer trickery and cunning. The *Chronicle,* almost alone of the dailies, deplored the advent of civil war, yet even the *Chronicle* closed its ranks once hostilities had begun. *The Pall Mall Gazette* (on which Milner had once served as assistant editor) felt that the Union Jack was a symbol that could not be unfurled in too many places. But, naturally, it was what *The Times* said that mattered, and never was that journal in better voice. President Kruger's ultimatum, in its view, was "an infatuated step." It had hoped to the last that the dispute could be settled without bloodshed and greeted the failure of the negotiations with "profound regret." Then waxing warmer, it called the Transvaal "a petty republic" whose mood was one of "studied and insolent defiance." "They have declared war on the British Empire. They must feel her arm and pay the penalty of their aggression." And as a final reinforcement *The Times* called up "the vigorous and characteristic sonnet" it had just received from Algernon Charles Swinburne:

> Patience, long sick to death, is dead. Too long
> Have sloth and doubt and treason bidden us be
> What Cromwell's England was not, when the sea
> To him bore witness given of Blake how strong
> She stood a Commonwealth that brooked no wrong.
>   . . . .
>   Speech and song
> Lack utterance now for loathing. . . .
> To scourge these dogs, agape with jaws afoam,
> Down out of life. Strike, England, and strike home.

"This poem is not copyright," the paper added.

*   *   *

So Britain was launched into war. Apart from the Crimea it was her first conflict for nearly a century against an enemy of European stock, but it seemed a very small enemy, and if anything troubled the public it was the thought of what rival nations might be saying. Germany, remarked the *Graphic* wistfully, had been every bit as much hated after the Franco-Prussian War: and in any case was not the world's hatred an envious tribute to the Empire's success? That the Boers could be a formidable foe, that they were working on interior lines, knew the country, were by far the more mobile, and had imported large quantities of the most modern artillery were not facts appreciated by the public or by a War Office that had no General Staff and had made no plans beyond the provision of an expeditionary force under the command of General Sir Redvers Buller, VC.

The hero's departure from Southampton for the war—immaculately dressed in frock coat and top hat—was the signal for one of those demonstrations that touchingly reveal the Victorian sunset. Sirens sounded and there was tremendous cheering as the general appeared on the liner's bridge:

> The shouts died away, and then there rose a gentle sound of women's voices first and men's voices later singing God Save the Queen. . . . It was a great and memorable scene. And then with a confused medley of cheers and all sorts of songs—Rule Britannia predominating—waving of handkerchiefs and tossing of hats, with wavings of little pocket Union Jacks also, the *Dunotta Castle* steamed off into the gathering haze of the evening. . . . Before the vessel was far down Channel the east wind began to blow with no common violence, but she is a first class ship, well found in every way, and there is nothing to be anxious about.

If only so much could have been said for the distinguished passenger she carried! Of all the generals who ever led British troops, Buller cared the most deeply for them and remained to the end the most beloved. As a commander of men he had every virtue except the ability to fight a battle, still less conduct a war. He had never wanted the supreme command; knew himself to be quite unsuited to it.

Under his limp direction in the autumn of 1899 the British armies in South Africa suffered three major disasters in one week as they battered themselves against the Boer defences. Stormberg, Magersfontein, Colenso, are now forgotten battles, but they loomed large enough to our grandfathers. The distinguished detective story writer, Margery Allingham gave Magersfontein as a Christian name to Mr. Campion's valet, Lugg, who must have gone to the font in "Black Week." No one in Britain could remember anything like it, and in the depth of national humiliation there was a great desire to put it all down to what one paper called "traps, ambuscades and crafty Boer circumventions," in other words to their unfair use of barbed wire and habit of entrenching themselves in hollows on the forward slopes of hills instead of on the skyline where honest Englishmen could shoot them.

After following the Jingo wave for a quarter of a century we are about to see it rise to its crest before breaking on the shore, and the spectacle was never more impressive. "Mummy, dear, I heard Papa say 'lots of infantry were going out to fight the Boers,'" says the six-year-old on its rocking-horse, speaking also for its two-year-old brother. "When shall *we* be old enough to go?" But even younger moppets were on the march:

> *Visitor to the Nursery:* "And has Baby begun to talk?"
> *Sister Elsie:* "Oh yes, but he can only say one word."
> *Visitor:* "What's that?"
> *Sister Elsie:* "BANG!"

The upper and professional classes who bought *Punch* were naturally committed by tradition to the war, and so were the middle classes who bought the *Mail* or the *Globe* and were now hastening to join the yeomanry or the volunteers, bound for the Cape along with the new overall commander, Lord Roberts, and his chief of staff, Kitchener, the victor of Omdurman. What the working class thought was only just beginning to seem of importance after the long proletarian slumber which had followed the fall of Chartism, but of course its members formed the rank and file of the professional army, and that even the man in the street was sound at heart was soon to be proved in a spectacular way.

Early in the war the Boers had besieged two exposed British garrisons on the borders of the rebel republics, one at Ladysmith, near the Orange Free State/Natal frontier, the other at Mafeking on Rhodes's railway in Bechuanaland. Ladysmith was eventually relieved by Buller after yet another disaster to British arms at Spion Kop. Mafeking, defended with great panache by Colonel Baden-Powell, future founder of the Boy Scout movement, had to wait till the late spring of 1900. It was an outpost of small military importance, and if it had fallen there would have been no massacre at the hands of a chivalrous foe. Yet the excitement caused by the news of its relief brought about scenes unparalleled in London even during the celebrations of the Diamond Jubilee. The whole town went wild —in *Vanity Fair's* words, "literally mad, delirious with delight." A huge crowd had gathered in front of the Mansion House, and when at 9:20 P.M. the Lord Mayor made the official announcement, the streets erupted. The news spread westward; drivers of buses shouted out the news as they clattered down Ludgate Hill; cabmen joined in with loud hurrahs; the newsboys gave away their papers gratis; the sight of any uniform provoked God Save the Queen; and even the postmen were cheered. Central London was "one dense, strident, jubilant mass," rich and poor mixing it like brothers, yet one remembers George Forsyte sardonically watching the display— "They want our goods." What were such people doing in the West End, in the heart of Clubland? Typically the War Office, taken by surprise as usual, had posted a "No News" bulletin outside its walls. The excitement infected the whole nation. Chester was reported "in ecstacies"; twenty thousand people took part in a monster procession at Leeds, thirty thousand in rival Bradford; in East Moseley they turned out the fire brigade; in Douglas, Isle of Man, they routed the mayor out of bed and made him make a speech; in Surrey even the gravediggers were *en fête.*

By a splendid irony Mafeking Night coincided with the unveiling of a statue of Mr. Gladstone on the anniversay of his death! What a headshaking there must have been in heaven. But the Grand Old Man need not have despaired, for there were straws in the wind. Already the *Standard,* a very Jingo organ, had called the bloodletting on the veldt "this costly and sanguinary war." What is more, the *Westminster Gazette,* remarking that it was in no sense "Little Englander" or anti-Imperialist in spirit, and agreeing that it was right that the British people, after all they had suffered, should rejoice over a victory, went on to add that certain manifestations which the war spirit had evoked might well cause uneasiness among sober people.

> The ready response when a statesman appeals to the instinct of revenge is not a pleasing sign. . . . Nor is it altogether well that we should make the music hall the centre of our congratulations and demonstrations.

It was time, thought the *Gazette,* to return to the principles of Gladstone, Cobden and Bright.

*   *   *

Two whole years separated Mafeking Night from the Peace of Vereeniging by which the enemy finally laid down his arms. After the first turn of the tide, which had led to the capture of Pretoria and the defeat of Kruger's field armies, they had been very unheroic years for Britain, in which the Boer commandos, fighting as guerillas, had been gradually broken by a system of blockhouse and wire and their families rounded up into concentration camps.

When the peace came there were celebrations which one Liberal organ thought were almost on the scale of Mafeking Night, certainly "enough to make the judicious grieve." But this was not the general press reaction, which was sombre and reflected a real change in the public mood. The news, wrote the *Nineteenth Century,* had caused one universal throb of joy and gratitude. "We have looked upon war with all its horrors in the face, and our most earnest prayer is that never again, in our time, shall we be confronted by that grisly spectre. The spirit of Mafeking Day hardly made itself visible at all." The *Westminster Review* thought that Imperialism itself had suffered a severe and deserved reverse; and no doubt this was true, for there was no longer Liberal support for a government which was widely held to have employed "methods of barbarism" in the closing stages of the war. Among the majority of Tories there was relief at the victory and gratitude for the help which the colonies had given to the mother country in a dark hour, but there was everywhere a realisation that the full strength of the Empire had had to be exerted to defeat an enemy of minuscule size. To have had recourse to so large a hammer to crack so small a nut, and to have taken so long about it, was a chastening thought after all the glories of the Diamond Jubilee. And by what methods had victory finally come? What had been achieved at so great a cost in blood and treasure and the loss of Britain's liberal image among the powers?

The British Empire was to grow much larger. The war itself had restored to it the two rebellious Boer republics. But the high noon of Jingoism was past. The bubble had burst. The "Greater Britain," "mightier and mightier yet," which lived on until the 1930s, was never to be supported by that fervour of the streets which for a while had transformed the Empire into a projection of the music-hall stage, as much a part of the daily life-blood of the British people as Dan Leno. The mood had been too emotional to last. In fact, it was to prove counter-productive, for the joint effects of the Jameson Raid (a failure) and the Boer War (a costly and questionable success) had created among the Liberals who were shortly to return to power at Westminster an attitude of such moral revulsion that they were to move, within a matter of a few years, to give back virtual independence to the Transvaal and the Orange Free State and thus, in effect, reverse the verdict of the fighting by ensuring Boer domination in the future Union of South Africa.

By doing so, with the best and most liberal intentions, the British government handed over the future dominion to peoples who were to reject Rhodes's vision of a multi-racial state. The "imperial factor" had been eliminated in one vital sector in a way that Rhodes himself would have deplored.

And the decline of Imperialism on a still wider front had been signalled even earlier, long before Joseph Chamberlain went to the Colonial Office to rescue an organism which had already begun to fall apart.

XI

The Goal of Imperial Federation

From the moment in the late 1870s when people began to re-assess the Empire's role in its world setting, the need for alterations to the old ramshackle structure became evident. Most theorists agreed that some kind of closer union would have to come, but how could it best be achieved? The more advanced and radical thinkers saw only one remedy—there must be Imperial Federation of the kind that had been achieved in Germany in 1871, with a federal diplomatic corps, a federal parliament, federal taxes, a customs union (*Zollverein*) and joint defence arrangements (*Kriegsverein*).

To popularise these views the Imperial Federation League had been founded in 1884 with distinguished support from members of both political parties at Westminster. The movement had spread to the colonies, particularly Canada, and for a while the highest hopes were entertained that this vision of one unified super-state could become practical politics within the lifetime of its sponsors. Under their impulse the highly successful Indian and Colonial Exhibition was staged in 1886, and the next year, to coincide with the celebrations of the Queen's Golden Jubilee, a concourse of over a hundred statesmen from all over the Empire were bidden to London to the first Colonial Conference.*

* See p. 132.

The Federalists were cock-a-hoop; they felt the tide of history was running with them and that the logic of their arguments must be seen by everyone. They had some grounds for such belief, for the Queen's speech at the prorogation of the parliamentary session had contained highly encouraging words—"I am led to the conclusion that there is on all sides a growing desire to draw closer in every practicable way the bonds which unite the various portions of the Empire."

"Practicable" was the operative word and one that should have sounded a note of warning to enthusiasts.

The Tory Prime Minister of the time, Lord Salisbury, was one of the shrewdest and most withdrawn of men, a patrician who was not always able to recognise the obscurer members of his own cabinet. Half-digested schemes were anathema to him—he saw the world around him as it was, not as what ideologues hoped it might become. To the gathering of magnates at the inaugural meeting he addressed words of sage advice. Imperial Federation was no doubt a "grand aspiration" which he had no wish to decry and which might come about when trends which were now nebulous had taken shape. The time was not ripe for it, and the same went for arguments for an Imperial *Zollverein* or Empire free trade area. The need of the hour was for none of these things but for a *Kriegsverein*, a joint union for defence such as Bismark's Germany had undertaken—this was the "real and important business" on which Lord Salisbury thought the conference should be engaged.

A writer in this field has likened the Golden Jubilee Conference of 1887 to a summons to vassals from their overlord, much as a mediaeval king might have sent for the barons. If so, the results were extremely disappointing, since all that the British succeeded in extracting from their Colonials in the way of defence contributions was a reluctant promise on the part of the Australians to pay some of the naval costs of warships stationed in their waters; and the one major contribution to the debates took the form of a South African plea for the levying of an Imperial customs duty on foreign goods, the proceeds to be devoted to defence costs—a breach of established principles almost as revolting to Lord Salisbury as a *Zollverein* itself.

Seven years later, in 1894, another gathering took place at Ottawa, supposedly to discuss Empire communications and in particular a cable link between Canada and Australasia. The Colonials used it for yet another assault on the Cobdenite tabernacle. "Who doubts for a moment," said George Foster, the Canadian Finance Minister, "that if Great Britain and her colonies could be formed into a commercial union whereby the trade between the different parts of the Empire would have a more favoured position than outside or foreign trade . . . who doubts but that immense benefits would immediately accrue to the Empire as a whole." This was a programme for Imperial Preference which flew in the face of British fiscal policy. Yet, had not Lord Salisbury himself admitted that an international tariff war was raging, in which free-trading Britain had stripped herself of armour and weapons? and was it not high time, the Colonials argued, that she answered the call of her Protectionist children in forming a common commercial front against her rivals?

The following year saw Joseph Chamberlain's arrival at the Colonial Office: a free trader by upbringing, but first and foremost an Imperialist in search of nostrums. On taking office, Chamberlain had told Lord Salisbury as one potentate to another that his intention was "to develop the estate" and strengthen a tie which seemed to him to hang by a thread of sentiment and sympathy so slender "that even a breath could sever it." At heart he was hankering after Imperial Federation, which he saw as a true prescription for unity, but it was not something that could be rushed. The Imperial Federation League, which had launched the notion on the world, had itself broken apart under its own internal dissensions between protectionists and free traders the moment it had been asked to formulate a definite programme; and in the colonies there was a deep reluctance to engage in anything that smacked of British domination or threatened their new-found independence. Since, therefore, he could not hope to get Federation at one bound, it seemed to Chamberlain that the sensible thing was to approach it by degrees; and in a speech to the Canada Club he put some of his cards on the table:

What is the greatest of our common obligations? It is Imperial defence. What is the greatest of our common interests? It is Imperial trade. And the two are very closely connected. It is very difficult to see how you can pretend to deal with the great question of Imperial defence without having first dealt with the question of Imperial trade. . . . If the people of this country and the people of the Colonies . . . intend to approach this question in a practical spirit, they must approach it on its commercial side.

To Chamberlain, who had watched the phenomenal growth of German industrial power, this seemed to point to a *Zollverein,* an Empire free trade area. The need and the challenge and the advantages to be won were all immense. "To organise an Empire, one may almost say to create an Empire, greater and more potent for peace and the civilisation of the world than any other that history has ever known—that is a dream if you like, but a dream of which no man need be ashamed."

But such a concept also raised great difficulties. If it entailed the erection around the Imperial free trade area of "protective" tariff walls, then this would be a defiance of Cobdenite principles which might please some Tories but would be deeply resented by the Liberal opposition and even by many of Chamberlain's own Liberal-Unionist supporters. Suppose, though, the barriers erected were not protective ones aimed at shielding Imperial industries from foreign imports, but were rather a species of *octroi* levied for revenue purposes with no intention of clogging trade channels? If this were the case, then arguably there would be no breach of the sacred canon, for free trade principles could be bent, and no less a person than Cobden himself had bent them when it had suited him.* But this raised a further difficulty, for the colonies were wedded to protection and had no intention of exposing their infant industries to competition from British or foreign exporters. To them a *Zollverein* was as heretical as protection was to British Liberals, and Chamberlain was reluctantly forced to recognise this fact.

When, therefore, he came to chair the Diamond Jubilee Conference of colonial premiers in 1897 he shifted his ground. A *Zollverein,* he admitted, seemed impracticable for the moment; and it soon appeared that any hope for Imperial Federation and an Imperial Parliament was likewise doomed. In a one-House chamber the Colonials would find themselves swamped: a two-House chamber,

---

* In his reciprocity treaty with France which had lowered the duties on French wines in return for French concessions in respect of British goods.

with equal representation in its Senate for colonies irrespective of
the size of their populations, was equally unacceptable to the mother
country. But were there not other ways towards closer union? Could
there not be, for instance, a "great Council of the Empire" to
which the colonies would send plenipotentiaries? The premiers would
not have this either—they were not prepared to delegate powers
to representatives far from home and the control of their parliaments. On the political front all the roads towards closer union
seemed to be barred. More might be hoped from a limited fiscal
approach to the problem—by an extension of the system whereby
Canada had recently granted a preference to British goods. Some
headway was made here when the other colonies promised to follow
suit, but this was the limit of the Conference's achievement. It
remained true, as Lord Salisbury remarked, that the government
was sustaining the Empire on the sole basis of goodwill and sympathy.
Commenting on these words, *The Times* observed that mutual
sympathy had better be translated pretty soon into mutual helpful-
ness, but it found few answering echoes in government circles
where the Prime Minister's pragmatic approach to problems set the
tone.

Before the next Conference assembled in London in 1902 the Boer
War had been won with the aid of thirty thousand Colonial troops.
In fact, their despatch had revealed deep cleavages in colonial
opinion as to the wisdom of such entanglements and sacrifices far
from home, and Lord Salisbury himself had not been deceived into
imagining, as some enthusiasts did, that these thirty thousand had
been so many proofs of the growth of an Imperial spirit in Quebec
and New South Wales. What he had observed was something very
different—the evidence of a growing colonial nationalism—and with
the coming Conference in mind he warned against any facile
assumption. "There is no danger that appears to me more serious,"
he told the Primrose League, "than an attempt to force the various
parts of the Empire into a mutual arrangement and subordination
for which they are not ready . . . and which may only produce a
reaction in favour of the old state of things."

When the Conference opened, the wisdom of these words became
apparent. "The days are for great Empires and not for little States,"
Chamberlain had declared in Birmingham Town Hall; and in this
spirit, adapting Matthew Arnold's lines about the "weary Titan" that

was Britain "staggering under the too vast orb of its fate," he called
upon the staid colonial premiers once again to take their place as
Atlases in a great "Council of Empire," which to begin with could be
advisory but in which he clearly saw the germ of eventual political
federation.

The idea was not even discussed. The most influential of the
colonial statesmen, the French-Canadian Sir Wilfred Laurier, had
come to London determined to discuss nothing but commercial matters, and the other premiers were much of the same mind. Indeed
Chamberlain himself, when urging his Great Council on his colleagues, had recognised that the initiative must come from them. At
heart he had become almost as certain as Lord Salisbury that the
pace could not be pressed. Yet in retrospect, if the Empire was to become a real empire and not the pretence of one, some kind of
federation had to be created, and created quickly before the disruptive forces lurking in the organism had torn it apart. Thoughtful
observers outside the Empire had already seen this, and in an article
in *The National Review* the American naval historian Captain
Mahan had posed the question of the hour: "Shall Great Britain
exist as an Empire or shall it fall to pieces by a series of willing or
tolerated secessions?" Closer union already had the appearance of a
losing cause. The colonies were too far from Europe, too well aware
of what Laurier called "the vortex of militarism" building up in a
Europe from which they hoped to disengage. Ideally they saw the
Empire in terms of trade and emigration: they were not Imperialists
but Emporiumists. And by a fortunate chance they found an argument ready to hand in a move the British government had just made
to re-introduce the old "registration" duty on imported grain and
flour which dated from Peel's time and which the Liberals, in a final
Cobdenite flourish, had dismantled in 1869. Why should not this
become the means by which Britain could offer reciprocal preferences
to her colonies in exempting them from this and other revenue
duties? Could it not form a starting point for a wider preferential
system?

After the great issues of Federation, *Zollverein* and *Kriegsverein*
this seemed at first sight a minor problem. Mr. Gladstone had for
many years been perfectly happy to live with a registration duty on
corn, and its re-introduction might not have been expected to arouse
too many sectarian passions. Yet it did. Nothing in British history is

more remarkable than the total commitment of free traders to their doctrine. Even the Tory government, which re-introduced the tax in a desperate search for revenue, became infected with a sense of guilt and, to the acclamation of the Liberal opposition, the hated measure was withdrawn.

Where political organisation was concerned, therefore, the colonies would not accommodate Britain: on the commercial front Britain would not accommodate her colonies. The conference of 1902 had converted Chamberlain to the knowledge that only by way of Imperial tariff preferences could any advance be made towards the goal to which he had dedicated his life, and his failure to convince all his cabinet colleagues of this fact brought him to the end of what he could achieve inside the government and the system. Out he went into the wilderness to preach tariff reform, and there in the wilderness he stayed. The country was not ready to follow the music this Pied Piper played—the boom of 1905 which followed the post-Boer War depression once more assured it that the free trade tune was best. "The Empire was composed not of complementary but of competing economic societies," wrote Elie Halévy, the great historian of the period, and because it was that kind of organism and would not evolve with tighter bonds, it had to begin to dissolve, just as the Federalists had said.

In the process, it was to find for a while a new identity in the conception of a "Commonwealth." "Elasticity" and "flexibility," said Asquith, were its hallmarks, and perhaps only by such means could any kind of association have been preserved at all. But the realisation of these limitations on the power and effectiveness of the Empire which the Colonial Conferences had revealed bit deep and played its part alongside the over-riding fear of isolation in a hostile world in turning the British from their self-sufficiency inside their cosy family circle and sending them scurrying post-haste in search of allies.

In the closing years of the Queen's reign all the talk had been of colonies and federation: the great crises had been in Africa. All this was to be changed, and it was now towards Europe and supremacy on the high seas that thoughts were turned. "I think Uncle Sam would be a good partner," muses poor Britannia at a ball, eyed lasciviously by prospective suitors as she sits (helmeted as usual in a delicious *Punch* cartoon) waiting for a dance—"so would little

Jap. I wonder if my cousin German William will ask me too?" But Kaiser Wilhelm, busy with his navy, never asked her, so in 1902 she formed an alliance with Japan. In 1904, after one of the most sensational diplomatic somersaults of modern times she formed the *Entente Cordiale* with her old enemy, France; and three years later signed a convention with Tsarist Russia. Triple *Entente* faced Triple Alliance of the Central Powers. After nearly a century Britain had once more entered the European power bloc system, and it was to take her, step by reluctant step, via a Balkan quarrel, into the maelstrom of the First World War.

XII

The Empire and the First World War

The decision to take the Empire to war was made by the British cabinet in response to a purely European and "great power" problem —there was no real consultation with the Dominions, let alone India or the other colonial territories on whose behalf the King Emperor declared war.

None of them had any quarrel with Germany; all of them had coastlines vulnerable to attack by raiders or fleets of the world's second greatest naval power and hardly a ship of their own to defend them. Yet, except in South Africa, where a small pro-German rising had to be crushed and a minority group was opposed to anything beyond "passive belligerence," the Dominions responded to the crisis almost as one man—even the French-Canadians of Quebec voted for once with the rest and ensured a unanimous vote of the Ottawa parliament.

This was the spirit in which the big circulation newspapers throughout the Empire greeted the coming struggle. As we shall have occasion to note, Sydney's *Bulletin,* most individual and trendy of the colonial press, had a few cold douches of its own to offer warmongers, many of them administered at the hands of that up-and-coming cartoonist, David Low. And an alleged tendency in certain Canadian (Conservative) circles to think that the dominion stood to gain by a general European war and could stand on the sidelines "with as much nonchalance as a crowd looks at a football game," had to be gravely rebuked by the *Quebec Daily Telegraph,* a Liberal party organ, which held up its hands in horror at the "dancing and prancing" of its opponents over the prospects of Armageddon on the other side of the garden wall. But this was just local in-fighting, like the tremendous circulation war which the *Ottawa Free Press* was waging with the rival *Citizen,* and by all accounts winning by most unfairly printing an 8 A.M. edition to catch the midnight news from London. On the issues that mattered, almost the entire Empire press, from *Cape Times* to *Auckland Star,* from *Quebec Daily Telegraph* to *Sydney Morning Herald* and scores of other journals besides, was united in one common front; in all of them we see the same belated, horrified recognition of disaster closing in, the same call to duty, the same steadfastness. Cynics might say what they liked—and in the *Bulletin* David Low produced one hilarious cartoon of politicians at a graveside burying the hatchet under a headstone,

HERE LIES
PARTY
GOVERNMENT
BURIED BUT NOT BURIED
VERY DEEP
BECAUSE THERE WILL BE
A
GLORIOUS RESURRECTION

—yet this closing of the ranks was real enough. In the New South Wales legislature the minority leader declared, "There is no Opposition now." In Canada, the Federal opposition proposed a political truce, and even the traditional antagonisms between the French- and English-speaking populations were for a moment stilled. If the test came, Canada's voice would be one voice its papers promised. In New Zealand, "England has the Empire solidly behind her," wrote the *Auckland Star,* and incredibly enough, apart from a few isolated pockets of disaffection, this was no more than the sober truth. Even in India the Hindu and Moslem press were falling into line, and the *Statesman* of Calcutta was declaring the intense loyalty of the nation. If anything, these Colonials showed from the start a greater awareness of what was at stake and of the realities involved in Britain's world position than did Britain herself. Whether the homeland could stand by and see France overwhelmed was a question posed by the *Sydney Morning Herald* and answered in forthright words. "There can be but one reply to this question in our opinion. She dare not. Her own existence is wrapped up in the balance of power." This was before news of the German invasion of Belgium reached Australia, and it was a firmer answer than Mr. Asquith's cabinet of all the talents had dared to give up to that time. These newly emergent nations, each busy with its problems thousands of miles removed from the cauldron, showed a remarkable understanding of their own involvement in a crisis which they had had no share in shaping.

To the desperate choice presented them they responded with resolution, with panache. Some greeted it more gaily, more zanily, than others. The *Montreal Daily Star* was announcing on August 3: "Thousands are eager for the fray." To prove it—to double prove it—under huge banners, RALLYING ROUND THE FLAG: CANADA'S MILITIA ARMY STANDS BY THE MOTHERLAND, the *Star* printed messages of "Loyalty and Patriotism" from the commanding officers of fifty thousand men. Bless its heart, the *Star* did have a tendency to embellish things. Its edition of August 5 confidently reported the German invasion of Switzerland, along with "a severe defeat" inflicted on the Junkers by the heroic Dutch. "Victories for France," it announced triumphantly. And next day the *Sydney Daily Herald,* which seldom lagged far behind anyone in optimism, was reporting from its Paris correspondent that the French Minister for War had accepted the generous offer from a Monsieur Turpin of a very remarkable invention which would greatly shorten the duration of hostilities: a weapon which would "render all defensive measures illusory" by annihilating all enemy forces on the spot. What happened to M. Turpin's invention was never subsequently revealed— perhaps it got filed away at Joffre's headquarters.

Not everyone, naturally, was as hopeful as all that. A recurrent theme in both Australia and Canada was the feeling that military preparations in the sister dominion far surpassed that to be expected at home. Announcements that Canada was ready and willing caused a certain anguish in Melbourne and Sydney: reports of expeditionary forces being raised in New Zealand and Australia and the immediate offer of Australian ships for service under the White Ensign wherever they might be required were held up by Canadian editors as illustrations of the grievous sins of Canadian politicians who had failed to provide any navy at all. Only the *Bulletin* questioned the ethics of going to war in a poem which deserves remembrance: a poem which appeared underneath a drawing of an aged and glittering figure in Generalissimo's uniform advancing in front of a stage curtain to announce the prologue of the play—the analogy with Death's soliloquy in *Everyman* is very clear:

> The curtain that I wait the word to draw
> Will show you not a drama but yourselves. . . .
> The action on the stage will spread to you:
> My shells will strike and rend the occupants
> Of gallery and stall and circle. You
> The actors and the victims of my play!
> You are the soldiers and the soldiers' wives,
> The little children waiting for their dad:
> You are the dying, the dismembered dead;
> And you the hungry and demented mob,
> And you the widows and the fatherless.
> The manager impatient grows, and loud
> The orchestra of slaughter sounds its paean:
> The curtain tautens. . . . Shall I ring it up?

We may take it that this was a very untypical reaction. The vast majority were eager to undergo what one paper inevitably called their "baptism of fire." But under the resolution and the eagerness to serve, the note of bewilderment, the desire to be informed, to *know* about this crisis in a far off land, was very plain. By August 4 the *Montreal Daily Star*'s entire issue of free war maps had been exhausted: another and revised edition was promised for the 7th, but where would the battle front have gone by then? And what should be the dominions' part in this crusade to which as Britons they had been called? How could they best help? No one had told them in black and white: the communications from London to the dominion governments, never mind the people, had been minimal. On this question a note of impatience can be discerned, but it is impatience with the local leaders, not with Britain. On August 5, with the Empire's war not a day old, the *Quebec Daily Telegraph* was com-

plaining in loud squealers: "NOTHING DECIDED ABOUT CANADIAN CON-
TINGENTS. GERMANS CROSSING FRENCH FRONTIER EVERYWHERE.
BEEFSTEAK 42 CENTS A POUND IN LONDON." There was even danger
at home, where reports were rife of an imminent invasion across the
undefended frontier with the United States by thousands of German
settlers in Milwaukee—a very choice war scare indeed—and what
was being done about it, apart from the voting of fifty million Canadian dollars for defence? As if this was not serious enough, the
Ottawa Free Press had a war scare of its own—were the Germans
using New York as a naval base? It rather feared so. In Australia,
the Prime Minister was playing it cool. "We have just got to sit tight
now and see the thing through," he counselled his compatriots. "Our
duty is quite clear, namely to gird up our loins and remember that we
are Britons." But more was expected, much more. A sense of dependence and of unpreparedness on a tragic scale had seeped through
to the public, touchingly reflected in a poem printed by the *Bulletin*,
no warmongering paper by any standards:

I never fired a gun in my life
There's nothing that I can do
To help myself, the kids and the wife—
And I am a young man too!
When shops close down and the desks are shut,
I'll only be in the way!
What sort of figure *do* I cut
In this thundring world to-day?

There'll be a gun for the baby son
If Britain and he shall last;
But where is *my* training and *my* gun,
Now trouble is coming fast?
Oh must I issue a High Court writ
And sit by a shot-lashed sea,
And match with powder my lawyer's writ
On a shore of lunacy?

We were fools, my friends! Let's still be fools!
While the tumult sinks and swells,
Let them hear *our* only fighting tools—
The idiot's cap and bells!

A High Court writ and a lawyer's grim
And a very frightful Fee,
And we stand on Armageddon's rim
Equipped as all fools should be.

This contribution, signed Mars Hannibal Smith, "An able-bodied member of the Australian Compulsory Peace Society—ever so many members and still swelling," can stand as evidence for the sense of helplessness that was prevalent at the time and might serve with honour as an epitaph on a whole generation drawn without warning into a world catastrophe. But there was determination behind it, a patriotic resolve and an idealism that found its way into many editorials. The war was not of Britain's making. She and her daughter states were entering it only to save themselves and civilised values, buoyed up by confidence in "a worthy cause."

*   *   *

To serve the cause, everywhere a flock of volunteers hastened to the colours to swell the rudimentary defence units and fit our expeditionary forces in answer to Kitchener's call. There was to be some backsliding—thus the huge province of Quebec, where separatism was a living issue, raised less than a tenth of the Canadian troops sent overseas, and even in loyal Australia conscription was defeated in two referenda—yet nothing can detract from the devotion that brought one and a half million Indians, well over half a million Canadians, half a million Australasians and 150,000 South Africans to join the six and a half millions recruited from the British Isles.

Of these, large proportions served as combatants far from their own shores in the various theatres of war—Canadians, Australians, South Africans, Indians, Gurkhas on the western front; Australians and New Zealanders in Palestine and at the Dardanelles; Indians in Mesopotamia; South Africans, white and black, in German "South-West" and East Africa; men of the Gold Coast in Togoland; Nigerians in the Cameroons; Australasians again in the Pacific, in Samoa, and aboard the fleets that drove German shipping from the seas. Even Newfoundland, whose forces at the outbreak of the war had amounted to 580 naval reservists and some Boys Brigade detachments, contributed, in the end, twelve thousand men and raised a six-million-dollar war loan. The Empire, including Britain, lost a million dead and far more than twice as many wounded and missing. It was an astonishing and moving performance from peoples far from bellicose, whose leaders had entered the struggle more from duty and idealism than any other cause.

The British High Command in Flanders and in Egypt was delighted to receive these spirited recruits; and as they came into the line, the press reports dwelt on their virtues and displayed them as a propaganda weapon, the living proof of the strength and solidarity of the Empire. The newspapers for the spring of 1915 were full of them—"Gallant Canadians" at Ypres; "Amazing dash and bravery" of the Anzacs (the Australian and New Zealand Corps) at Gallipoli; "the brilliant and rapid success" of the Springboks in their campaign in German South-West Africa, and later, on the Somme, their heroism at Delville Wood. No one in Britain, wrote *The Times* proudly, ever had the slightest doubt that all the young nations would show their breeding and uphold the honour of race and flag.

Yet the tone of surprise between the lines is unmistakable. Professional soldiers—perhaps even editors—had had their doubts about the usefulness of untried troops, and in the reports from the front there lingered a sense of wonder at the quaintness of it all. "These Colonials are extraordinarily cool under fire," wrote a war correspondent with the Anzacs at the Dardanelles. "One of the strangest sights of all was to see them bathing in the sea with the shrapnel bursting all around them." Another correspondent spoke touchingly of "a passion of enthusiasm and a great joy of anticipation" in these "young troops."

As the war went on and the contribution from the colonies grew with it, bringing into the line tens of thousands of now seasoned men, this air of patronage died away, to be replaced with a feeling of true respect, whose impact may perhaps be dated from the Battle of Arras in April 1917, when the Canadian Corps was assigned the task of capturing the Vimy Ridge where earlier French assaults had failed at the cost of 150,000 casualties. "A formidable undertaking," notes the *Official History of the War,* for the site was trenched like a fortress and shell-holes provided the attackers' only cover from the German field of fire.

By 7 A.M., the *Official History* goes on, the Canadians had taken the entire enemy front line system. German accounts likened the advance "to the irresistible flood of the incoming tide," and as it flowed to the crest of the ridge the assault troops could look down, as no other troops had done for nearly three years of war, on the unravaged villages of the Douai plain under a blue spring sky. "Soundness of plan, thoroughness of preparation, dash and determination in execution, and devotion to duty" had been the ingredients of the victory, noted the Army Commander, General Horne, who expressed his high appreciation of this "splendid work" and his conviction that it had marked a heroic day in the history of the Empire.

It was a false dawn, of course, but the Canadians, along with the Australians, were now recognised as crack troops whose presence in the line was one of the signals of a coming offensive and had to be carefully hidden from the enemy—together they formed the spearhead of the great attack outside Amiens in August 1918 that smashed through the German entrenchments south of the Somme in "one irresistible surge," to quote from Liddell Hart; and a few days later it was the Canadians again who broke the Drocourt-Quéant switch, forcing the enemy back to the old Hindenburg Line.

"The graveyard of Canada in Flanders is large," *The Times* had written three years earlier after the German gas attack at Ypres. "It is very large": and this was true, for 51,000 of those who landed in France never returned and 150,000 were wounded—figures very similar to those suffered by the Australians, whose graveyards also lay in Palestine and in barbed wire enclosures on the Gallipoli peninsula below the heights of Sari Bair.

To the war the Australians had brought their own special qualities of jauntiness, dash and sardonic humour. In *The Seven Pillars of Wisdom,* T. E. Lawrence, who came across them at the capture of Damascus and did not like them, noted the swagger of their "quick bodies, all curves and never a straight line . . . with the disquieting suppleness of blades half drawn from the scabbard." Though himself a rebel against authority, he mocked at their casual discipline (". . . a complaint from Chauvel that some of the Arab troops had been slack in saluting *Australian* officers!" he records with scorn) and their open-handedness with looted Turkish money in the captured town—one trooper he saw gave the equivalent of a five hundred pound note to a lad who held his horse for three minutes.

How typical! These were the men who after suffering fearful

losses on the hills and beaches of Gallipoli sent their congratulations before leaving to "Johnny Turk" for being a clean fighter at the game. The despatches of the British general commanding them, full of high-flying tributes to their heroism, must have earned a few horse laughs in the pubs of Woollahra and King's Cross. "Give it to the Yarra, it needs it more than I do," says the wounded Sydneysider in the desert, handed a mug of water by a Melbourne man, both in derision at that muddy little river that flows through the "Queen City of the South" and at the whole knightly epic enshrined in the old tale of Sir Philip Sidney's death at Zutphen. The anti-hero was a Digger concept long before it entered English literature in our own time. Yet for all that, the deeds that were done at Gallipoli became part of Australian folklore—and New Zealand folklore too, among a people far less volatile than their cousins north of the Tasman Sea: the most sober, the most dogged, the most "English" of the colonials, who sent one in every five of their white population to the war.

"Just as faith moves mountains, so valour can carry them," reads the official despatch recording one New Zealand attack on the hill called Table Top inland from Suvla Bay—a mushroom-shaped height whose summit seemed to bulge outwards over its stem. "There are moments during battles when life becomes intensified, when men become supermen, when the impossible becomes simple—and this was one of these moments. The scarped heights were scaled, the plateau was taken. . . ."

Sir Ian Hamilton's despatches on this series of battles for the straits dividing Europe from Asia at the Dardanelles, which ended in a defeat on the pattern of Dunkirk, should be read by all those who want to understand what the Empire still meant during the First World War. Since by this time the colonies were making a very real contribution to the sinews of war, the gratitude expressed is quantitative and a response to practical benefits in men and munitions. But the emotional content is of still greater importance, both to Britain and her colonies. "Never while men speak our tongue can the blood spent by the Canadians at Ypres and by the Australians and New Zealanders at Anzac be forgotten," wrote *The Times* in a valedictory leader to the dead. "That rich tribute of love and loyalty to the highest ideals of our race has not been wasted, far from it; when this war is done there will assuredly spring a new and closer unity of all the British peoples." And indeed it did seem for a while that the bonds had been strengthened by that "moral unity" which *The Times* saw as forged by the sacrifices of those who had fought and died together.

*   *   *

When with their aid the war was finally won, it remained for King George V as the visible symbol of the Empire to express both his valediction and his hopes for the future. On November 11, just after the historic scene in Marshall Foch's railway coach in the forest of Compiègne, he sent his congratulations to all participants in the victory, from the Emperor of Japan to the President of Cuba, and then turned nearer home.

> At the moment when the Armistice is signed, bringing, I trust, a final end to the hostilities which have convulsed the whole world for more than four years, I desire to send a message of greeting and heartfelt gratitude to my oversea peoples, whose wonderful efforts and sacrifices have contributed so greatly to secure the victory. . . .
>
> The outbreak of war found the whole Empire one. I rejoice to think that the end of the struggle finds the Empire still more closely united by the common resolve held firm through all vicissitudes.

This was for the benefit of the white dominions, while India, which itself had provided more recruits (if less active combatants) than the rest of the Empire less Britain put together, received a parallel message cabled to its Viceroy:

> On signature of Armistice with Germans. . . . I desire to congratulate your Excellency, Princes and peoples of India on success which has attended our united efforts. Struggle now so happily ended has demanded unprecedented sacrifices from us all, and in responding to the call upon her for men and resources, India has played a part worthy of her martial qualities and high traditions. She has fulfilled my faith in her single-minded devotion to my

person and Empire; she has vindicated my confidence in her destiny. . . .

In this period piece it does not need a very perceptive ear to distinguish the variation in tone and pitch from the message sent to the dominions. Some colonies were more Colonial than others. On November 20 the King returned to the theme in an impressive ceremony in the Royal Gallery of the palace of Westminster in the presence of a representative gathering of Empire leaders:

> Not less prompt (than Britain's) was the response of the splendid troops which eagerly hastened to us from the dominions overseas, men who showed themselves more than ever to be bone of our bone, inheriting all the courage and tenacity which have made Britain great. A hundred battlefields in all parts of the world have witnessed their heroism, have been soaked with their blood, and are for ever hallowed by their graves.
>
> I shall ever remember how the Princes of India rallied to the cause, and with what ardour her soldiers sustained in many theatres of war . . . the martial traditions of their race. Neither can I forget how the men from the Crown Colonies and Protectorates of Great Britain, also fighting among novel and perilous scenes, exhibited a constancy and devotion second to none.

No one can say that the decencies were not observed and a kind of justice done to every participant in the great struggle according to his degree. The King was deeply and sincerely grateful, and this gratitude still sounds through the official words. "How is the Empire?" he is said to have asked on his death-bed two decades later—truth or myth, it makes no matter, for at least it was in character with a lifetime of concern both for his people and for an ideal.

In November 1918 that ideal seemed everywhere triumphant. But some could see beyond the pageant of flags and the cheering crowds in the streets. On the night of the Armistice of November 11, the Prime Minister, Lloyd George, spoke at the Lord Mayor's Banquet in Guildhall in the midst of a scene of splendour and pageantry from which only the carvers of the traditional baron of beef were absent, by order of the Food Controller, and in this speech of the greatest orator and keenest political intelligence of his time we can discover both a tribute and a warning:

> We must not forget in this old country what we owe to these sturdy children of ours beyond the seas, who have set up free households of their own and of their own free will came to the aid of this land. Their share in the victory stands conspicuous, and they must have a voice which is equal to their sacrifice in the determination of the terms of the peace. . . . I say without hesitation that the British Empire never stood higher in the councils of the world than it does to-day.

Then he added:

> Victory has its snares and its burdens as well as defeat. . . . The next few years are charged with the fate of Britain and her Empire, and I appeal solemnly in this great hour. Let us banish faction until the Empire has been thoroughly restored.

To banish faction—what a splendidly artful prescription for the leader of a coalition government who had waged almost unceasing war with his own generals and had come to power through a palace revolution involving intrigue of almost Byzantine complexity.

Yet oddly enough faction had greatly declined since 1914, and the nation that came out of the struggle with the central powers was a far more homogeneous one than had gone into it racked with labour unrest, the Feminist revolt and the "Home Rule" crisis which had split Ireland into two armed camps and had affected even the loyalty of the British Army.

By November 1918 almost everything except Ireland had apparently changed for the better.

The Feminist revolt was over, simply because by their full and eager share in the war effort women had proved themselves indispensable in more than the traditional way. The case for women's suffrage no longer had to be argued. Ladies no longer padlocked themselves to railings outside Buckingham Palace—they had chained themselves in large numbers to machines: they were part of the national labour force.

And that labour force itself had shed its old syndicalist leanings. It had done very well out of the war, and rosy prospects of plenty for everyone seemed to be opening in the trade boom that followed it. Only in the mines did the old bitterness live on.

On the political front the heat seemed to have gone out of the political battle also. The Prime Minister of a government dependent on Tory support was that same Liberal ex-Chancellor of the Exchequer who had introduced a system of National Health Insurance, had challenged the old Establishment, humbled the House of Lords, won the war, and now promised "a country fit for heroes to live in." In the process, he had split the Liberal party which had won the landslide victory of 1905, but the resulting in-fighting between the two factions did not seem of great importance to the nation, nor did the growth of a Labour party raise any threat to public order or to the government. No great issue divided the parties. In 1914 they had been at each other's throats over Ireland—in 1918 they merely wondered if they could try the Kaiser and get reparations out of Germany.

If this was the picture at home, it was still more promising abroad. With the defeat of Germany and her collapse into chaos Britain's main trading rival in Europe had been removed from the arena. That threatening fleet, which for years had obsessed English thinking and which at Jutland had dared dispute the passage of the North Sea, was now interned in Scapa Flow. France had been bled white by the war with appalling losses in men and material: Russia was in the throes of a revolution which for the time being at least had crippled her militarily and industrially.

Britain herself had lost three quarters of a million dead and one and a half millions disabled by wounds or gas, but the capacity of her labour force was virtually unimpaired. On paper she was a creditor nation. New markets were opening in former German territory in Africa which she had occupied and was soon to acquire in the form of "mandates" to round out the imperial estate which now stretched uninterruptedly from the Cape, via the Rhodesias, Uganda and Tanganyika, to the Sudan and Cairo. Yet if these were important gains, they were nothing beside the new status Britain enjoyed in the Levant as a result of her victory over Turkey, which had placed her in company with France as one of the inheritors of Turkish suzerainty in what had once formed the heart-land of the Arab Empire of the Caliphs. Where Coeur de Lion had failed, General Allenby had succeeded: Jerusalem, Damascus and Baghdad were in British hands, and it had become possible for visionaries like T. E. Lawrence to dream of a new "brown dominion" in lands soon to reveal a fantastic wealth in oil.

What might equally have impressed British statesmen at the Armistice was the condition of Empire unity which had apparently come about. Lord Salisbury and Joseph Chamberlain had worked for a *Kriegsverein*—now it existed. Dominion troops were under British command in many quarters of the globe: dominion ships were under Admiralty orders. A committee, a so-called Imperial War Cabinet consisting of premiers and ministers from Britain and the white dominions, had been called into existence to supplement the British War Cabinet which itself included one committed colonial Imperialist in the person of General Jan Christian Smuts, and if Federation was impracticable as political doctrine, it looked very much as though many of its benefits had been achieved by this *ad hoc* control of the Empire's resources which had grown up almost by accident during the emergency.

At the 1921 Imperial Conference, which was in effect less a conference than a post-war sitting of the Imperial War Cabinet, that "Cabinet of Governments" as Sir Robert Borden had described it, Lloyd George at his wiliest spread his net in full view of the birds— "We shall also welcome any suggestions which you may have," he said to his assembled colleagues, "for associating yourselves more closely with the conduct of foreign relations. . . . There was a time when Downing Street controlled the Empire; to-day the Empire is in charge of Downing Street." And the dominion Prime Ministers agreed under these blandishments that they should have one common foreign policy, to be propounded, of course, by the British Foreign Office, which at that time meant by Lloyd George himself.

Only General Smuts had seen the need for new appreciations of Empire: his paper on this topic was not even debated by the delegates. When reminded that there was talk of a special conference to determine the future constitution, Mr. W. M. Hughes, most splendidly Churchillian of Australians, remarked that he was at a total loss to understand why such nostrums were needed. "Is it," he asked, "that the Dominions are seeking new powers? . . . What remains to us? We are like so many Alexanders. What other worlds have we to conquer?"

Indeed on every front, from imperial unity to the factory floor, the omens for the Empire seemed good. Yet many aspects of this engaging picture had their more sombre side and shortly most of the hopeful auguries of 1918 were to be falsified.

*   *   *

The fall of Lloyd George in 1922 and the rise of Labour to power two years later changed the whole political climate by introducing a decade of balancing between three rival parties and its concomitant of weak minority government. From every other viewpoint, however, Labour's advent was beneficial; the political temperature stayed down; and though Socialism's Trade Union wing was in more militant mood than were its representatives at Westminster, industrial unrest even at the height of the general strike of 1926 never quite approached the bitterness of the immediate pre-war years. Similarly, the inflation caused by the wartime government's refusal to balance its budget by covering more than a quarter of its expenditure, its borrowings at exorbitant rates of interest, its large printings of paper money and inability to peg wages had no long-term social ill-effects and was never allowed to reach anything like the panic proportions that destroyed the German mark and the German middle class along with it. By mid-1919, though the cost of living had doubled, real wages were back to 1914 level and the worst was over. The true damage to the economy which the war had wrought or had at least accelerated was more complex.

Britain's capital investments abroad before the war had formed one of the bulwarks of her international trading position, bringing in a stream of dividends amounting in 1913 to £188 million from mines, ports, railways and factories around the world from China to the Argentine. In order to finance the war, however, she had been forced to sell some 10 per cent of these assets and had also lost by confiscation a further 4–5 per cent.

This was a very obvious loss; less so was the gradual change in the savings habits of the population, partly due to the levelling of incomes owing to the tax needed to pay for the increased national debt, which left the rich with less money to invest, and partly to the "live for the day" philosophy born of the war which had put everyone in a spending mood. Although appreciable amounts were still invested overseas, the levels were not up to pre-war in real terms. Other invisible exports were also decreasing. London still remained one of the main financial centres, but an indication of the challenge to her position can be seen from the fact that whereas in 1910–13 loans raised there for investment in overseas countries other than the British Empire amounted to an annual average of £100,570,000, by 1926–1930 this had fallen to less than half that sum. Britain's invisible earnings from shipping, which until 1870 had been greater than her income from capital investment overseas, was never to advance on the income earned in 1914; and though by 1925 her merchant shipping tonnage was once more on a pre-war level, she had failed to maintain her proportion of the world's total —this had been 44.2 per cent in 1915: by 1925 it was down to 32.1 per cent. Similarly the Empire's share of the world's carrying trade had declined from 47.5 per cent in 1912 to 39.5 per cent in 1931, largely in face of competition from the United States and Japan.

Alongside this stagnation or decline in invisible earnings from investment income, shipping and the services of London as a financial centre, there was also a growing problem of unbalance caused by the great increase of imports without a comparable rise of exports. This was a problem which was cloaked both by invisible earnings and by low food prices and did not become critical until 1931. Nevertheless, by 1924 imports had exceeded the 1913 level: by 1929 they were 20 per cent greater—an alarming rise in five years. And the situation was made still worse by a fall in re-exports amounting to about 5 per cent over the same period. As compared with this, the volume of exports between the wars never rose to more than 84 per cent of the 1913 figures. Britain's share of world exports had also fallen from 13.1 in 1913 to 11.1 in 1927 and by 1937 was to drop below 10 per cent. This was mainly due to two closely allied factors: the continual pre-occupation with old-established industries, such as textiles and coal, and a failure to concentrate on the manufacture of goods which were increasingly in demand in newly industralising countries—machinery, machine tools and goods which demanded in their production an advanced expertise which Britain was peculiarly fitted to provide. Instead, she continued to manufacture unsophisticated goods for unsophisticated markets—even in 1913, 70 per cent of her exports went to largely agricultural countries, a process which was not reversed. Coal, with the increased use of oil, was a declining industry. Exports from the mines fell from 61.7 million tons in 1924 to 35.9 millions in 1938, only about half of the 1913 export tonnage. Exports of cotton goods also declined, and in the mid-thirties, largely because of the rapid industrialisation of India and Japan, amounted to only one third of those in 1924.

In spite of great strides in the steel, electrical and automobile industries Britain had failed to adapt herself sufficiently to the changed marketing conditions or to appreciate where her true interests lay. Thus, by the beginning of the 1930s, probably for the first time, invisible exports failed to make good her losses on the balance of trade.

It was bad enough that Britain in her post-war euphoria had failed to appreciate the real nature of her problem. Yet it was worse than that, for the trading problems were global, and as the most global of powers, Britain was particularly vulnerable. What the post-war world needed was financial leadership such as had been provided throughout the Victorian and Edwardian eras by the City of London. The City was no longer in a position to give this leadership on a sufficient scale, and there was no other power willing to take on the job. The free-trading system which had been the glory of Victorian Britain had collapsed under the strain of national greed and international rivalry. A rigorous system of military alliances had led to 1914. A lack of economic alliances and of any real economic system at all was one of the main causes of the great Depression of the thirties, and by a series of doom-laden steps led to the rise of Nazism and the renewal of global war in 1939.

*   *   *

Even the Empire's colonial gains were double edged. On the map the occupation of ex-German territories in Tanganyika, Togoland and the Cameroons* looked impressive, and the fact that they were

---

* The Mandate for Southwest Africa went to the Union government, whose troops had conquered it.

not absolute possessions, but were to be classed as "mandates" in trusteeship to the newly formed League of Nations made little actual difference in terms of sovereignty on the ground. But like most of the other British colonial territories in Africa they were peopled by backward races whose potentialities as markets were not large but who were very demanding of the capital required to work them. Any go-ahead company would have classed them as liabilities.

At first glance this would not have applied to Britain's rich new gains in the Levant, where she acquired mandates over Iraq, Transjordan and Palestine carved out of territories conquered from the Turks in the huge quadrilateral bounded by the Mediterranean, the Persian Gulf, Asia Minor and the Arabian peninsula. Since she already controlled the Suez Canal, had turned Egypt into a Protectorate, aspired to turn Persia into another, and was paramount in the future "oil" sheikdoms along the Gulf and the Trucial Coast, she had become by far the most important of the Middle Eastern powers. The oil wells around Mosul she managed to detach from Turkey by the Treaty of Lausanne, incorporating them in her Iraq mandate, now raised into an Arab kingdom alongside another similar satellite creation in Transjordan. Honour as well as self-interest seemed to have been served, for the princes chosen for these thrones were members of the Hashemite family, descendants of the Prophet, sons of the Sherif of Mecca who had been the nominal head of the war-time Arab revolt against the Turks, and both of them had fought in the Bedouin armies in the desert advance which had finally reached Damascus. The British, with their traditional fondness for aristocratic regimes in colonial territories, could hardly have been blamed for mistaking as usual princes for peoples and assuming that they had satisfied Arab aspirations by providing a couple of kings and a few advisers to organise the finances and train the local levies. But they did worse; for not content with paying one debt of honour they embarked on another, and in a spirit of mixed humanitarianism and "politiking" unique in history, complicated an already chaotic situation by planting on the liberated Arab soil of Palestine a "Jewish National Home" which was to grow into the State of Israel.

Out of this Pandora's Box two implacably hostile forces were released—and all with the best intentions in the world. Divide and Rule was never a British precept: the British merely practised it.

Under the stresses of war, and in order to encourage allies or potential allies, they had made so many contradictory promises in the Levant—to the French, to the Arabs, to the Jews—that they had probably lost count. But at least some of them had been honoured and a whole backward area brought into the twentieth century.

Too effectively. The firing on the main battle-fronts of 1918 had barely stopped before it broke out again throughout the lands that the British fondly believed they had pacified—rioting by Egyptians against the Protectorate that was so good for them; the refusal of the Persians to ratify the 1919 treaty and become "protected" in their turn; an Afghan invasion of India; rebellion in Iraq; the sudden resurgence of Ottoman pride which brought Mustapha Kemal to power in Ankara, and at Chanak, on those same straits between Europe and Asia where the Anzacs had fought, threatened to bring about a renewal of the war between Britain and Turkey.

Certainly the oddest thing about this chain reaction of rebellion across the Middle East is that it should have occurred not when the British were being defeated but when they were everywhere triumphant. That French-dominated Syria was not spared similar disorders suggests that this was simply a stirring of Arab nationalism in response to the belief that at Geneva a new world order was being born in which the rights of small nations as well as large ones would be guaranteed. Persia's defiant rejection of the treaty her representatives had signed with the "protecting" power might fit into this pattern—but what of Afghanistan's astonishing attack on the Indian Empire, a pygmy hurling itself on a giant? In such an action one senses something so wholly irrational and instinctive that one is tempted to see in it a subconscious knowledge that beneath the gilt and the glitter the British had lost their will to rule and that the days of the *Raj* were ending. Had not the same thing happened fifteen centuries earlier with the first stirrings of the barbarians around the frontiers of the Roman Empire when the Legions were still the most formidable military force in the Mediterranean world?

In the West the symptoms of British decline were more straightforward, arising out of changed attitudes caused by the war. Just as in Britain, the tremendous impulse of patriotism, which had brought into being the First Hundred Thousand and filled Kitchener's armies which had died on the Somme, was followed by the emergence of a less quixotic generation in less of a hurry to reach the front, so even in the white dominions the first flush of brotherhood did not quite survive the strains which showed themselves as the years went by and the casualty lists mounted. The Australians, the most dashing of the Colonials, twice proved unwilling to accept conscription. In Canada this was forced through Parliament, but only at the cost of political division and riots in Quebec, while in Ireland the attempt had to be given up altogether in face of public hostility. The armies that ended the war were very different from those that began it, for a whole code of chivalry had perished on the Somme and in the Flanders mud as the romantics who responded to Rupert Brooke were replaced by men shocked into cynicism by the suffering they saw around them, so that even the war songs of the later years reflected the change from the mood of *Tipperary*.

> If you want the Sergeant Major
> We know where 'e is,
> We know where 'e is,
> We know where 'e is,
> If you want the Sergeant Major
> We know where 'e is,
> 'E's 'angin' on the front barbed wire.

It was a question of scale. The men in the trenches had ceased to regard life as meaning much beyond what they could see and hear from the parapet: their world was bounded by the Battalion and the letter from home, and this was a habit that was catching. Everyone felt it. The Prime Ministers or deputies from the dominions who had served with the Imperial War Cabinet and dealt with the future of the world returned from London to their own capitals, where they were at once caught up in the problems of how to win votes in Montreal and Adelaide. All were determined to press the claims of their own nations which had contributed so much to the struggle—Canada's contribution in manpower alone had been more than fifteen times larger than the British forces Wellington had commanded at Waterloo—and for these services they demanded, and received, a voice in the peace making, not only as part and parcel of the British Empire package, but also in their own right as New Zealanders, Australians, Canadians, South Africans, soon all to be accepted as individual members of the League of Nations along with India, which was not even a dominion.

At the height of mutual co-operation during the war the Canadian Prime Minister—a conservative devoted to the British connection— had found it necessary to complain of the absurdity involved in treating nations which had mobilised half a million men as though they were "toy automata" to be manipulated by Whitehall. This may have been no more than an isolated outburst, but it represented —whether correctly or not—a very real suspicion among dominion statesmen and public that in some way they were being used. A mutiny of Canadian troops at Rhyl in Wales in 1919, caused by demobilisation delays and put down at the cost of several Canadian lives, was another straw in the wind. The Colonials were sick and tired of commitments far from home. Isolationist sentiments, particularly in Canada, always the leading dominion, had made rapid strides since 1914—previously such sentiments had been confined solely to Quebec. There was a great distrust of Europe—a feeling that Canada could survive by herself. "We live in a fire-proof house far from inflammable materials," a leading Senator had cried. The 1921 Imperial Conference in London which was to agree to one common Imperial policy in foreign affairs was a "sport" and in effect reflected more the opinion of the loyalist dominions of Australia and New Zealand than the more realistic separatist trend already evident in Canada and soon to be dominant at the Cape. Not even all the Australasians were wholly satisfied with Britain. At large within the Empire was a real disenchantment with central direction from London or indeed from anywhere outside the national boundaries. Idealists—always in a very small minority—might lean towards loyalty to the new supra-national body of the League of Nations at Geneva, but though proud at being invited to be signatories of the League's charter, most dominion citizens had a thoroughly ambivalent attitude towards it and half feared that it might entangle them in problems that were not their own.

The dominions, in fact, had become very parochial. After four years of war they wanted no more alarms from Europe but peace in their own time and place. If they too had any understanding of the Empire's failing powers, this was not what chiefly concerned them, but rather a fear of the too meddlesome nature of British imperial policies which twice in a generation had dragged them into war.

*   *   *

Judge, then, of their concern when within four years of the Armistice the call went out again over an obscure seaport on the map of the Middle East almost equidistant from Canada and Australia.

To explain the Chanak crisis is like trying to précis the *Iliad* or to make sense of the Wars of the Roses, for involved in it were echoes not only of the struggle that had ended with Turkey's surrender in 1918, but also of the clash of interests in the Middle East between the victorious Allied Powers, the still farther-off reminders of the Balkan Wars and even of Turkish massacres of Christian populations in Armenia.

This complicated history had escaped the British public which neither knew nor cared that at this barren spot on the Asian shore of the Dardanelles, defended by a few Allied battalions, the Armistice lines had been drawn to keep the Turks out of Europe while their future frontiers were decided by the victors. Only a few diplomats remembered—and even they were frequently confused by the results—that just as in the outlying Arab provinces once ruled by Turkey the Allies had divided and partitioned the spoils among themselves, so under the stress of wartime and in order to encourage Russia and Italy to fight Germans, a number of promises had been made which had come home to roost in the (unratified) Treaty of Sèvres, which had the effect of partitioning Turkey proper; in fact, of carving her up like the traditional bird on the Christmas table or at Thanksgiving.

The response, which should surely have been expected, was a wave of militant Turkish feeling under a new national leader, Mustapha Kemal, who had been one of the victorious commanders in the fighting at the Dardanelles in 1915.

Neither the British nor the French, still less the Italians, were prepared to resume where they had left off in 1918—the only available Allied army on the spot was the Greek army, which was willing to adventure in territories on the Asian mainland around the port of Smyrna which had once been Greek and indigenously still largely remained so.

So far, so good. But as the situation worsened, these Greek armies were encouraged by the Allies to advance from their entrenched lines at Smyrna into the heart of the Anatolian plateau, and there, at the very moment when they looked like routing the Kemalists, they were halted by a veto placed on their further progress by the French and Italians, who had come to regard them jealously as agents of British ambitions in the Levant.

The result of this sad falling-out among friends was wholly disastrous—for the Greeks, for the British and, finally, for Lloyd George, whose rash opportunism was far in advance of public opinion. The Greek armies in Anatolia melted away under a Kemalist counter-attack; the French and Italian governments meditated a complete change of sides; and at Chanak the thin screen of troops along the Armistice lines found themselves faced with the triumphant forces of a re-born Turkey intent on crossing into Europe and re-covering its lost territories in Thrace.

No one in London had bothered to consult the dominions about all this. Greek armies at Lloyd George's beck and call had been launched here and there, had been marched up the hill like the Grand Old Duke of York's command and had been marched down again, with appalling consequences in massacres at Smyrna, and the British themselves were now in the firing line at Chanak—all without a word of enlightenment to Ottawa or to the Australians and New Zealanders who had died in their thousands just across the water in 1915 at Anzac Cove and Suvla.

Then, at the first appearance of the threatening Kemalist armies, the cries for help went out. Would the dominion governments desire to be associated with the steps Britain was taking, and in that event, would they wish to be represented by "contingents"? a nice euphemism for a new Anzac Corps.

As in 1914, so in 1922, New Zealand at once responded. "I had hoped," her Prime Minister wistfully remarked, "that the Empire would have recovered from the last war before being called upon to take part in another"; but he was nevertheless in no doubt where his duty lay; 11,000 recruits came in within a week; and the Maoris sent an encouraging—perhaps too encouraging—message: "I will go. Be brave, O father!"

In Newfoundland, which disputed with New Zealand the title of the most loyal dominion, the response of the Prime Minister, Sir

Richard Squires, might have been an echo of this robustness—"New-foundland does not want the British Empire to get into another row, but if there is one she wants to be in it."

Australian reaction was more guarded and varied from state to state. South Australia and New South Wales were much readier to support Britain than the cautious men of Melbourne. Also it varied from party to party. The Labour representatives in the federal Parliament were wholly unwilling to send even a platoon to Chanak until a referendum had been held, basing themselves on the fact that Australia, in their opinion, had not recovered from "the recent disastrous war."

Thus the federal Prime Minister, Mr. Hughes, had to tread warily. Australia, he announced, was ready to work with Britain in any steps that might be necessary for the defence of the neutral demili-tarised zones at the Straits, yet his government "could only view with despair" a war arising out of the clash of Turkish and Greek ambitions and would in no wise take part in "filibustering expedi-tions." Australian reluctance at this tidal drag towards war and Aus-tralian suspicions of the motives at work behind the scenes among the European powers can be sensed in every guarded word and can be read in the strong protest against lack of consultation which was sent to London. Yet at the end, as the tension mounted and it really seemed that the Kemalists were set on breaking through the neutral zones, Hughes came down firmly on the side of the Empire —"Whoever else fails to stand by Great Britain," he declared amidst cheers in the House, "we shall not. If war comes we shall be with Great Britain!"

In South Africa the news that the Union had been appealed to was received with bewilderment. Prime Minister Smuts was away on a tour of Zululand, from which, as a statesman of refined percep-tion, he showed himself in no hurry to return; but his finance minis-ter, speaking of all places in the loyalist stronghold of Natal, was quoted as confessing that, though not unpatriotic, he could not raise much enthusiasm for any appeal for men. The influential *Cape Times,* more forthright, declared that in South Africa's name the Union government must insist that the whole issue of the Straits be referred "for honest settlement" to the League of Nations instead of to some Conference "dominated by intriguing European powers."

"SOUTH AFRICA SEEKS MORE LIGHT," read the headlines in the London *Times*. "NO BLANK CHEQUE FOR MR. LLOYD GEORGE."

The whole incident was, of course, a grave embarrassment to the Empire-orientated Smuts government and a heaven-sent blessing to the Boer nationalists as a stick with which to beat their opponents. But Smuts still managed to outwit the opposition, since by the time he returned to Cape Town the crisis was so far past its peak that he could answer the British invitation and silence every critic with the reply that the active participation of the Union was no longer necessary.

The Liberal Prime Minister of Canada, Mr. Mackenzie King, had not been prescient enough to be visiting his own Zululand in Saskatchewan or Hudson's Bay; he had got no further than his constituency of North York. But he too was able to treat the London invitation with impressive calm by announcing that the news he had received was not informative enough as a basis for any action. He too had his Boers in the French press and voters of Quebec who were thoroughly opposed to intervention, as indeed were most Canadians except the Veterans' organisations in the English-speaking provinces which found their natural mouthpiece in the *Toronto Globe*. Mackenzie King had received the official message from Lloyd George several hours *after* the Canadian papers had printed a somewhat emotional press release from Downing Street announcing that the dominions had been invited to send troops to Chanak in the defence of soil "hallowed by the immortal memories of the Anzacs." It made him extremely cross. He forthwith cabled a complaint to London and noted in his diary: "I've thought out my plans. . . . No contingent will go without Parliament being summoned in the first instance. . . . I am sure the people of Canada are against participation in the European War." The British government, in fact, made no fewer than four separate attempts to get Canada to commit itself to some sort of diplomatic or military support. Yet all these failed, and Mackenzie King was later to declare that if war had come out of Chanak it was extremely unlikely that Canada would have sent troops.

Fortunately for all concerned, the crisis ended without hostilities in an armistice with Kemalist Turkey which later grew into the Treaty of Lausanne, displacing the Sèvres agreements. But the damage had been done. The blow to dominion confidence in the mother country had been severe. "Peace is our purpose. Peace is our object . . . we are not establishing (on the Straits) a sort of British Gibraltar," Lloyd George had told a group of newspapermen. But from Ottawa and Cape Town, even perhaps from Melbourne, it had looked very much as though "peace" in such hands was a variable commodity and that the old imperialist Adam was again at work. Under the veneer of diplomatic language the sense of irritation felt by the dominions was extreme. Mr. Hughes of Australia, most pro-British of statesmen, had protested; General Smuts had prevaricated; Mr. Mackenzie King of Canada had been outraged. "If membership within the British Empire," he remarked, "means participation by the dominions in any and every war in which Great Britain becomes involved, without consultation, conference, or agreement of any kind in advance, I can see no hope for an enduring relationship." Yet it was probably not the lack of consultation that really troubled him but the way Canada's isolationist leanings and her pacifism had been affronted. That the crisis had outraged the British people also and in the end brought about a revolt of the Tory party from the coalition government, bringing down Lloyd George in the process, was small compensation for the embarrassments which had been caused all round by miscalculations and follies in distant London. Had not *The Times* declared in a magisterial leader during the crisis that Britain and her other allies, whether they liked it or not, should remember that history had constituted them trustees for the Balkans? Yet what were the Balkans to Canada or Canada to the Balkans? Far too many questionable assumptions seemed to be made in London, and even *The Times,* which admittedly recognised that things were in flux and that the dominions had taken their place "at the council tables of the world," still continued to regard them with a proprietary and patronising air. "Although the dominions may speak with many voices for themselves as individuals," it had written during the Chanak crisis, "they speak as one when the time comes to speak for the Empire."

This did not correspond with the facts: it was purest fantasy. The Empire had not spoken with one voice. There was no longer unanimity towards commitments made in London which in many colonial eyes were dangers which had increased, were increasing, and ought to be diminished. Chanak was merely one visible proof of trends working below the surface; the dominions' presence in the League of

Nations was another, and so was Canada's signature in her own right of the Halibut Treaty of 1923 with the United States without recourse to the British Ambassador in Washington. The appearance and reality of the Empire no longer coincided. Could the circle be squared, the necessary adjustment made?

* * *

As early as 1917 the subtle and enquiring mind of General Smuts had applied itself to the search for some new definition of this strange organism which he believed to be unique in history. It was not a state but a system of states, not a nation but a community, a "Commonwealth of Nations," and the one great question he foresaw was how so loose a thing could be kept united. He was, of course, propounding a mystery worthy of St. Athanasius. How could the dissoluble be made indissoluble, the divisible indivisible without losing its divisibility?

At the 1921 Imperial Conference, though Smuts's exploration of this ground was only circulated as a private paper and not debated, it really seemed that agreement had been reached on the need for one common foreign policy. Yet at Chanak these hopes dissolved in dust, and by 1923 the dominions were in full retreat from the idea. When the 1926 conference met in London it was soon clear that these separatist trends had grown. Britain herself had recognised them when at Locarno she had specifically excluded the dominions and India from her guarantees of the non-aggression pacts between France, Germany and Belgium by which convalescent Europe had been patched up and supposedly pacified. But if this was a somewhat novel doctrine of exclusion, Canada had already anticipated it by refusing to ratify the peace treaty which Britain and her allies had signed with Turkey at Lausanne. This whole incident had been rich diplomatic comedy. Britain had moved heaven and earth to get Canada invited to the party. The French had refused—if Britain insisted on Canada and her other dominions, France would call up hers, starting with Tunisia and Morocco. This rejection of the cherished child caused dismay in the British camp. The Canadians, however, were delighted at not being asked. "Thank God we weren't!" one minister exclaimed with fervour. No invitation; no signature. No signature; no obligation—certainly not of the active kind that might be involved in guaranteeing the status of the Dardanelles, though the Canadians were rather prepared to think that they might ratify the actual peace.

Such was the trend of Empire relationships in 1926. And if the Canadians were difficult—they came to the conference hopping mad over a constitutional wrangle between Prime Minister and Governor-General which seemed to reflect on the whole principle of "Dominion Status"—what should one say of the sternly nationalist delegation from Ireland or of South Africa, where the pliable Smuts had been replaced by General J. B. M. Hertzog, a politician in the mould of the Boer intransigence of Kruger's day? The Empire was in extraordinary confusion. The Australians and New Zealanders wanted things left as they were—an undefined and instinctive relationship which sprang from ties of blood. The South Africans and the Irish felt no such sentimental attraction. General Hertzog wanted instead a declaration of autonomy which would divide the Empire into lots in private ownership: a kind of notice of sale which would establish in his words "the fundamental facts of the dominions' independent status and make these facts known to the world."

Where should one find a formula to satisfy these mutually exclusive views? There was a South African draft and a British draft; Mr. Mackenzie King of Canada was called in to suggest amendments; and from it all emerged Mr. A. J. Balfour's famous definition of the status of dominions:

> They are autonomous communities within the British Empire, equal in status, in no way subordinate to one another in any aspect of their domestic or external affairs, though united by a common allegiance to the Crown and freely associated as members of the British Commonwealth of Nations.

Neither the ideology nor the phrasing of this much-praised definition were new, for at the time of the American War of Independence Dr. Richard Price had wanted a voluntary co-operative of self-governing states, Granville Sharp a free commonwealth with the crown as its link, while Major John Cartwright had actually used several of the words that Mr. Balfour was to borrow.

Yet, derivative or not, the Balfour draft was a remarkable diplomatic feat, a splendid juggling with words which used "Empire" and "Commonwealth" as interchangeable. "It was all things to all men," Mr. W. M. Hughes of Australia was later to remark of this "almost metaphysical" document. "Every Prime Minister went away perfectly satisfied—Mr. Bruce because it altered nothing that affected Australia, Mr. Mackenzie King because it taught Lord Byng* where he got off, and General Hertzog because he was able to assure the burghers that the King of England was no longer the King of South Africa, although it was true that the King of South Africa was also King of England." Was this not indeed "the apotheosis of colonising genius" that a later enthusiast was to dub it? Yet there have been others, including a Prime Minister of Australia, who have believed it "a grave disservice" to the Commonwealth, a misguided attempt to reduce to writing something which was a matter of spirit.

These were afterthoughts. In 1926 Mr. Balfour's draft was accepted because it had become necessary that the indefinable should be defined, though the more impenetrably the better. No one but a philosopher of Balfour's standing could have risen so nebulously to the occasion. And certainly no one but parliamentary draftsmen acting on the instructions of a Commonwealth committee could have produced the end product of all this anguished cerebration in the Statute of Westminster of 1931 which spelled out in remorseless detail relationships which generations of British and dominion statesmen had judged better unsaid.

In its preamble it declared that laws affecting the succession to the throne or royal titles should require the assent of all dominion parliaments. Mr. Hughes's witticisms were not misplaced—the King of England was no longer King of South Africa, though George V (who also happened to be King of England) *was*. He was also King of Canada, of New Zealand, Australia and the Irish Free State, where he would probably have been shot if he had landed, and was bound to accept the advice of each Prime Minister where the affairs of the individual dominion were concerned, so that the-

---

* Lord Byng of Vimy, Governor-General of Canada, had refused Prime Minister Mackenzie King a dissolution of the Canadian Parliament. Shortly afterwards he granted a dissolution to King's Conservative successor. It caused great offence in Canadian Liberal circles.

oretically he could receive six sets of mutually destructive advice
to the point of actually being at war with himself, as Colin Cross has
most amusingly pointed out is his book, *The Fall of the British
Empire*. This actually happened during the fighting between India
and Pakistan after independence.

The main provisions of the statute were less spooky and more
mundane: a clearing-up operation to bring all the dominion parliaments into line as equally sovereign bodies except where they themselves deliberately asked for restrictions on their powers.* Dominion
Status was defined in much the same terms that Hertzog had demanded five years earlier. From now on, no British legislation should
apply to a dominion except at its request, and no dominion law
should be deemed invalid because it conflicted with British laws.
The Colonial Laws Validity Act was thus repealed, and any dominion parliament could cheerfully have re-instituted slavery within
its borders if it wished—critics of *Apartheid* could argue that this
in fact has happened, and happened moreover before South Africa
left the Commonwealth.

The Statute of Westminster was a necessary piece of legislation.
It recognised realities. It gave legal effect to a separatism which
had long been growing within the Empire and could no longer be
either resisted or ignored. Its few demonstrable absurdities—mostly
connected with the "divisibility" of the Crown which were so to
embarrass the monarchy, particularly at the time of Edward VIII's
abdication—were certainly outweighed by the good sense of its
general provisions which were in line with current thought and ac-
curately represented the shift in emphasis which the war had underlined. It was widely acclaimed for a while as a charter for the Commonwealth, but more recent generations came to be impatient of
even these tenuous ties. The Act of 1931 took the brake off a vehicle
which had begun to run downhill. In Australia and New Zealand
the passengers wanted to stay aboard—years passed before they
claimed the benefits of the Act's provisions. In Ireland, always the
examplar of anti-Imperialism, it was simply assumed that the whole
run-away coach was headed for the scrap-yard.

* Thus Canada requested that the provisions of the 1865 Act protecting the
status and separate culture of Quebec should remain entrenched and altera-
ble only by the British Parliament.

XIII

John Bull's Other Island

In a sense every nation has its "Ireland," the problem that defies solutions. Italy's Ireland is in Sicily, Iraq's in Kurdistan; France's was Algeria, America's the South; and even Ireland now has its own Irish problem in the six counties of Ulster.

There was therefore nothing particularly new or distinctive about the relationship existing between Britain and her sister island; two neighbours, one rich, one poor; one dominant, one in a state of resentful subjection; tied together by geographical and economic factors yet divided by acute social and religious differences.

From this uneasy partnership, however, important results were to flow. Ireland was to be a testing ground for revolutionary concepts among the governed and for repressive techniques among the governors. At the time when the Old Thirteen had been in revolt against the Empire, events in Ireland had helped point the way to independence; and a century and a half later, when Ireland herself finally broke clear, her example found a response even further from her shores, by the Bay of Bengal and the Gulf of Guinea. She was the exemplar of anti-Imperialism, both in theory and practice.

But was Ireland even in the Empire except as one component of the British Isles? Right to the end of the connection her exact status was a matter of dispute, and indeed still is, for even now that she is independent of Britain her citizens working "across the water" are still popularly regarded as being different from other immigrants and almost as British as the British themselves. Who and what are the Irish? and what is Ireland?

In the eighteenth century she was clearly a colony with representative government, if of rather a peculiar kind; but the activities of the "Volunteers" and the enlightened self-interest of the Rockingham Whigs at Westminster resulted in the "Constitution of 1782" and the Renunciation Act by which Britain formally declared the Irish parliament and judiciary independent "for ever," though of course subject to the same Crown. "Ireland is now a nation," Henry Grattan had cried. Yet a striking anomaly remained: her executive was headed by a Lord Lieutenant appointed in London.

Within twenty years of this declaration the Irish parliament had been induced to vote itself out of an existence which had lasted for five hundred years. The bribery and pressure had been expertly applied. The rising of 1798 inspired by Wolfe Tone and his "United Irishmen" and supported by French arms had gravely alarmed the British government, which once more saw Ireland as a springboard for European enemies as in the time of Elizabeth and William III. Just over a century later the same threat, this time from Germany, was again to bedevil Anglo-Irish relations at a critical time. Ireland's physical closeness to Britain and the emotional and political distance she tried to keep were both arguments for absorbing her; and on the first day of the new century the thing was done and the United Kingdom of Great Britain and Ireland came into being.

Grattan's nation thus no longer existed on the map: it had become part of a new multi-national body and, presumably, an equal part. But in that case why was there still an English Viceroy and Chief Secretary in Dublin? There were no such functionaries in Edinburgh. And there was another and greater anomaly at work, for where else in the Empire but in Ireland did an established Church serve a tenth of the people, and a minority of Protestants hold sway over a Catholic population deprived of all political rights?

Pitt had hoped to sugar the pill of Union with a programme for Catholic emancipation, and if he had succeeded, it is possible that Ireland might have adapted itself to its new status. The Scots, after all, had had their own religious differences with the English as well as a long and proud tradition in which England had been for centuries the "enemy," yet the marriage of convenience had worked and the two nations had settled down amicably enough to the business of running an empire. Why should not Ireland do the same? In some respects she had been treated at Union with surprising generosity: she had to pay no more than two seventeenths of the running costs and had been given a much larger representation in parliamentary seats at Westminster than had come Scotland's way. Unfortunately, the religious question in Ireland had deep social undertones in the gulf between Protestant landlord and Catholic tenant. It concerned land hunger, injustice, the struggle of the dispossessed; and when Emancipation was at last conceded by the Wellington Ministry in 1829 the day for gratitude had gone and an Irish patriot leader had appeared in the person of Daniel O'Connell, whose Catholic Association had immediately to be suppressed.

Concession and coercion were the unhappy Siamese twins of the Anglo-Irish connection. It is easy to blame English statesmen for their lack of generosity and vision, but the truth was that the sense of Irish nationalism which Grattan had expresed for the Protestant few, O'Connell had shown to the Catholic many, and with its coming something irreconcilable had entered the argument.

The terrible events of the famine of 1845–49 caused by the failure of the potato crop revealed the fatal division which had opened up and the bare subsistence line at which the vast majority of eight million Irishmen existed. During these years a million people died of starvation and disease and as many emigrated. The figures in themselves are bad enough, but the panic that accompanied the emigration in the "coffin ships" left behind it a legacy of bitter hatred both in Ireland and in the New World against a government which had failed even to feed its people.

The history of Ireland abounds in ironies. So terrible a calamity —a continuing one in the sense that massive emigration continued for the next fifty years and halved the population by 1900—should have had at least one compensation in providing more land for those who were left. But, in fact, the reverse occurred. There was a crying lack of capital, small-holdings were swallowed up in large estates, tillage gave way to cattle-raising and the land hunger of the peasantry grew into the central Irish grievance that persisted till the end of the century. Even to-day as you drive through the green and empty countryside you can see the evidence—the great houses of the "Ascendancy," some of them still in ruins from the "Troubles," the cottages at the park gates, the absence of ploughed fields, the acreages of grazing in the rather bumpy Arcadian landscape between the mountains and the bog. This was the land of the "Whiteboys," of the Fenian Brotherhood, where "Captain Moonlight" walked— a land in the grip of creeping civil war whose scars were burning homesteads and the sudden gunshot from ambush under the trees. "My mission is to pacify Ireland," said Gladstone, taking office as Prime Minister for the first time. But though he disestablished the Irish Protestant Church and by his Land Act of 1870 removed the worst hardships of eviction, he failed to conciliate the people and had to fall back like his predecessors on a Coercion Act to deal with agrarian crime. Indeed, by the time he returned to office in 1880 the situation had got worse; a majority of the Irish members at Westminster had formed themselves into a tightly disciplined "Home Rule" party under the leadership of Charles Stewart Parnell; the Land League had been formed, and the countryside was in the grip of a terrorism so intense and widespread that no landlord's life was safe, no tenant dared take on a farm from which another had been evicted for fear of "boycotting," of social ostracism, in a society where, in the words of a popular jingle,

Moonlight's the law of the League,
And Moonshine's the law of the land.

In the general chaos of the times even the Irish leaders had lost control of the situation. Parnell was gaoled under the provisions of a new Coercion Act and the all-powerful League of which he was president was suppressed—his release, after a bargain with the government in which he pledged himself to calm the country, was promptly followed by the assassination in broad daylight in Dublin's Phoenix Park of the new Chief Secretary for Ireland, Gladstone's own nephew by marriage, along with the Under-secretary, Thomas Burke.

Seldom among civilised nations has a whole society been plunged into such anarchy as Ireland at this time. Every kind of crime was rife. Gangs like "The Invincibles" who had carried out the killings in Phoenix Park were organised along Mafia lines; their crimes were rehearsed down to the last detail of the alibis they would produce in court, vouched for by witnesses who were bribed or terrorised into compliance. Perjury was raised to an art. There were few arrests and even fewer government informers—theirs was not an occupation that promised a long or peaceful life. And even if the criminals were caught, juries for similar reasons would not convict them. A low property-qualification introduced in 1871 had resulted in a new class of jurymen, called in derision "The Wild Flowers of Tullahogue" after the name of a locally manufactured scent, and one can well believe the story of how a jury of these worthies, when told to take their usual places, scrambled with one accord into the dock. "Boycotting" itself was a cruel and dreadful thing when administered by the Land League "courts." "Do you know what a boycott in Ireland means?" Sir Edward Carson was to ask a half-incredulous public meeting in England. "Do you know that a mother cannot get milk for her dying babe; and that it will be allowed to die, simply, forsooth, because the father or mother is under a boycott? . . . It is a state of savagery." A boycotted man could not be sure that his family would be allowed the wood to make him a coffin. Parnell himself had introduced the system, which he had called "Christian and charitable," presumably compared with even worse things; and that a man of such calibre and a normally compassionate people should have lent themselves to such horrors is the yardstick by which we can judge the depths of emotional hatred that existed for the "Ascendancy" and all its works. Every act of apparently insensate cruelty—from the murders in Phoenix Park to the mutilation of cattle in obscure areas of Connaught—was to some degree proof that Catholic Ireland had rejected the Union of 1800; and in this light they had come to be regarded by the most powerful of English statesmen, the Liberal Prime Minister Mr. Gladstone, who had convinced himself that only in the granting of Home Rule and the reversal of Pitt's Act lay escape from an intolerable problem.

Unfortunately, at just this moment the Irish Protestants, who formed a majority in the northeast of the island, had won the support of the Tories at Westminster and a sizeable number of Mr.

Gladstone's own Liberal followers for a precisely opposite conclusion —that the Union must be maintained.

*   *   *

In Grattan's time the Irish northeast, the Protestant province of Ulster, had led the campaign for an independent Irish parliament and judiciary; the celebrated "Constitution of 1782" had been a Protestant triumph in which the submerged Catholic mass of the people had played little part. For years the inhabitants of Belfast and County Down had been just as distrustful of Britain and as revolutionary in spirit as the southerners of Dublin and County Cork.

But while the south had sunk into depression after the great famine, the northeast with its abundant flow of capital and its textiles and engineering industries had flourished through the British connection which opened world markets to its goods; and as the southern Catholics under O'Connell's leadership found themselves a voice and became more militant, the "Orangemen" of Ulster took fright and began to look around for allies against the far more numerous "Papists" whom they and the minority Protestants in the southern counties had dominated since "King Billy's" victory over James II at the Battle of the Boyne. Gladstone's land reforms of 1881, which assured to tenants "the Three Fs" demanded by the Land League—Fair rent to be assessed by arbitration, Fixity of tenure, and Freedom for the tenant to sell his tenancy at the best market price—still failed to pacify the south, but in the north they brought about a revolution in political thinking by which the wealthiest and most industrialised Irish province turned its back on Ireland and looked to Britain for support.

This change in political patterns had been noted by acute minds at Westminster, and when in 1886 Mr. Gladstone introduced a Home Rule Bill, it was defeated in the House of Commons by an alliance between the Tories, the Ulster "Orangemen" and a number of Liberal supporters of the Union; and that these by and large represented the will of the British electorate was proved when Gladstone appealed to the country, only to find himself routed at the polls. Six years later he returned to power and got his second Home Rule Bill through the Commons. The House of Lords incontinently threw it out; and this time even that iron-willed old man accepted what seemed to be the inevitable verdict.

Of course, we can see now that Gladstone was right and that between 1886 and 1894 a great opportunity was missed of knocking Irish heads together before they had wholly parted company. The fateful division we are still witnessing, with its terrible legacy of bloodshed, was then only in the making and might have been checked by a generous gift to Ireland of what even Ulstermen had for centuries been demanding—the right to run their own affairs. Ireland was a special and peculiar problem, the nearest home and in a sense the furthest away, quite different from other imperial problems. The failure of the British people to recognise the nature of the need—and it was largely a selfish and headstrong refusal to face facts—not only denied the vast majority of Irishmen the Home Rule which was due to them, but it encouraged those revolutionary elements that looked back for inspiration to Wolfe Tone and the rebellion of 1798—elements which rejected Home Rule as completely as they rejected Union with the hated "Saxons."

This factor—too long ignored or unperceived at Westminster—was to introduce a complication which sometimes baffled the Irish themselves. The Home Rule agitation seemed to have created two Irelands, north and south, but in fact there were four. Southern Ireland—the future "Free State" which is now Eire—was soon to be split between the moderates, the Home Rulers, who were prepared to settle for a status rather lower than Canada's inside the Empire, and the militants of the growing party of Sinn Fein who demanded at the very least a dual monarchy such as existed in Austro-Hungary under the Habsburgs: while the Ulster province in the northeast was split between the hard-core Protestant areas around Belfast and those Ulster counties on the fringe where Catholics were either in a majority or in balance with the Orangists.

Such a situation seemed made for civil war, and when in 1912-13 the Liberal Prime Minister, Mr. Asquith, forced the third Home Rule Bill through the Commons, only to find it rejected by the Tory House of Lords, its coming was signalled to everyone.

In 1911 the Lords had lost their power of absolute veto over decisions of the lower House, and their treatment of Asquith's Bill could only impose a limited delay. But it was a highly dangerous one. Passions on both sides had been aroused. The Tory party at Westminster had taken up Ulster's cause: for ideological as well as political reasons it had come to regard any attack on the Union or any attempt to coerce Ulster as a sacrilege which must at all costs be resisted. "Ulster will fight, and Ulster will be right," Lord Randolph Churchill had declared some years earlier, giving the movement its rallying cry. Lord Randolph was now dead, but Ulster had found itself a leader—Sir Edward Carson. Since this was an Irish problem, it was natural that this champion of the north should be a southerner by birth who sat for a Dublin seat. But the situation had passed out of the realms of comedy, for both sides were arming. Two hundred thousand Orangemen at monster rallies in Belfast signed the covenant binding themselves to resist Home Rule, and in April 1914, 25,000 rifles and three million rounds of ammunition were smuggled ashore—a gesture followed in the south by a slightly more modest landing of guns at Howth in Dublin Bay. It would have spelt war if that August the whole Liliputian problem had not been overtaken by Germany's invasion of Belgium and the outbreak of Armageddon itself.

* * *

For two years thereafter almost everyone behaved beautifully. Asquith's Home Rule Bill, which in fact promised the Irish a status within the Empire well short of that enjoyed by Canada, Australia and the other "dominions," was placed on the statute book with a clause suspending it till hostilities with Germany were over, and as such was accepted gratefully by the southern Irish, if not by the Ulstermen. In the meantime there was a rush to the colours, and the whole island began to prosper economically from the struggle engulfing Europe. There remained the irreconcilable Sinn Feiners, for whom even world war was an irrelevance.

On Easter Monday in 1916 their armed forces seized the centre of Dublin in a lightning *coup* and proclaimed an Irish Republic. If the British at this point had realised how little backing the rising had, if they had understood the apathy or active hostility most Irishmen felt for it and had acted with restraint towards the small band of mutineers whom they had broken within six days, the events of Easter Monday might have joined the other failed movements of Irish history. By shooting the captives in batches by British firing squads the government turned conspirators into martyrs, and when under the stresses of 1917 it attempted to impose conscription on the English model on a people who had never shirked a fight, it declared itself an alien dictatorship.

In 1918, in the first post-war elections, the Sinn Feiners swept the board in southern Ireland, with seventy-three members as against six supporters of a now outdated and discredited Home Rule. In the north, twenty-six Ulster Unionists were returned. The war with Germany and her allies had changed the face of the world, but it had not changed "the state of Ireland" or its endemic tendency to disagree. In January 1919 the Sinn Feiners, disdaining the parliament at Westminster to which they had been elected, proclaimed themselves a sovereign assembly—*Dail Eirean*—and in the following year a war of liberation broke out between its irregular armed forces and the irregulars the British employed against them which in its horrors equalled anything the Germans were supposed to have committed in Belgium in 1914. This was the war between the Volunteers of the Irish Republican Army and the "Black and Tans" which is enshrined in Irish legend under the immortal euphemism of "The Troubles." The choice for Britain, said Winston Churchill, was between "War with the utmost violence and peace with the utmost patience," but there could be no doubt what the war-weary British people most desired. It was peace at any price. By the Government of Ireland Act, Ulster was offered (and accepted) Home Rule with a parliament at Belfast of its own: and when the south rejected this recipe for its own future it was offered something even better—full dominion status, complete autonomous self-government, which even Parnell had never asked for and which even the Sinn Feiners might have accepted if it had been offered before the rising of '16.

This the south accepted in the Anglo-Irish Treaty of 1921. But it accepted it under duress, under a British threat of more hostilities, and the settlement was totally rejected by almost half the population, who were prepared to fight yet another bitter civil war with their own more accommodating countrymen for the principle of total separation from Britain and her Empire.

These militants in fact lost the war: but they were not slow to win the peace that followed. They had become in spite of themselves a dominion, the Irish Free State—very well. The trappings could be shed. In 1933, having become the government in Dublin, they did away with the Oath of Allegiance to the monarch; in 1936 they

sent the Governor-General packing and cut all references to mon-
archical links still existing in the constitution. In 1937 the Irish Free
State took unto itself a new name—Eire. In 1939 it stayed
neutral in Hitler's war. In 1948 it withdrew from the Commonwealth. In 1949 the Irish Republic was officially proclaimed, and
there was an end to what was deemed the "long and tragic association with the institution of the British Crown."

*   *   *

What then were the lessons to be drawn from these events by a
Britain which had now emerged victorious on the world stage after
four years of herculean effort, only to be rebuffed in her own back
yard?

The first was that British concessions to Ireland had always been
too little and too late. Emancipation had been granted the Catholics
twenty years after any gratitude could be collected. The land problem
had been solved, the land hunger of the peasants appeased, but by
that time the Irish had found themselves other grievances. Similarly,
Home Rule had been delayed, first by prevarications inside the
government and then by the appalling mischance of world war.
When it was conceded, no one in southern Ireland wanted it. So
the offer was upgraded into one of dominion status, and by then
few people in Ireland wanted *that*.

Was this simply another "Irishism," the result of association with
a brilliant but too mercurial people? The British certainly had no
means of knowing, because not for a century and a half had they
been involved with another such popular insurrection by people of
their own kith and kin; but in India, their most cherished possession,
they were faced with a situation which bore disturbing resemblances
to Anglo-Irish history.

What should be made of it? What *could* be made of it? It was a
pertinent question. Because if Ireland had been divided into north
and south, Protestant and Catholic, so was India divided into Muslim
and Hindu. Might its peoples diverge, just as Ulster and Eire had
diverged? Here was a ready-made warning. Also a ready-made
temptation to those who hankered after the old precept of Divide
and Rule, the best Roman prescription for running an Empire.

XIV

The Struggle for Swaraj

If in 1918 the white dominions meant "Commonwealth," the Empire meant colonial territories in every continent but pre-eminently it meant India, that legendary land of rajahs and elephants, durbars and tiger shoots, which as the war had shown was also a reservoir of manpower and capital ensuring Britain's place among the great powers.

To protect India's frontiers and the route to her, Britain had established herself in Egypt and the Sudan, in Malta, Cyprus and Mauritius, at Aden and the sheikdoms of the Persian Gulf, in the Horn of Africa and at the Cape; had occupied Burma, the Straits Settlements and Ceylon; alternatively supported and fought Turks and Afghans; fended off Russia; tried to "protect" Persians; and extended her diplomatic presence to Tibet and the Himalayan kingdoms on the roof of the world. Large chunks of the Empire, in fact, had not been picked up in any "fit of absence of mind": they had been quite deliberately acquired to bolster up the continuing British presence in India: the *Raj*.

Pliable where the white dominions were concerned, the British kept a firm autocratic front towards this, their most prestigious possession. What they had, they held. "You cannot apply constitutional principles to a conquered country," the Viceroy, Lord

Dufferin, had declared in 1888, thirty years after the Mutiny. "We cannot give the natives what they want," a Secretary of State had echoed in London: "representative institutions and the dimunition of the existing establishment of Europeans is impossible." India was too vital a possession to be put at risk. She was necessary to Britain as a power base, a training and recruiting ground for armies, a market for British goods, a field for capital investment and for the employment opportunities she afforded for British officials, bankers, traders and entrepreneurs. Moreover, Britain was necessary to India—almost everyone, including most educated Indians, was agreed on this. In 1885 was founded the All India Congress, that future scourge of the *Raj*. It was founded by a retired British official, A. O. Hume, and its first session ended like some school speech day with Three Cheers for the Queen Empress, repeated over and over again in a gale of loyal applause. It was "a merciful dispensation of Providence," one leading figure was to declare, that Britain had become the paramount power to rescue India from internal strife: it had been God's doing, said another, for India's own salvation.

God-given or not, to both British and Indians the *Raj* was a reality and an immensely powerful one. Half the land area of the sub-continent containing three quarters of the population formed "British India," directly administered through a chain of command which ran from the parliament at Westminster, via a Secretary of State in London, a Viceroy/Governor-General with his Executive Council in Calcutta, downwards through the Provincial Governors or Lieutenant-Governors and *their* Councils, to the Collectors and District Officers who brought law and administration to the myriad villages of plain and jungle. The rest of the country—"Indian" or princely India—was formed of a patchwork of semi-autonomous states, some larger than Ireland, some smaller than an English parish, in treaty relationship with the "Paramount Power" which was responsible for their external affairs but left domestic matters to the ruling rajahs or maharajahs whom it could at a pinch depose.

Such a system obviously lent itself to autocratic management. India was not one but several; even British India was federal rather than unitary—and there could be no "Indian opinion" as such. But these political divisions were nothing in comparison with the racial and religious ones. The small dark-skinned Dravidians of the south were as different from the inhabitants of the north and west as Egyptians were from Scotsmen, and their languages were equally diverse. Most vital of all was the division between those who practised Hinduism in its various forms and the Muslim descendants of those followers of the Prophet who in the sixteenth century had swept down over the Khyber under Babur and in the great days of the Mogul Empire of Akbar and Aurungzeb had ruled the country to the borders of the Deccan.

Not all the Muslims of the late nineteenth century were direct descendants of these invaders. The Moguls had made converts among the conquered, and racially members of the two groups often resembled one another. But Islam is a very durable faith and its devotees had come to form a quarter of the total population. In some areas—in the Punjab and Sind in the northwest and in East Bengal—they were a majority bloc; but communities of them were scattered through every province and town of consequence, sometimes in near parity with the Hindus, sometimes forming only a minute percentage of the dominant majority group whose ancestors had ruled the land a thousand years before Babur at a time when Britain had been a Roman province.

The results of this cheek by jowl existence of neighbours who tolerated one another for most of the year but at times of religious festivals could lapse into homicidal rage at every imagined insult were as inevitable as Moonlighting in Galway in the heyday of the Land League; and after every Hindu-Muslim riot at "Holi" or "Muharram," with its tally of dead, and burnt or desecrated temples or mosques, the British officials deplored these insensate outbreaks provoked perhaps by the ill-treatment of a cow or the height of a pagoda in a procession. How barbaric, how absurd! How childish also the pretensions of some rajah in one of the princely states demanding an increase in his ration of ceremonial guns while he oppressed his peasantry and ignored the good offices of the British "Resident"! These complaints over a sundowner at the club were heartfelt. But, of course, it was precisely *because* of these divisions that the *Raj* had remained unchallenged for so long. The British had been in no way responsible for these communal tensions. All the same they benefited. In so divided a country there could be no common front against them. The villagers on the whole were satisfied—and India was still a land of villages. For the man at the plough and the woman at the well the *Raj* was at least no worse than "Mogul or Mahratta," those other tyrants from the past. Muslim opinion at the end of Queen Victoria's reign had no acknowledged spokesman, while the Hindu moderates in Congress still looked gratefully to the *Raj* for benefits received and in hopes of further crumbs from the imperial table in the way of more Indianisation of the Indian Civil Service and in the government itself. As for the British, they concentrated on the practical: built roads, railways, schools and hospitals, did their best to suppress dacoitry, brought law and order to the villages, promoted irrigation, and even introduced the rudiments of an elective system at municipal and provincial level.

For thirty years after the Mutiny the country lay passive under this treatment; then from the 1890s onwards native opinion began to harden. There were several apparent causes—among them the damage to white prestige caused by the Abyssinian victory over the Italians at Adowa, the upsurge of Asian pride which followed Japan's still more startling defeat of Tsarist Russia, the example of the Sinn Feiners in Ireland, and the bitter unrest springing from the famine followed by outbreaks of plague which affected vast areas of the country in Diamond Jubilee year—but essentially these stirrings marked the birth of a sense of nationhood such as had not existed in India since the Moguls. For the first time voices were raised in Congress demanding freedom from all foreign control, to be won if need be by boycott and other Irish practices, and though the moderate majority easily headed off these prentice steps in revolution, they too had shifted their ground to a demand for self-government within the empire. "I say we are British citizens," one speaker declared, "and are entitled to and claim all British rights."

This message from India was not lost on Mr. Asquith's Liberal administration which had taken office in London in 1906. The Secretary of State was Lord Morley, Mr. Gladstone's chief lieutenant during the battles for Irish Home Rule. With such a background his mind turned naturally towards conciliation. "Reforms may not save the *Raj*, but if they don't, I don't know what else will," he wrote to his like-minded Viceroy, Lord Minto; and by the reforms associated with the names of both these statesmen, as embodied in the Indian Councils Act of 1909, steps were taken not only to associate Indians with the Executive Councils of the Viceroy and the Provincial Governors, but also greatly to extend the elective principle on a franchise which, though very limited, would greatly increase the number of Indians elected to the central Legislative Assembly and in the Provincial legislatures would actually provide Indian majorities of elected and "nominated" members over and against the caucus of government officials.

These measures were well short of full representative, let alone responsible, government. The Viceroy and his Executive Council in Calcutta, the Provincial Governors and their Executive Councils at the periphery, remained autocrats. The Indians in the elective legislatures might argue and debate, but that was the limit of their powers. Yet the reforms were still far too much for British Imperialists to stomach, and a storm of indignant protest broke out over this toying with notions of Indian self-government which one ex-Viceroy described as "a fantastic and futile dream." All conservative opinion was abusing poor Lord Morley, oblivious of the fact that Lord Morley himself, like Lord Minto, heartily agreed with them that India was totally unfitted for democracy. In fact, in one sense his reforms were as reactionary as any backwoodsman could wish, for with the best of intentions he had in his Indian Councils Act played the Anglo-Irish game to perfection by providing separate electoral rolls for Muslims which would return a larger number of the minority group to the assemblies than their numbers warranted. Divide and Rule? Neither Morley nor Minto had intended anything of the kind. They had tried to protect minorities and take a small step forward—nothing more.

Such concessions, which if granted in the 1880s would have been rapturously received by everyone, fell coolly on the ears of a Congress which, while praising Lord Morley's efforts to introduce what it called "a fairly liberal measure of constitutional reform," was highly critical of the details and, in particular, of the pro-Muslim bias which underlay it. In certain restrictions and disqualifications placed on candidates for election, Congress claimed, in fact, to see nothing helpful to Indian aspirations but rather an attempt by the bureaucracy to penalise the educated classes in favour of conformist elements. A mood of disillusion and resentment seemed to be spreading through the country. But there was still an immense fund of respect and even of affection for the *Raj* and for the person of the King-Emperor, whose visit to India in 1911 did much to restore harmonious feelings; and when in August 1914 the Empire went to war with Germany the results astonished the British themselves—like George V at his Silver Jubilee they had not imagined themselves beloved.

Almost as one man, Indians of all groups closed ranks. "We sink our differences," wrote the *Bengalee* of Calcutta, "and offer all that we possess in defence of the great Empire with which the future prosperity and advancement of our people are bound up." "The people of India," agreed the *Indian Patriot*, "will be prepared to bear any responsibility and any burden," while the *Amrit Bazar Patrika*, a nationalist organ usually highly critical of Britain, came out with a leader which went far to prove what the *Times of India* and the *Madras Mail* were saying, that the Indian press acclaimed the loyalty of an entire nation.

Was all this nothing but words? Mr. Nehru later wrote in his autobiography that beneath the high-sounding phrases there was little true sympathy with Britain but rather a desire to see her humbled. Yet these words were written much later at a time of increasing bitterness, and they hardly square with the speeches, the letters, the actions of a time when tens of thousands of recruits were drilling and almost every town produced its demonstration of fervent loyalty. In London on August 8 Mr. Gandhi, greatest and most generous of future antagonists of imperialism, hoped that India would "think imperially." "It is certain," wrote Sir S. Subramania Iyer, who was to be chairman of the Congress reception committee that year, "that no thinking man in this country fails to appreciate at this moment how indissolubly the interests of India are bound up with the integrity of the British Empire." And on August 12 the revered figure of Dadabhai Naoroji, confessing that all his life he had been more a critic than a simple praiser of British rule, expressed the idealism which had underlain a whole generation of Indian statesmen: "If ever India expects to attain again her former glory on the advanced character and scale of modern British civilisation, of liberty, humanity, justice and all that is good, great and divine, it shall be at the hands of the British people and with the British people as self-governing members of the British Empire."

Mr. Nehru was certainly mistaken, for even Congress had pledged its "unswerving allegiance" and "firm resolve to stand by the Empire at all hazards and at all costs." The devotion and self-sacrifice were real, and perhaps the most remarkable tribute ever paid to an empire by its subjects since the Britons of the fifth century petitioned Rome for the return of the Legions. But the tributes all had a valedictory sound, and mixed up with them was expectation merging into a demand that loyalty's debts should be paid. If after the termination of the war the constitutional position of India remained unchanged, warned a group of notables in the central Legislative Assembly, bitter disappointment and discontent would result and enthusiasm would be replaced by "the painful memory of unrealised expectations." The national mood, in fact, was becoming very fluid; an increaing restlessness was in the air, affecting not only the Hindus, always the most vocal critics of the *Raj,* but the Muslims also, as more and more Indians crossed the seas for the battle-fronts and the casualty lists mounted.

Late in 1916 by the Lucknow Pact the incredible happened and Hindu-dominated Congress and Muslim League came together in one common demand that Britain should make a declaration of intent to advance India to self-government along dominion lines.

The days had long passed when such demands could be ignored. They could sometimes be deferred, and in fact the British cabinet managed to put things off for the best part of a year before coming up in the summer of 1917 with an answer which at first sight might have delighted the Delphic Oracle:

The policy of His Majesty's Government, with which the Government of India are in complete accord, is that of increasing association of Indians in every branch of the administration, and the gradual development of self-governing institutions, with a view to the progressive realisation of responsible government for India as an integral part of the British Empire.

"Increasing association," "gradual development," "progressive realisation" all sound like splendid shots out of the diplomatic locker, and indeed it seems clear that the ex-Viceroy Lord Curzon, who had a hand in the drafting, deliberately put in the phrase "responsible government" for what he believed to be its vagueness, apparently unaware that the words had acquired the very definite meaning of a promise of full self-government—in which light it was undoubtedly regarded by the entire Indian press and public.

The Secretary of State, Edwin Montagu, had not intended to be devious. A true friend of India, he had set out to give her all that was politically possible at the time, and by his Government of India Act of 1919, which put into law the reforms he had worked out in conjunction with the Viceroy, Lord Chelmsford, a new concept of "Dyarchy," double government, was introduced into the provinces, by which certain matters affecting justice and law enforcement were "reserved" to the Governors, while domestic matters were "transferred" to Indian legislators and ministers responsible to them, so that a measure of self-government was created, with the promise of a further review in ten years' time.

This was of course a great advance on anything that had gone before and should have assured Edwin Montagu and Lord Chelmsford the kind of place in Indian history that Durham and Lord Elgin had won for themselves in Canada eighty years earlier. The Congress moderates, though disappointed that Dyarchy had not been introduced at the centre, were still prepared to work the scheme and enjoy office. Far different was the reaction on the Congress "left" where the reforms were greeted as "the contemptible device of a bankrupt statesman to stave off the evil day"; and this vision of the *Raj's* real intentions was borne out by an ill-judged attempt on the Government of India's part to keep in being war-time emergency powers after the war was over.

The country's response in its mood of doubt and frustration was threefold. Mr. Gandhi, making his *début* as a national leader, proclaimed his *Satyagraha* movement of non-violent opposition to a regime which seemed to him set on bad courses but which he thought could be "shamed" into good ones; his less patient followers interpreted this as a call to revolution; while mobs in the cities and bandits in the countryside joyfully turned to derailing trains, arson, looting and the murder of officials.

In the spring of 1919 throughout the Punjab, which had stayed quiet through the troubles of 1857 and by its loyalty saved the *Raj,* the fires of another mutiny year were burning. At Amritsar, on April 11, five Englishmen were killed, houses were burned, the railway station attacked and the telegraphic communications cut. The riot was handled by the British with what the *Times of India* called "patience and forbearance," but when two days later a huge and potentially menacing crowd gathered in a square known as the Jallianwalla Bagh the British officer in charge, Brigadier General Dyer, ordered his troops to fire, killed 379 of them and wounded over a thousand.

At the time Dyer certainly believed, if mistakenly, that he had taken the only possible action to save Amritsar and the Punjab from full-scale revolution, and if his actions had ended there, and had been promptly explained to public opinion in India, the events of Sunday April 13 might have been accepted as the painful but necessary cauterisation of a dangerous wound.

Dyer and the civil power went further. In an alley in the city an English lady had been attacked—Indians passing the spot were ordered to do so crawling on their bellies, while throughout the Punjab a regime of stern repression was imposed. Worse still, though the Liberal press expressed its horror when the full details of events at Amritsar finally reached London after eight months' delay, a sizeable group in the Commons and an actual majority in the House of Lords acclaimed Dyer's actions, while in India itself the official Hunter Commission, set up by the government to examine the affair, came out with a report (from which its Indian members dissented) blaming Dyer merely for an error of judgment and condemning *Satyagraha* as an illegal conspiracy.

Far more than the shots in the Jallianwalla Bagh, it was this cool, contemptuous treatment of India's wrongs that really outraged public opinion throughout the country. It was a turning point in the lives of many Indians, and perhaps an excuse for as many more who had already crossed the line dividing loyalty from rejection of the *Raj* but found in it a convenient justification.

In Congress the President, Pandit Motilal Nehru, father of one future Indian Prime Minister and grandfather of another, broke into impassioned verse:

O for our land, woe,
Arise and for coffin and cerements go!
O for our land, woe.
With the blood of our men killed in this pursuit
Hill, plain and garden blood-red glow.
O for our land, Woe.

In Mahatma Gandhi's words "iron had entered the Pandit's soul." Gandhi's own reactions were more complex. He felt a measure of guilt over his part in the Amritsar tragedy, for it had been his attempt to enter the province as a *Satyagraha* and the government's refusal to admit him that had sparked off the riots at Lahore, Amritsar and Ahmedabad. As a passionate believer in non-violence, he had regarded the outrages committed in his name as disgraceful to himself; "a rapier" run through his body. He had promptly suspended the civil disobedience campaign. He had, he said, underrated the forces of evil in this his "Himalayan mistake": if the Viceroy and the Governor of the Punjab and General Dyer were to be condemned, Indians must also condemn themselves.

Gandhi had served the *Raj* with loyalty and distinction in South Africa and later in India in 1914. This "half-naked fakir," as Winston Churchill was so ludicrously to describe him, had won British campaign medals for his work with ambulance units during the Boer War and the Zulu risings. He had believed that British rule was "on the whole beneficial to the ruled," and that British administrators, though "insular and dense," had honestly intended that India should take an honoured and equal place as a dominion within the Empire. "Hardly ever have I known anybody to cherish such loyalty as I did. . . . It is my knowledge, right or wrong, of the British Constitution which has bound me. . . ." After Amritsar his attitude changed. "Experience has made me wiser. I consider the existing system of government to be wholly bad and requiring special national effort to end or mend it. . . . I can take no pride in calling the Empire mine or in describing myself as a citizen. On the contrary, I fully realise that I am a pariah untouchable of the Empire." In August 1920 after the Hunter Report and the exoneration of Dyer in the House of Lords, the Mahatma returned his medals to the Viceroy.

*   *   *

Under such auspices Dyarchy began. At the December meeting of Congress in December 1919, mid-way between the Punjab rising and the publication of the Hunter Report, Congress had agreed to co-operate in working the Montagu-Chelmsford reforms if only with the object of reforming them. This triumph of moderation and reason had been entirely Gandhi's work; but with his estrangement from the British, Hindu opinion among all but a section of moderates on the Congress "right" fell away, and was matched among the Muslims by the outburst of religious fury against the *Raj* which followed the Allied attempt by the Treaty of Sèvres to dismember Turkey, the seat of the Islamic Caliphate.

This Muslim belligerence was not destined to be long lasting, since the Kemalists in Turkey soon removed the dynamic behind it by themselves abolishing the Caliphate, thus leaving their more fanatical Indian brethren without a figurehead or a cause. From the mid-1920s onward the Indian Muslims began gradually drifting back into their old hostility to the Hindus and dependence on the *Raj*. But for a while the unnatural alliance held between the Khalifat party extremists at one pole and Hindu intransigence at the other in the shape of Mr. Gandhi's new non-co-operation movement; and between this upper and nether millstone the experiment of Dyarchy was to be ground into the dust.

In 1920, as indeed in 1940, the Mahatma was a moderate set on revolutionary courses—his love-hate relationship with the *Raj* was lifelong, though in it there can be no doubt that love predominated. To him, as to everyone in Congress, the course for India was set towards *Swaraj*, self-rule.

But what was *Swaraj*? To the extremists on the Congress left it meant quite simply independence. In the words of S. R. Mehrotra, the example of the Sinn Feiners in Ireland had become for these zealots "a perennial source of inspiration . . . a running lesson in tactics and strategy." But to Gandhi, using the same word for his ideal, *Swaraj* was to be attained by peaceful means and meant no break with the British connection unless it were forced on India by the harsh logic of events. "It is derogatory to national dignity to think of the permanence of the British connection at any cost," he said at the Nagpur conference of the Congress in 1920. "We are labouring under a grievous wrong which it is the personal duty of every Indian to get redressed. . . . If the British connection is for the advancement of India, I do not want to destroy it. But if it is inconsistent with our national self-respect, then it is our bounden duty to destroy it."

Thus it was perhaps more to help Britain towards right-thinking actions than to end an old alliance that Gandhi launched his movement in August 1920, shocked though he was by the brutalities, almost reminiscent of the Mutiny, with which the central government had reacted to the Punjab disorders culminating in the deaths at Amritsar. If only Britain would co-operate and see where her true interests lay! But if she would not, if she would behave like "Satan," like Satan she must be treated. There could be no co-existence with evil.

Therefore, India must put on the pressure; she must dissociate till repentance came. Indians must to a man refuse British honours, withdraw their sons from government schools and universities, boycott courts, refuse service in the Army or on the municipal, provincial and central councils, and indeed refuse all government salaried posts. An element of sheer unworldliness had clearly intruded at this point, and one may remark in passing the comment of an old Khan Bahadur who, when urged to return the honours and medals conferred on him by the *Raj*, replied that he would do so when the Congress lawyers returned their briefs, which, like lawyers the world over, they showed no great inclination to do.

Even in Congress circles voices were soon raised protesting that by this practice the dynamic India of the future was being strangled in its cradle and its leaders deprived of the education which was their birthright. Did Gandhi share this view? He was in many respects a saint who cared nothing for modern technology, but he was also a politician as well as a thoroughly humane man, and when in 1923 a number of policemen were hacked to death by a mob at Chauri-Chaura he called off the whole campaign to the dismay of his more militant lieutenants. To the young Jawaharlal Nehru he wrote: "The foetid smell of violence is still powerful. . . . The movement has consciously drifted from the right path. We have come back to our moorings"—sentiments which some years later Nehru himself interpreted in political terms as meaning that the Mahatma had sensed that the movement had temporarily run out of steam.

Right or wrong? Who even now, when all the speeches and debates are published, can speak for a character so complex as that of the man who finally sent the *Raj* packing? That Gandhi wanted Dyarchy to fail is evident, for Dyarchy had long since been overtaken by events. He was a nationalist using methods as devious as his principles were clear and achieving a synthesis—as in his address to the court when he was finally brought to trial some months after Chauri-Chaura—far more baffling than anything that Britain had encountered even in the Celtic twilight of Ireland:

I wanted to avoid violence. I want to avoid violence. Non-violence is the first article of my faith. It is also the last article of my creed. But I had to make my choice. I had either to submit to a system which I considered had done an irreparable harm to my country, or incur the risk of the mad fury of my people bursting forth, when they understood the truth from my lips. . . . I do not ask for mercy. I do not plead any extenuating act. I am here, therefore, to invite and cheerfully submit to the highest penalty that can be inflicted upon me for what in law is a deliberate crime and what appears to me to be the highest duty of a citizen.

So the justification was the crime itself, and the jury was public opinion both in England and India. It was a situation full of anomalies, and the address of the presiding magistrate, matching in courtesy Gandhi's own words to him, was an answer in kind which paid tribute to the moral grandeur of this unique antagonist of the *Raj*, just as the swingeing sentence of six years' imprisonment reflected the knowledge that even the Mahatma's most moral acts were also political ones.

After two years the prisoner was released on health grounds. His hold on the imagination of his countrymen was as strong as ever, and so was his willingness to work with the British if they would show some understanding of the changing tempo of events and of the way his moderate colleagues were being outflanked by the growing militancy of the younger members of Congress. But in England Edwin Montagu had resigned, and the Secretary of State in Mr. Baldwin's Tory government was the Earl of Birkenhead, who had privately let it be known that he could see no way in which Britain's "trust" over India could safely be abandoned.

By 1926, under these discouragements, Dyarchy was effectively dead if not buried, the moderates in despair, and Motilal Nehru had walked out of the central Legislative Assembly with words reminiscent of Cromwell's dismissal of the Rump of the Long Parliament:

> Sir, the co-operation we offered has been contemptuously rejected and it is time for us to think of other ways . . .

Such was the innate conservatism of the older leaders, including Motilal and Gandhi himself, that the demand they formulated and got Congress to accept was still self-governing dominion status: and this after the incredible ineptitude of the home government in sending to India an all-white committee of enquiry to investigate and report on the needs of the hour, as though Indians had not been shouting them from the housetops for years. But it was only with difficulty that Gandhi and his friends could hold the militants who had been enraged by this "insult" to the nation. The commissioners under Sir John Simon were met by an almost total boycott. Tempers were rising—not improved by the appearance in London of a book called *Mother India* dwelling on such topics as child marriage and the old practice of *suttee:* on which innocent but ill-timed volume even the Mahatma felt impelled to fall with a scathing review headed "Drain Inspector's Report." It was one more embarrassment in his struggle to keep the temperature down and stop Congress from passing meaningless resolutions along "Quit India" lines. And even here he had to give ground; had to shorten the period of postponement of a new civil disobedience campaign from two years to one, during which time the British must pledge themselves to an immediate grant of dominion status. Would the government never respond?

In the summer of 1929 it did. Shocked by the deteriorating situation, the ceremonial burning of foreign cloth by huge crowds in Calcutta and a bomb outrage in the Assembly, the Viceroy, Lord Irwin, took the unusual step of returning to London for consultations.

In October he was back bearing gifts. An immediate grant of full dominion status? A pledge of it within a stated time? No—it was a declaration that the promise of dominion status had been implicit in the Government of India Act ten years earlier! Also a Round Table Conference was offered.

* * *

So what had everyone been waiting for and doing all that time? Officially, trying to make Dyarchy work. The proof of how much goodwill for Britain yet remained in India is shown by the way the Congress was still prepared to welcome this almost comically belated peace offering and accept the proposed conference, provided some start towards full Responsible Government could be begun forthwith. Gandhi himself gave the plan a cautious welcome—he was prepared, he said, to wait for the dominion status constitution if he could get some prepayment "in action" and if there existed a real desire on Britain's part to see India as a "free and self-respecting nation."

Unfortunately, Congress had also made it a condition of acceptance that there should be a predominance of its own members among the conference delegates. This was hardly likely to appeal to Muslim opinion, though the League was by no means yet the force in the land it was soon to become. Still more unfortunately, Lord Irwin's declaration was very badly received indeed in British right-wing circles as the full implication of what he had said came through. For since 1917, when the Montagu pledge had been given, "dominion status" itself had changed. The Balfour draft of 1926 had greatly enlarged its meaning—it amounted now to virtual independence. And as the Viceroy began to back pedal under these pressures from home and told the Indian leaders that nothing could be done till the Round Table Conference had met and the British Parliament had legislated, total and complete independence was what Congress chose to claim. "We are now entering," said Gandhi, "upon a new era." Independence was India's immediate objective, not just her distant goal—and on the stroke of midnight on December 31, 1929, in a resolution which he himself sponsored, this demand for full *Swaraj* was given official form.

For the thoughtful colloquy with Britain which Gandhi had desired, there was now substituted a dialogue of the deaf.

On January 25, blandly ignoring Congress's extreme demands, the Viceroy repeated the government's firm desire to do everything possible to conciliate India and collaborate with her in search of a solution of the present "difficulties." He spoke not of independence but of dominion status, and even here there must be slow constitutional advance. "No sensible traveller," he said, "could feel that a clear definition of his destination was the same thing as the completion of his journey." To travel hopefully was evidently better than to arrive. In reply, Gandhi was prepared to put off civil disobedience if eleven demands were met, including a call for total Prohibition and the abolition of the Criminal Investigation Department! Even his luminous and rational self had become infected by the national malaise—"We refuse to be satisfied with the airy peace; we would rather risk the dark anarchy." In a letter to the Viceroy addressed "Dear Friend," he told him that he held British rule in India to be accursed, though he did not consider Englishmen in general to be worse than any other people on earth. And when the Viceroy replied to these threats regretting that the Mahatma should be contemplating actions clearly illegal and dangerous to the public peace, Gandhi remarked: "On bended knees I wished for bread and I have received a stone."

On March 12, 1930, he began his famous 241-mile salt march to the sea at Dandi.

*   *   *

For twenty-four days the lengthening columns straggled from village to village, while through its newspapers the nation watched enthralled; then on April 5 the small wiry figure, after a morning bathe, bent down on the sea-shore and picked up a lump of natural salt.

A great shout of exultation went up. The government salt monopoly had been broken: in this one symbolic act Gandhi had marked the nation's final rejection of Britain.

As a propaganda gesture it was tailor-made to the occasion. No one else could have thought of it. Nowhere else but in India would it have been meaningful. Against no other opponents but the British could it have imposed any kind of sanction.

As with all Gandhi's actions, non-violence was meant to be the key. To collect salt from the beach, to urge villagers to collect and sell it—what could be more peaceful? The Mahatma had not really learnt the lesson of Chauri-Chaura, or perhaps he had ignored it.

He must surely have known that the mass demonstrations he was calling up would lead to violence. On April 18 the police armoury at Chittagong was raided: six days later Peshawar was in the hands of the mob. On May 4 the Mahatma was arrested. His salt marchers, whose objective was now a salt depot in Bombay province, fell in behind a new leader, Mr. Tyabji. On May 11 Mr. Tyabji was arrested. His place was taken by a Mrs. Naidu, who led a non-violent demonstration against the depot to such effect that 320 of her supporters were injured in clashes with the police and she herself removed to gaol. On June 30 Motilal Nehru was arrested and the Working Committee of Congress was declared an unlawful association. During the next month sixty-seven nationalist newspapers were closed down under the censorship.

In most countries, between most opponents, it must have led to civil war. The British were still too powerfully entrenched to suffer such a thing to happen, and too liberal-minded not to search around for some constitutional remedy. They pressed on with their Round Table Conference in London, and when in the absence of the Congress leaders it was clear that no real progress could be made, they released Gandhi from gaol, also the dying Motilal Nehru. On February 17, 1931, the Mahatma, clad in his usual garb, ascended the steps of Viceregal Lodge for conference with the Viceroy.

Commenting on these events far off in London, "It is alarming and also nauseating," said Winston Churchill, "to see Mr. Gandhi, a seditious Middle Temple lawyer, now posing as a fakir of a type well known in the East, striding half naked up the steps of Viceregal palace while he is still organising and conducting a defiant campaign of Civil Disobedience to parley on equal terms with the Representative of the King-Emperor."

Actually, Viceroy and rebel got on extremely well, as the British government had guessed might happen when they sent a devout Anglo-Catholic to India as Britain's answer to a Hindu guru. Towards the end of their two weeks of bargaining they had reached the stage of joking even about Winston's purple prose. As the Mahatma was leaving one day without his shawl the Viceroy with elephantine humour called him back—"Gandhi, you haven't so much on, you know, that you can afford to leave this behind." The agreement finally reached by these two remarkable delegates for their countries was so fair that it caused misgivings among the militants on either side. Imperialists feared—and with much reason as the future was to show—that it meant the loss of India, and without India Britain would be a second-class power. Congress was dismayed by the way (as it seemed to members) that the Mahatma had been outmanoeuvred by the enemy in agreeing to attend the London conference and call off civil disobedience without obtaining anything of substance in return. "For a settlement of this kind," said Gandhi himself, "it is not possible or wise to say who is the victorious party. If there is any victory, I should say it belongs to both." He had, of course, obtained—first of all Indian statesmen to do so—a position of equal negotiating partner with the *Raj,* even if his final victory was delayed for sixteen years.

*   *   *

Under the surface antagonisms which troubled their relationship, the British government and Gandhi had shared a similar vision for India. Of course each side placed a different emphasis on it. Gandhi wanted independence without delay: the government envisaged a step-by-step advance, and among its more imperially minded members and many of its agents on the spot the day of reckoning was seen as a very distant objective indeed. Yet even Churchill had seen that the day must come, and when it came it must be for an India far more unified than the tortured and fragmented country that John Company had taken over from the Moguls. Towards this "ideal" India the British had always aimed, and they were now to work for it at least as faithfully as the Mahatma and with a far better understanding of the complexities involved. If they seemed to drag their feet, it was because they knew the treacherous nature of the ground and that the way across it was beset on all sides by voices calling out very contradictory instructions from the woods. For their would-be guides were not only Hindu Congressmen, but also Liberals, Muslims, Sikhs, Christian communities, Princes, Untouchables, who were agreed on only one thing, that the traveller must hurry. "But do not say 'You shall march so many paces,'" said the Liberal leader, Sir Tej Bahadur Sapru. "The time has long since passed when India could be told to hold its soul in Patience." There must be action not to-morrow, "but-to-day, now, this minute," declared Maulana Muhammed Ali for the Muslims.

Hastening slowly at the first session of the London Round Table Conference in 1930, in the absence of the Congress representatives who were in gaol, the government got some measure of agreement for its plans based on the despised Simon Commission's Report. To partition the country was never, of course, considered; it would have been to flout the vision of everyone concerned. Even the Muslims disclaimed any notion of making themselves another Ulster. "I say we are one India," said Sapru, appealing to the princes to think as patriots. "India," responded the Maharajah of Bikaner, "is a single geographical unit and we are all members one of another." But this did not mean that such a jig-saw of competing interests could be welded into one unitary state like Britain herself, for the country was too vast, too diverse, and even those who paid lip service to the ideal of unity knew that it must be a qualified one. As a Muslim spokesman put it: "The centrifugal and centripetal tendencies are so well balanced in India that we are bound to have a federal system of government there. . . ."

This was the plan favoured by the government—a federation of self-governing provinces of British India and of the princely states, with a central government which itself would advance towards autonomy as the scheme took shape—and it was a plan acceptable in principle to the moderates among the Hindus, though with reservations and warnings well expressed by Sir Tej Bahadur Sapru: "It will not do for you to take a provincial view and offer provincial autonomy . . . unless you couple it with a decided and clear change in the constitution of the Central Government. You must make that responsible to the Legislature." It would not, in his view, make for harmonious action if responsible government in the provinces was combined with "irresponsible" government at the centre.

By "irresponsible" government Sir Tej meant, of course, official, non-representative government by the British over Indians. But it was "irresponsible" government in its more popular meaning of wayward, tyrannical rule that princes and Muslims feared at Congress's hands. That the princes should have agreed to discuss Federation at all was a triumph of moderation, for they had been perfectly happy with their old treaty relationships with the *Raj* which guaranteed them honours, decorations, ceremonial guns, favoured treatment at Viceregal Lodge and the minimum of interference in their affairs. How much of this they would be able to preserve in an

India dominated by a Congress packed with lawyers whom they despised and in a climate of democracy which they feared was questionable. No doubt they believed, as autocrats themselves, that the British would not be fools enough to quit India or allow the kind of Home Rule at the centre for which Congress and the Liberals were clamouring. At all events they showed themselves surprisingly ready to fall in with the government's scheme. "By far the larger proportion of the States," declared the Maharajah of Patiala, "will come into the federal structure at once, and the remainder will soon follow." Similarly, the Muslims seemed willing to sink their differences with the Hindus for the common good. "For the first time in India we are going to introduce majority rule, and I, belonging to a minority community, accept that majority rule," said Maulana Muhammed Ali. It was a remarkable concession, and it was shared by the man who was about to take on the mantle of Muslim leadership, Mr. Muhammad Ali Jinnah. All that seemed needed was some generous response from the Congress both to the British plan and to the minorities.

At the second session of the Round Table Conference in the autumn of 1931 this response was delivered by Mr. Gandhi in person, recently released from gaol under his pact with the Viceroy. It seemed to have been designed to offend:

I said at one of the preliminary meetings . . . that the Congress claimed to represent 85 per cent of the population of India, that is to say the dumb, toiling, semi-starved millions. But I went further: that the Congress claimed also to represent even the Princes . . . and the landed gentry, the educated class. I wish to repeat that claim and I wish this evening to emphasise that claim.

All the other parties at this meeting represent sectional interests. Congress alone claims to represent the whole of India, all interests.

If that took care of the minorities—and to such purpose that the princes did not re-appear at the third session of the Conference in the following year—the Mahatma had saved his most Parthian shots for his old opponent, the *Raj,* from whom he demanded "very respectfully" in Congress's name the grant of immediate responsible government at the centre, including control over the armed forces and foreign affairs.

He himself had probably little hope that any such thing could or would be conceded, and he returned to India to yet another round of civil disobedience and imprisonment for himself with, "the greatest joy." Perhaps he was truly happiest in this role and in this relationship with his British friends and oppressors whom he knew would not remain unmoved at India's plight—"I want to make you suffer because I want to touch your hearts." By the end of that year sixty thousand were in gaol.

* * *

Deserted by the militants and with dwindling Liberal support, the British pressed ahead and in 1935 got their new Government of India Act through the Westminster Parliament.

By this statute, which came into force in 1937 on April Fool's Day, the provinces of British India were freed absolutely from official control and given responsible government, the only check being that the governors retained certain reserve powers in order to protect minorities should the need arise.

Dyarchy, abolished in the provinces, was to be transferred to the centre. A Federal government composed of provinces and princely states was envisaged, with defence, foreign affairs and "safeguards" similar to those in the provinces reserved to the Viceroy, the rest of the administration being in the hands of ministers responsible to the bi-cameral legislature. This Federation of India was not to come into being until a sufficient number of states with a population equalling half the total population of the states had adhered to it. The franchise was greatly extended to include some 35 million voters.

This enormously complex and exhaustive measure seemed to have taken account of everything since time began—the only thing left out of it, said Mr. Clement Attlee, was the Indian people itself. He thought it a constitution overloaded with conservative interests, a document full of "mistrust and inequality."

But these conservative interests in India were just as hostile to the measure as Mr. Attlee, if for precisely opposite reasons. "The Bill cannot be regarded as acceptable to the Indian states," announced the princes before it even became law.

For them the government had shown itself far too revolutionary. The All-India Muslim League, on the other hand, found the Act "fundamentally bad" because of its reactionary and retrograde nature and its tendency to favour the princes at the expense of British India. Strangely enough the League, which thirteen years later was to play a leading part in wrecking all hopes of a united nation, complained in particular of the Act's refusal to allow complete responsible government at the centre, and at its Bombay session in April 1936 the president, Sir Sayed Wazir Khan, anathematized it in memorable words:

> A constitution is literally being forced on us by the British Parliament which nobody likes, which no one approves of. After several years of Commissions, Reports, Conferences and Committees a monstrosity has been invented. . . . It is anti-democratic. It will strengthen all the most reactionary elements in the country, and, instead of helping us to develop on progressive lines, it will enchain and crush the forces making for democracy and freedom.

"Enchain"? League and Congress were for the last time working in unison even down to the metaphors they used, for that year the Congress President, Pandit Jawaharlal Nehru, called the Act " a new charter of slavery." Even the National Liberal Federation, most moderate of bodies, found shortcomings in the Act. No one loved it. No one of influence, for the time being at least, was prepared to work it.

*   *   *

So once again it seemed that all the "Irish" mistakes had been repeated. Dominion status in its restricted pre-war sense would have been received with rapture by the Congress in 1909. Instead, India was given the Morley-Minto Reforms. It would have been accepted with acclamation in 1919: and all India got was Montagu-Chelmsford and Dyarchy in the provinces. The fuller dominion status as defined by Balfour in 1926 would have been acceptable to most Indians at that time: and they got the Simon Commission. Even the 1935 Act did not grant a dominion constitution but merely removed

Dyarchy from the provinces to impose it at the centre. Meanwhile, the forces making for disunity, which could have been scotched if taken in time, had been allowed to grow and were to continue to grow—Hindu extremists, Muslim extremists, the princes jealous for their prerogatives.

The pace had been too slow—perhaps because deep down in the English subconscious lay the conviction that Britain's prosperity depended on India and that the ties between them could somehow be kept.

But if this inhibited successive governments—even Labour ones until Mr. Attlee's administration of 1946—they always consciously aimed to reach that "proudest day" Macaulay had dreamed of when through British exertions India would be free and able to govern herself. Slowly, clumsily, sometimes grudgingly, always well behind events, they had worked to create such an end, and the Government of India Act was to be the keystone. When Dyarchy was dead its achievements lived on. In spite of all her errors, Britain had produced the structure for a national state and a training ground for India's future rulers. It was one of her glories as an imperial power, and its monument is the Indian democracy of to-day. Those who accused her of a policy of Divide and Rule deceived themselves—very fatefully, as it turned out, for it was their errors, not Britain's which ensured that when the time for independence came it had to be granted to two countries, not one.

XV

The Goal of Empire Unity through Trade

Any colonial thinking that was done in Britain during these years was taking place against a background of public indifference. The crowds that had flocked to the great Empire Exhibition at Wembley soon found themselves plunged into a world depression with two and a half million unemployed. In its grip departed the last vestiges of Jingoism, along with much of that optimism and sense of adventure which had peopled an empire. The man in the street was losing interest, and significantly these inter-war years saw a steep drop in emigration and in the number of candidates coming forward for the Indian Civil Service.

But then imperialism, even as a theory, had long been in decline. Influential thinkers like the economic theorist J. A. Hobson had pronounced it unprofitable, "a huge business blunder," and in an industrial society one could hardly say worse than that. Hobson and his followers, however, also took a moral view of its shortcomings—imperialism abroad drained off capital and stunted the growth of social welfare at home.

Thus, for the first time since Gladstone's day children in progressive homes and schools were being taught to regard the red patches on the map not with pride but with suspicion, a sense of guilt. A new spirit was in the air, a yearning for equality between all classes and races. The Christian ethic was still strong, though church-going was rapidly declining. But it was a Christian ethic in process of change, and already a "red Dean" of Canterbury had been appointed, the first of a long line of turbulent priests whose views found echoes among the missionaries and colonial clergy. There were few "muscular Christians" on the Victorian model left among them. Humanism was on the increase—there seemed little place for God in a world which had seen the sufferings of war and depression. Along with it went a strong vein of pacifism which reached its height in Oxford's famous "King and Country" debate and in the Peace Pledge Union's mammoth ballot.

An unlikely climate, one might say, for imperialist exercises. Yet it was during these years when the foundations of their world seemed to be collapsing around them that British statesmen made the last serious attempt to rationalise the Empire. The Statute of Westminster and the Government of India Act were two illustrations of it. Equally important—more important if Cecil Rhodes had been right and the Empire was a bread-and-butter affair—were the government's activities in the economic sphere which resulted in the Ottawa Conference of 1932, "the most momentous conference in the history of the British nations," *The Times* called it, not without reason. For Britain now had a new weapon in her armoury. Eighty-six years after the repeal of the Corn Laws she had turned her back on free trade and gone back to protection.

*   *   *

Such a reversal could hardly have happened without the slump and the monetary crisis which brought down Ramsay McDonald's second Labour Government in the autumn of 1931. In 1923 the Tory leader, Stanley Baldwin, had chosen to fight an election on a protectionist platform and lost. But since that time the nations and parties had been running for cover to save themselves from the economic blizzard. Any port in a storm. The crisis of confidence which had been sparked off by the Wall Street crash of 1929 had spread round the world in narrowing witches' circles of recession. Restrictive monetary policies which refused credits to producers had led to a flood of primary goods in the world markets, then to a chain reaction of deflation, falling prices, unemployment, rumours of currency devaluation, bank failures, the freezing of foreign assets by European governments and, finally, to a run on the gold and foreign reserves of the Bank of England which could only be met by the immediate raising of large loans in New York and Paris. These loans were made conditional on the imposition of cuts in British government spending as proof of a desire for a balanced budget and financial orthodoxy. The economies demanded could not be met without cuts in unemployment benefits which the Labour Cabinet as a whole was unwilling to make. On this rock it broke, to be replaced by a coalition under McDonald's leadership of Tories and those Socialists and Liberals who were determined to "save the pound." This was the National Government which duly went to the country on its programme of retrenchment, won a landslide victory, went off the gold standard it had been elected to preserve, and introduced protection in the following year.

If it was not as yet a wholly Tory government, certainly its measures were Tory measures and the "Doctor's Mandate" it had asked for and received had Tory labels on the bottle. This ensured the overwhelming triumph of protection which went through Parliament almost without a murmur—even the Labourite and Liberal free traders on the government front bench did not resign but merely "agreed to differ," to a chorus of mildly ironic back-bench witticisms about these "martyrs for the old faith" who hoped by special arrangement to enjoy the martyr's crown "without the natural discomforts." Thus free trade ended, not with a bang but with a whimper. Cobden and Bright must have turned in their graves.

For the Tories, of course, this was the day of deliverance, eighty-six years after Peel had split the party, nearly forty after Joseph Chamberlain had raised the banner of Imperial Preference and Tariff Reform. By an agreeable coincidence the new Chancellor of the Exchequer was Neville Chamberlain, the reformer's younger son, and loud were the ministerial cheers when at the end of the introduction of his Import Duties Bill the tributes of filial piety were paid—and most justly paid—to a statesman who had "counted for something in his day and generation"—"I believe he would have found consolation for the bitterness of his disappointment if he could have foreseen that these proposals, which are the direct and legitimate descendants of his own conception, would be laid before the House of Commons which he loved in the presence of one* and

* Joseph's elder son, Austen, who was also in the House that day.

by the lips of the other of his two immediate successors by whom his name is carried on."

This was true in a very exact sense, for just as Joseph Chamberlain had seen protection as a first step towards imperial preference and closer economic union, so did his son regard it. Now that Britain was protectionist she had advantages to offer to protectionist dominions in return for benefits to be enjoyed herself; she had something to bargain with. And for this reason the Chancellor chose to act, as he said, "in the true spirit of Imperial unity and harmony" by exempting the dominions from paying his new import duties, pending the decisions of the conference soon to be held in Ottawa where the real bargain might be had.

The need to do *something* was all too evident. World trade had shrunk by two thirds since 1929, and within the Empire things were hardly better. Falling prices threatened to ruin primary producers of wheat, wool and dairy produce in Canada and Australasia. The total value of India's overseas trade had been halved between 1925 and 1931, the annual fall for the last two years of that period being in the order of £102 million. By 1925 Britain had seemed to have recovered from the war and to be set for expansion. If we take the trade figures for that year and compare them with those for 1931, we can judge the magnitude and widespread nature of the problem. British imports from Canada dropped from £70.6 to £32.6 million; from Australia, £72.6 to £45.7 million; from South Africa, £25.1 to £13.1 million; from New Zealand, £51.3 to £37.8 million. Similarly British exports to Canada over this period fell from £27.6 to £20.6 million; to Australia, from £60.2 to £14.5 million, a catastrophic fall; to New Zealand, from £23.1 to £11.2 million; to South Africa, from £30.6 to £21.9 million.

In the face of such figures and the remorseless grip of the depression, it took a sanguine statesman to believe that Ottawa would provide some magic formula. But the need of the hour was there to see, and Mr. R. B. Bennett of Canada who chaired the conference expressed it very well:

When we reach an agreement by which our products pass more freely from one Empire country to another, we drive clear channels through the stagnant pools dammed up by the world upheaval, and naturally we will carry past the boundaries of the Empire and, to its benefit, establish once more throughout the world that commerce which is its very life blood.

Similarly, Mr. Baldwin who led the British delegation expressed the conference's aim: "the expansion of Empire trade, brought about by the lowering of trade barriers as between the several members."

Lowering of barriers: Empire priorities—Mr. Baldwin in his own person perfectly exemplified that mixture of Gladstonian and Joseph Chamberlainite thinking which had led him to bring in protection and yet remain as firmly opposed as John Bright himself to "stomach taxes" on the people's food.

So what could come of Ottawa once the euphoria and eloquence were over and the conference got down to business? An agreement to lower tariff barriers for which Bennett had called (on behalf of an electorate in Canada which had elected him to raise them)? This had never been likely because of the conflicting needs of Britain and the dominions—needs which could only be reconciled by an increase in tariffs. There remained that other aim of Empire unity, a common economic policy. Neville Chamberlain's biographer, Keith Feiling, is clear that Chamberlain himelf, for all his devotion to his father's memory and ideals, had not pitched his hopes unduly high: he was prepared for many setbacks, so long as he could set the Empire on the path of preferential trade. But that his leader Stanley Baldwin saw the possibilities in more Messianic terms is evident from his opening speech, which might have been made by Joseph Chamberlain himself in the hey-day of his hopes:

The real importance of Ottawa lies in the fact that it marks the point where two roads diverge, the one leading to the development of purely national interests, the other to closer Imperial unity. . . .

During this speech the words "Empire" and "Imperial" were often on his lips, and for the two Pacific dominions this was a chord they knew. Mr. Coates of New Zealand thought the conference would be "a great adventure in imperial co-operation": Mr. Bruce of

Australia believed its aim must be "a closer economic union between the British nations."

But alas! for others this was heresy of the deepest dye; and when the Conservative Canadian Prime Minister was tactless enough to tell his own parliament that an "imperial policy" on trade was now in being (which was almost grotesquely untrue), the opposition Liberal leader rounded on him with the tart reminder that there was no such thing as an "imperial policy" and that nowhere in the Empire was there a cabinet authorised to create one. "This is an endeavour to create a *Zollverein*," he angrily exclaimed. "It is an endeavour to make out of the British Empire an economic unit. . . ." Clearly, he could find no more damning accusation.

He might have spared himself, for so far from creating one policy for the Empire, the Ottawa Conference did not result even in an imperial treaty; it took the form of a number of bilateral trade agreements between the various parties. These proved helpful up to a point. Certainly Ottawa played some part in the gradual and mysterious revival of trade that was finally hastened by rearmament on the eve of the Second World War. *The Times,* which thought the conference "a great achievement," had little doubt which of Mr. Baldwin's "two roads" the Empire had chosen—the better one of Empire unity. Looking back with the benefit of hindsight we can see for how long the dominions and India and indeed Britain herself had actually been marching along the other.

*   *   *

At Ottawa the Empire's statesmen had tried to solve a world crisis in trade parochially. It was certainly no more illogical than the way in which on the international front they idealistically rebuked aggression by giving in to aggressors. Pacific by nature, worn out by the struggles of four years of war, it was not surprising that their response to the "Axis" powers was inept. Their very failures speak for their good heart. They believed in the League of Nations. They had to: their electorates insisted on it. With the Japanese invasion of Manchuria this idealism was put to its first test, and dismal was the failure that resulted. Manchuria was far away, but not so far from Australia that Australians did not show a strong inclination to play the crisis down to avoid antagonising the Japanese. Abyssinia, on which Mussolini's Italy had designs, was much closer to the centre of world affairs. And over Abyssinia it was Britain herself that chose to betray the League's principles in the notorious Hoare-Laval Pact, a proposed partition of the country along the bad old colonialist lines which the dominions hoped had died with the abortive carve-up of Turkey by the Treaty of Sèvres.

This *débâcle* went far to destroy the credibility of the League. When all was over and the Italians were in possession not of half of Abyssinia, but of all of it, no one could decide who had been the more culpable: the British and French governments for their cynical sell out of League principles, or the League apparatus itself which had been impotent against an armed aggressor.

Sanctions had failed. They were irrelevant to the reality facing the world, which was simply that force could only be contained by force. Yet this was the element which all those who were hottest for action by the League were determined to prevent. As early as 1925, a decade before the Peace Ballot emasculated it even further, the British government had rejected moves to put teeth into the Geneva protocol on the grounds that the League's business was peace, not war; and this attitude, which implied a ban on armed resistance to aggression, was adopted in full by the most influential of dominion spokesmen, Mr. Mackenzie King. Seldom tiring of stressing Canada's adherence to the "fundamental aims and ideals" of the League and his determination to make it the cornerstone of his foreign policy, he always managed to avoid being taken at his word. He had found much that was "attractive and persuasive" in the concept of "a world united to prevent by force a breach of the peace by an aggressor." The concept had obviously not persuaded *him,* for in almost the same breath he went on to add that unfortunately this was a dream which had no relation to the actualities; and later, at the 1937 Imperial Conference in London, he abandoned it altogether, declaring that the League's failure had been so absolute that he could no longer base Canadian policies upon it.

South Africa, often Canada's twin in these dominion dialogues, had been much stronger for action under the Covenant during the Abyssinian crisis, which was after all an African crisis. However by 1937 its Premier, General Hertzog, pronounced the League to be dead and buried: to rely on it was like relying on rotten wood. This was the time when Hitler's propaganda on the injustices of the

Versailles Treaty was nearing its height, and no doubt it was the traditional Boer fondness for Germany as much as fear that led Hertzog to define his government's policy as "this high object of world appeasement," a year before the Munich surrender of Neville Chamberlain gave notoriety to the word. Even the Australians, with one eye cocked uneasily on Japan, were reluctant to take any risk that might stir up trouble for themselves. No one had grasped the totalitarian threat, or if they had, no one was prepared to take active steps to resist it by the only effective means. Hitler was allowed to advance into the Rhineland, to carry out the *Anschluss* with Austria, to seize the Sudeten borderlands of Czechoslovakia, a far-away country as Neville Chamberlain said, a quarrel "between people of whom we know nothing."

"Resolved only to be irresolute . . . adamant for drift"—Winston Churchill's famous words were an indictment of a whole empire with the honourable exception of New Zealand which had stood steadfastly by the League throughout. "Sagittarius" in the London *New Statesman and Nation* attacked the Sudeten betrayal in caustic words,

> Opening as from to-day
> as Chamberlain et Daladier,
> Messrs. Hoare-Laval successors
> For doing business with aggressors. . . .

but this was the voice of a left-wing minority itself unprepared to fight. The diplomatic exchanges at the time of Munich make melancholy reading—the Canadians, South Africans and Irish were more certain than Chamberlain himself that nothing must be done to provoke a war for which no one among the democracies was ready. If Britain had gone to war with Germany in 1938 the dominions might well have stayed aloof. If Hitler had been content with the Sudetenland and had turned to the economic exploitation of eastern Europe instead of raping Prague and attacking Poland, few in the Western World could have been found to thwart him. His apologists in London, in Ottawa and Cape Town could always have justified inaction by reference to the unfair terms of that "monster treaty"

of Versailles* which so obsessed their thinking. How close he came
to destroying the last vestiges of Empire unity, even in the moment
of his most wantonly warlike acts, can be seen in the fact that in
September 1939 the Irish decided for neutrality and only by a hair's
breadth did South Africa not do the same. Far off in India, Mr.
Gandhi was addressing to the Führer sage advice on the uses of
non-violence as a political weapon. Can one wonder that the new
Attila and prophet of the Thousand Year Reich thought the moment
ripe to defy the pretensions of that rival organism he professed
to admire; to shake that house of cards.

* * *

He should have known better. In the summer of 1939, during
the first Test Match of the series against the West Indies, the home
captain appealed over the loudspeaker to the crowd at Lord's.
"England and Cricket are in danger," he declared.

And when the testing day finally came the response of the Commonwealth could hardly have been more "British." An attempt by
the Australian Lawn Tennis Association to recall the victorious
Australian Davis Cup team before it had competed in the United
States championships at Forest Hills had to be reversed after indignant protests from the public. There was time to finish the game
and beat the Germans too. "It is my melancholy duty to announce,"
said the Australian Prime Minister to his people, "that in consequence
of German persistence in her invasion of Poland, Great Britain
has declared war, and that as a result Australia is also at war."
A day earlier he had declared: "There is unity in the Empire ranks
—one King, one flag, one cause. We stand with Britain"—and this
was largely true. "With gratitude for the past and confidence for
the future we range ourselves without fear beside Britain," said
the New Zealand Prime Minister, Mr. Savage, in a broadcast from
his sick-bed. "Where she goes we go; where she stands we stand."
In India the Viceroy simply announced his government's belligerency
—this caused great offence in some Congress circles, but Gandhi
for one was more realistic. "I am not thinking just now of India's
deliverance. It will come, but what will it be worth if England and
France fall?" Even South Africa by some miracle of fate managed

* The phrase was General Hertzog's.

to shed its neutralism, and by a majority of eighty to sixty-seven in the House at Cape Town, Smuts returned to power in place of Hertzog and took the Union to war. Canada delayed her decision for a week to enable her Parliament to meet, when the choice for war was made without a vote being taken.

The response of the dominions was striking. *The Times* felt that it had even exceeded that of 1914, because on this occasion not even moral pressure had been exerted on them to conform. They could have stayed out. Ireland *did* stay out, placing its nominal head King George VI in the odd position of being at war with Germany in London and at peace with her in Dublin. "A United Empire" was the message of *The Times* leader on the morning after Canada came in, but perhaps the truth was that the dominions, now fully adult and independent, had judged the crisis for themselves. "If Hitler and the forces of evil should win the war," said the Canadian Prime Minister, Mackenzie King, "there can be no neutrals, and isolation for North America will prove a myth. In that event, life on this continent will not be worth living."

In 1914 the dominions had hurried with splendid and unselfish devotion into a war that was only marginally their own. They had had no particular quarrel with the Kaiser. With Hitler they had, and Mackenzie King's remarks on the declaration of hostilities were as much addressed to the United States as to his own compatriots. The people of the dominions saw as clearly if as belatedly as Britain herself that the values of civilised life were at stake. So was their own existence at stake as it had never been before, and they reacted accordingly—even the Sydney *Bulletin*, which had remained solidly anti-militarist, closed ranks with the rest, declaring that the defence of the Empire and the need for a firm and enduring peace were Australia's priorities. One may note of these priorities, however, that the dominions were now more inward-looking and self-concerning than in 1914. Since there was never any Nazi threat to the American continent, the Canadians reappeared in Europe much as they had done a quarter of a century earlier, and their exploits at Dieppe and in the Normandy *bocage* repeated the triumphs and tragedies of Vimy and the Hindenburg Line. The Anzacs and Indians similarly came back to the Middle East—without them Egypt would certainly have been lost. But with the Japanese entry into the war the Australians were pulled back to defend their own homeland, and in their hour of trial it was to the United States rather than to Britain that they and the New Zealanders looked. Indian troops were similarly withdrawn. The South Africans, who this time had no German "South West" to conquer, played a relatively minor role, and some of the ruder of their allies in the Desert War against Ròmmel did not let them forget it.

> There are too many Springboks in the old Transvaal and f. . . all at Mersa Matruh,

they sang to the tune of that trusty Afrikaner favourite "Sarie Marais."

It was an altogether different war from its predecessor, and after the first years the Empire's role was relatively smaller. Nevertheless, in 1940 it alone had held the gate against barbarism, and its total contribution was still immense. In the United Kingdom nearly six million were mobilised; two and a half million Indians joined the colours, close on a million Australians, over 700,000 Canadians, 200,000 South Africans and the same number of New Zealanders; the dependent colonial empire provided 400,000, and there were many volunteers from Eire. As before, they fought on all the major battlefronts. And triumphantly the results were the same. In London there was again dancing in the streets. The irrepressible Winston Churchill had himself driven down Whitehall on the roof of a car and conducted the crowds as they sang "Rule Britannia." King George VI made speeches almost identical with those his father had made and received similar congratulatory addresses from grateful parliaments. In Sydney, Melbourne, Auckland, Montreal and dozens of Commonwealth cities there were similar scenes of mass rejoicing, and two decades of history seem to roll back as we read the victory leaders and the letters in the press. Many, it seems clear from their tone, had found themselves moved by the King's speech to his peoples as they remembered that other broadcast in September 1939 and found reassurance in the continued strength of the Crown, both as a symbol of unity and as an active force making for the spread of high ideals. In the moment of triumph there seemed a very close parallel with the events of that other global war whose scars were barely healed. The victory had been rather longer delayed. But just as in 1918 the enemy had laid down his arms and collapsed into apparent ruin, so did the Germans and the Japanese on VE and VJ Days. It had been a near thing. But it was the same clean sweep as before.

*   *   *

The lost were recovered. Burma, Malaysia, Hong Kong, New Guinea, returned uneasily to the fold. At Singapore, the scene in 1942 of the greatest single disaster that had ever befallen British arms, the British Supreme Commander in Southeast Asia took the surrender of the Japanese armies in that theatre in a ceremony far more glittering than Field Marshal Montgomery had allowed himself a few months earlier with the Germans on Luneburg Heath. It took place in the colony's Council Chamber under a portrait of the King-Emperor recovered from the Raffles Museum, and the Union Jack that was triumphantly hoisted was the identical flag that had been carried by the British delegation at the surrender in 1942. The symbolism was deliberate, since this was the East where loss of "face" was a serious matter. For this reason Admiral Mountbatten, before calling on the Japanese to make their formal surrender, went out of his way to stress that this was no mere negotiated laying down of arms but an abject "submission" to force in the shape of the 100,-000 troops ashore on Singapore island whom he commanded. Representatives from every country involved in the campaign were present, prominent among them a strong detachment of Indian troops in jungle green, for this was meant to be an Empire occasion.

A few months earlier, after the end of the war in Europe, Winston Churchill in his broadcast to the nation had struck the same keynote in words very reminiscent of Lloyd George's oration at Guildhall in 1918:

> . . . sustained by the entire British nation at home and by all our fighting men abroad, and with the unswerving co-operation of the dominions from across the oceans and our Empire in every quarter of the globe, it became clear last week that things had worked out pretty well and that the British Commonwealth and Empire stands more united and more effectively powerful than at any time in its long romantic history.

How did these confident predictions represent the realities on the ground?

*   *   *

In the January before D-Day Lord Halifax, the British Ambassador in Washington, went north into Canada to address the Toronto Board of Trade. "I often think that to the outsider the British Commonwealth must surely appear as an almost inexplicable freak of nature," he remarked in the course of an otherwise encouraging address. It was a case of true things being spoken in jest, and even to some of its major components inside the organism, never mind outside it, the Commonwealth had begun to look like an irrelevance.

To see what it really amounted to through sharp colonial eyes one can hardly do better than glance at the speeches of the Canadian Premier, Mackenzie King, who in the same month as Lord Halifax's Toronto speech addressed himself to the Ottawa Parliament. "I am one hundred per cent," he declared, "for closer consultation, for close co-operation and effective co-ordination in all matters of common concern between the different nations of the British Commonwealth. By all means let us within the British Commonwealth be as united as we possibly can. . . ." It is fascinating to read the reservations between the lines of so subtle a spokesman. "We are certainly determined to see the closest collaboration continue between Canada, the United Kingdom and other Commonwealth countries. Nothing I am saying should be construed as supporting any other view than this. . . . When, however, it comes to dealing with the great issues which determine peace or war, prosperity or depression, it must not, in aim or method, be exclusive." Addressing a joint session of the British Parliament later that same year, in the very course of giving the Commonwealth a puff, he let drop some Freudian words which illuminate his real opinion of that organism:

> "Visions of youth sometimes
>   die away
> And fade into the light of common day."

He went on: "Let us, by all means, seek to improve where we can. But in considering new methods of organisation we cannot be too careful to see that, to our own people, the new methods will not appear as an attempt to limit their freedom of decision or, to peoples outside the Commonwealth, as an attempt to establish a separate bloc."

Yet what else but a bloc, an exclusive club, had the Commonwealth been in its hey-day? Canada was now walking backwards out of it as fast as she decently could. She had a double vision. She hankered for a far wider membership in a world order at the United Nations and for increasing non-alignment with old friends—a process we are still witnessing in Mr. Trudeau's Canada today—yet at the same time she was developing parochial instincts and wanted not to enlarge but to concentrate her national force and genius. Since her inception as a nation, her citizens had been first and foremost British citizens and only secondly Canadians (at least in law.) There had been one common citizenship for the Empire: Indians, Nigerians, Australians, Malayans, all had been British—theoretically the whole population of India could have emigrated to London and voted for the Westminster Parliament. Yet hardly had the Second World War ended than there was passed through the Canadian Parliament (to the general astonishment of its dominion partners) the Canadian Nationality Act of 1946 which stood this principle on its head by insisting that it was not British nationality which from now on would profit a man or qualify him when he came to be born, live, vote and die within the territory of Canada, but *Canadian citizenship,* a totally different and novel concept of national status. "The responsibilities of this country are greater than ever before," said the Canadian Secretary of State during the debates on the bill. "For a young nation Canada has done great things. . . . We can afford to hold our heads high and be proud of the fact that we are Canadian. And it is time we know what a Canadian is."

Canada, like Ireland in another context, was always an imperial trend setter. On the argument she was advancing—and it was one which in the circumstances was bound to be followed elsewhere—Australians must likewise first and foremost be Australians, and New Zealanders, New Zealanders. Even the British in their home islands found it necessary to follow suit and introduce in 1948 a citizenship for the United Kingdom and the dependent colonies. It was a logical process. But clearly an Empire (or a Commonwealth for that matter) which had been forced to recognise this kind of differential between its members was no longer a legal or practical unity. *"Civis Romanus Sum"* had once been its model—Palmerston in his great speech in the affair of Don Pacifico* had been explicit about it and cheerfully prepared to start a war to right the alleged wrongs at foreign hands of one highly dubious Levantine. Whatever had happened to that doctrine, one thing was certain—it had been profoundly changed where the new British communities were concerned. The extent of that change was nowhere more evident than in the communiqué issued after the first post-war meeting of the Commonwealth premiers in the spring of 1947. "Informal exchange of views . . . common cause . . . devotion to kindred ideals . . . flexible methods of consultation . . . efficacy of free and constant cooperation . . . steady development . . . increasing mutual confidence . . ." If any commercial concern had issued such a report there would have been a rare old rumpus among the shareholders at the next annual general meeting. At the very least it would have been assumed that the company was in dire need of new articles of association and perhaps a new board of directors.

*   *   *

As it happened, however, this translation of white dominions into fully self-automated nations (reflected in the banishment of the very word "dominion" from the vocabulary of Commonwealth consultation) was only the last stage in a process which had been evolving for so long that everyone in Britain had become resigned to it. No real loss of power seemed to have resulted, because Britain's hold over these elder children had been more moral than actual, a flexible bond which had been recognised as such ever since the days of Lord Durham. In any case, the white dominions, however important in themselves, represented only a part of British power—in both world wars the contributions from the home country and India had greatly out-

* Don Pacifico, a Jewish Gibraltarian by birth, had suffered damage to his property in a riot in Athens and, as a British subject, called on the Foreign Office to enforce his claim against the Greek government. The Greeks were prepared to be reasonable: Don Pacifico was not. His optimistic claims for compensation were taken up by Lord Palmerston who sent a British fleet into Greek waters to enforce them. A vote of censure was moved on him in the House of Commons. "Pam" triumphantly defeated it. The Greeks paid up.

weighed them, and the colonial dependencies on the second occasion
had provided as many recruits for the armed forces as New Zealand
and South Africa combined. It was still Great Britain which had
emerged triumphant from Hitler's war, and British commanders,
who on Luneburg Heath and at Singapore had taken the surrender
of vast enemy forces.

Yet this too was really an illusion. It had only been by permission
of the Americans that the Japanese surrender in Southeast Asia had
been conceded to the British at all, a fortnight after the main ceremony in General MacArthur's presence aboard the *Missouri* in To-
kyo Bay. If Britain remained formally one of the "Big Three" in
1946, it was by courtesy of the United States, which had only in the
sketchiest sense "consulted" her when the decision had been taken to
drop the atom bomb on Hiroshima. It was not Britain's armed power
but the moral prestige she had won by resisting Hitler in 1940 that
kept her a seat at the conference table at Yalta and Potsdam, a deserving old-age pensioner.

And instinctively the British sensed this, even in the intoxicating
moment of victory. In spite of the VE Day celebrations, in spite
even of Winston Churchill's well-earned exuberance on his car roof in
Whitehall, the national mood had been far more serious and reflec-
tive than in 1918. A nightmare was over: that was all. "To-day we
give thanks to Almighty God for a great deliverance," said the King
in his victory broadcast, and that was the whole tenor of his speech
which reflected what Britain had dared and suffered during those
traumatic six years. Wrote *The Times* on VE Day: "The British
people went to war for the second time in a generation with a stern
and sombre resolve. The exalted mood of 1914 was not recaptured."
And on May 14 it underlined the lesson of the day:

> We must ponder on the means of our escape. We escaped by
> coalition with 'the numberless millions of the Russian people' and the
> 'immense superiority of the power used by the United States.'

The words it had quoted were Churchill's own—who knew better
than he that only by the skin of its teeth had the country survived?
The Times went on:

Only by upholding boldly and frankly the military and other responsibilities of continued coalition with mighty powers . . . will this country still be able to say with certainty, we shall be able to breathe; we shall be able to live.

It was not in such humble and dependent terms that Britain had spoken when she had held to the "two-power standard" of naval superiority over the next two largest of her rivals. In 1922 she had accepted parity with the United States, but those times too had passed and the Royal Navy was now only a poor relation of that fleet with which Admiral Nimmitz had swept the Japanese from the Pacific. Her land forces could comfortably have been accommodated on one small sector of the Russian front.

This shrinking of a whole scale of values had not gone unrecognised in the British dependencies where prior to 1914 the mystique of the Empire's invincibility had been taken for granted. The difficulties Britain had experienced in defeating the Kaiser's Germany, and still more importantly Turkey, had changed all that. The failure at the Dardanelles and the surrender of British forces at Kut el Amara had cut the *Raj* down to size. It was not omnipotent: it could be defeated. In 1942 at Singapore it had been disgraced. £60 million had been spent during the thirties in creating a vast naval base as an assertion of Britain's claim to be a great Asian power. Twenty-one square miles of dockyard had been fashioned out of a swamp and given the protection of an air base and the most modern artillery. This huge and supposedly impregnable fortress defended by 100,000 men had surrendered a week after the first assault by Japanese troops. That the defending guns faced the wrong way, to repel invasion from the sea rather than from the land, was unlikely to be accepted as much of an excuse by the astonished witnesses of the disaster. *The Times* attributed it largely to green troops and the debilitating effects of the climate on Europeans, but this too was double edged, for if it was so unhealthy for the British in the East, why were they there? In London, Winston Churchill, facing things more robustly, had called it "a heavy and far-reaching military defeat." He added: "It is an Imperial defeat."

And so it was, in a wider sense than he intended. Even when the Japanese in their turn were brought to surrender in the autumn of 1945, the events of February 1942 lived on. "It has done a little to wipe out the past three and a half years," a British ex-prisoner of war remarked as he watched the victory celebrations in the recaptured city. A little, certainly, but not enough. Everyone present knew that though the Fourteenth Army had recovered Burma and Malaya in a brilliant jungle campaign, it was the American atom bomb at Hiroshima that had really settled the war beyond argument. The loss of prestige was all the more serious because of the widespread Asian belief that both America and Russia, the real victors, were anti-imperialist powers. The full extent of the fall from grace was not yet fully appreciated in Britain. But then no one there appreciated either the equally serious fact that the country, in addition to all its other troubles, was on the verge of bankruptcy.

*   *   *

Though the supremacy of sterling had been undermined by the First World War, Britain had unwisely returned to the Gold Standard in 1925 at the pre-war parity of 4.86 dollars, an over-valuation of the pound which meant that her exports were not competitive, and in 1931 the Gold Standard had to be abandoned. Countries had then to decide whether to keep their currencies stable in terms of gold or of sterling, and those who chose sterling formed the Sterling Area. This entailed a double system which made the pound vulnerable and would have inevitably led to a sterling payments crisis if the greater calamity of war had not arisen first. Immediately it broke out, steps were taken to protect the pound. A regulation of September 3, 1939, forbade payments to residents outside the United Kingdom, but did not apply to countries that kept their currency reserves in sterling and operated an exchange control system similar to that announced in Britain. These countries formed a new sterling bloc which was defined in July 1940 and included the United Kingdom, the Dominions, the colonies, the dependencies and mandated territories, Egypt, the Sudan and Iraq.

All Britain's resources were to be poured into the war effort. Thirty-five per cent of the cost was to be financed out of her accumulated capital. Altogether £1,118 million was raised by the sale of overseas investments, and all £564 million of her Sterling Area investments were realised. But this was not enough, and since most of the goods needed had to be bought in the United States, dollars were urgently needed. The United States was unable to give credits because Britain was still in debt to her and legislation on Capitol Hill had insisted on down payments from defaulters. To carry on the war, Britain was thus forced to dispose of her gold and dollar reserves, which in 1939 had stood at £600 million. To meet additional needs, it was also agreed that the dollar earnings of the whole Sterling Area should be put at Britain's disposal and the sterling equivalent paid out to the individual countries by Britain at the end of hostilities. These "sterling balances" accumulated in London, and though at the time they relieved a critical situation, they laid up many problems for Britain in the post-war world by sharply reducing her investment in her own Sterling Area. India, for instance, used her credit balances to buy up British investments in India, and in spite of this Delhi's sterling balances had risen to £1,321 million by the end of 1945. In effect, the debtor position of India and Great Britain was reversed in the Second World War as the roles of Great Britain and the United States had been reversed after the first.

This desperate dollar shortage was alleviated in 1941 by Lease Lend. Yet indirectly even this imaginative gesture, which was meant to help Britain, proved harmful to the British export trade which came to be regarded as of secondary importance now that the imports for war were guaranteed. By 1945 British exports by volume were only 40 per cent of the 1938 level. Britain's Lend-Lease liability when the system was wound up was fixed at £162 million, in itself a formidable burden of debt, but because of the balance-of-payments gap further help from America was needed and 3,750 million dollars (£937 million sterling) was borrowed at 2 per cent, repayable in fifty annual instalments from 1951: a deal which was scathingly attacked by *The Economist* seven months before it was finally signed by President Truman in the summer of 1946:

> . . . our needs are the direct result of the fact that we fought earliest, that we fought longest, and that we fought hardest. . . . For that we shall pay 140 million dollars a year for the rest of the twentieth century. It may be unavoidable, but it is not right.

Thus, Britain had her debts to America to pay off, she had to be prepared to pay out the accumulated sterling balances amounting to

£2,732 million, and by the agreement with the United States in 1946 faced the covertibility of sterling in the following year. This indebtedness had to be met by a Britain with sadly shrunken resources. In addition to the sale of overseas capital which had lessened her income from invisible earnings, shipping losses, amounting to 30 per cent of the mercantile marine, had depleted her income from this traditional source. Once the great exporter of coal, she now had insufficient for her own home needs. Hancock and Gowing in their *British War Economy* have estimated that her invisible income had probably shrunk from £248 million in 1938 to £120 million in 1946, while her deficit on visible trade had probably grown during the same period from £300 million to £650 million. The balance of payments position showed a deficit of £750 million in 1946.

The reduced circumstances of the country had not been fully grasped. The need was for retrenchment at home and for the reduction of imports, for the modernisation and diversification of industry, combined with an export drive particularly aimed at America, matched by wage restraint so as to make this competitive. However, this was not at all how the British people in the aftermath of war saw the situation. They wanted a comfortable and decent living for everyone, more education, better schools, better housing, a free health service, comprehensive pension and social insurance schemes. The Beveridge Plan, which embodied these hopes, had made the Welfare State a possibility once the government in May 1944 had committed itself to a full employment policy. And certainly these longings for the good life had to be met. After their sufferings and exertions during the war the British people *demanded* that they be met. It was because they instinctively felt that Churchill was no longer the man to provide them that they sent him packing in 1945.

His successor, Mr. Attlee, felt confident that Britain could shoulder financial burdens while providing social services at home and undertaking large schemes for the recovery and social welfare of the colonial territories. His government embarked on this comprehensive programme believing that the loan from America would tide it over until more normal conditions were restored and increased exports reduced the dollar gap to manageable proportions. But there were no cuts on dollar imports, the Sterling Area continued to drain off the sterling balances, and the deficit in Great Britain's gold and dollar reserves rose from fifty million dollars a month in the first three-quarters of 1946 to 200 million dollars in February 1947, to 500 million in July when the convertibility of sterling came into force. On August 20 convertibility was suspended, the loss of dollars in the week previous to this having amounted to 237 million dollars, as much as the total deficit for the whole of 1946. A new policy of austerity set out to reverse this process, giving priority to exports, then to capital investment in industry, and leaving the needs and comforts of the family at the bottom of the list. But the respite obtained was only temporary. The necessity to cut dollar imports drastically had been faced neither in Britain nor in the Sterling Area as a whole. Everyone wanted dollars, either to supply their consumer demand after the deprivations of the war years or to industrialise. It only needed a recession in America and the cutting of her imports from the Sterling Area to precipitate another crisis, which resulted in a massive 30 per cent devaluation of the currency in September 1949.

The genuine idealism of Mr. Attlee's government secured, in spite of these difficulties, the Welfare State which the British people had been demanding. But this idealism did not stop at home. Though anti-imperialist by instinct and tradition, British Socialists could not divorce themselves from the empire they had inherited. In the early days the party's Fabian wing (which had included such formidable intellects as Sidney and Beatrice Webb and George Bernard Shaw) had been distinctly imperialist at times, even J. A. Hobson, the most important twentieth-century writer on the subject, had accepted that in undeveloped territories there was room for the benevolent guardianship of a colonial power, provided it acted on good Socialist principles and prepared the way for freedom. This line of thinking, which appealed to Labour's deeply ingrained compassion for the under-privileged, provided also a new platform for the useful exercise of power after years in the political wilderness: everything combined to make Mr. Attlee's administration far more conscious of the needs of its dependencies than its Tory predecessors had been. Huge colonial development grants were cheerfully shouldered, amounting to £450 million between 1946 and 1955, a severe drain on resources needed at home for capital re-investment and modernisation of industry. Britain was not to prove incapable of meeting these responsibilities; these debts of honour. But they reduced her capacity to compete with reviving industrial nations in Europe and Asia unhampered by such commitments and thereby significantly reduced her national "weight." Certainly they left her with no reserves to deal with colonial problems over and above the provision of cash or welfare aid. She would no longer have the power to put down insurrections or fight a holding action for long against nationalist movements, and still less did she have the will to do so or that "capacity for imperialism" on whose loss Pandit Nehru was to remark in 1949. Colonel Blimp was dead: unlamented and without descendants. The British Empire would in future have to depend—as theoretically it had always depended—on the consent of the governed. Its testing ground as usual would be India.

XVI

India, from Dyarchy to Independence

In their Government of India Act of 1935 the British had finally prepared the way for their own withdrawal, but few saw any likelihood of it taking place for several years—the responsible ministries had to be set up in the provinces; Dyarchy had to be introduced at the centre (itself only a first step towards full "responsibility" there) and the princes cajoled into the federal scheme. Only optimists at Westminster believed that such a training programme could bring independence within another two or three decades: indeed, in a way it seemed farther off in 1935 than ever before, if only because of the complexity of federation and the size of the infrastructure that was now being run up. As late as 1939 the Viceroy, Lord Linlithgow, could still write in terms which earlier proconsuls like Curzon would have found familiar ". . . that there should be any impression . . . that public opinion at home, or His Majesty's Government, seriously contemplate evacuation in any measurable period of time, seems to me astonishing."

If these were perhaps surprising words to come across four years after the Government of India Act and two decades after the Montagu-Chelmsford reforms, the continued coyness of the princes to come into the federal scheme and to work the central provisions of the Act bore out this forecast of a long haul ahead. However, the

British, who were certainly anxious after their fashion to make their brainchild work, found themselves agreeably surprised by the success it began to enjoy at provincial level. The leaders of Congress, and to a lesser extent of the Muslim League, might declare the 1935 provisions unacceptable: the mass of Indian politicians of all classes and creeds longed, like sensible men, to enjoy power when it was offered them. So it happened that after the elections for the provincial legislatures had been held and the successful candidates found control was theirs for the asking, it became impossible for the zealots to hold them, and the rush to the ballot box was succeeded by an even fiercer scramble of politicians for office.

The elections themselves had given Congress large majorities in the five Hindu-majority provinces, and in a sixth, in Assam, they formed the largest single party. In the North West Frontier Province the dominant Muslim "Red Shirts" were Congress-allied. In Bengal, the Punjab and Sind, Muslim governments were swept to power. But these governments were not Muslim League subsidiaries; they were coalitions of independent Islamic groupings, and in the Punjab in particular the victorious Unionist party under Sir Sikander Hyat-Khan was resolutely anti-League. Ironically enough, it was not in the Muslim-majority provinces but in the *Hindu* ones that Mr. Jinnah and the League had had their best polls. There they had certainly done well enough to expect to be invited by the Congress to share in coalition governments. All that was needed for co-operation between the races was generosity from the victors.

It was not forthcoming. Perhaps there had never been any real chance that it *would* be forthcoming. As far back as the time of Queen Victoria's Golden Jubilee a Muslim leader, Sir Sayed Ahmad, had prophesied that the two nations of India would never share the same throne, but that one would inevitably dominate the other and thrust it down. In 1935 in British India (putting aside the 90 millions in the princely states) 300 million Hindus faced a Muslim population less than a third of their size. And whereas the Hindus formed substantially one party, the Muslims were split into many, and Jinnah's League, which claimed to represent them all, had won a majority in no single province. The Congress leaders, proclaiming as a matter of faith to represent all Indians and despising Jinnah as an ex-Congress renegade, saw no reason to allow his claim to share in coalitions in provinces which they had carried by massive majorities—if he wanted office, let him renounce the League and accept Congress discipline, or else look to his own and try out his wiles in the Muslim provinces, where he was also likely to get a dusty answer.

Just for a moment—a very fleeting one—there had gleamed a real ray of hope for the creation of one united India, beginning at provincial level. The Viceroy, Lord Linlithgow, had publicly urged it: "I am convinced that the shortest road to that fuller political life which many of you so greatly desire is to accept this constitution and to work for it for all it is worth. Of their nature, politics are ever dynamic."

No truer word was ever spoken, and Congress's failure was to appreciate just how dynamic, how mobile and fluid, the situation was. At that time, after the elections under the Act, Congress enjoyed British goodwill; the Muslim League was a client for its favour; the Muslim provincial governments were either allies (as in the North West Frontier Province) or in the hands of moderates; and even the princes were under constant pressure from the Viceroy to accept the realities of their position and join with British India to make federation work.

Unfortunately Congress, for all the idealism of its claims as the standard-bearer of Indian independence, was sectarian at heart, a Hindu party which had just achieved a resounding victory at the polls over its self-proclaimed rival, the League. Contemptuously it refused Mr. Jinnah the share of power he had expected. And by doing so, not only did it outrage and grossly underestimate that cold, egotistical and ambitious man, but it flouted and alarmed *all* Muslim opinion throughout India, even in those provinces where Jinnah's writ had not run. It was to make a national leader of him.

The Congress rejection of the League was really a piece of politicking. No one at that time could have foreseen that it would lead to a partition of the country, which not even Jinnah then really desired. Far more than Europe, India was geographically one unit— this huge pear-shaped mass bounded by the ocean and the highest mountains in the world. The Moguls had managed to impose one rule over most of it; and their British successors, for all their tolerance of a mosaic of provinces and princely states, had drawn the bonds of unity much tighter with a network of railways and trunk roads linking the historic centres of population. "Whom God hath joined . . ." But alas, in India there were many Gods, and the British, who had also brought their own deity with them, had provided in their cherished federal scheme almost as many elements of discord as there were divinities in the Hindu pantheon.

Perhaps if there had been no war in 1939 and India had not been drawn into another struggle, she would have found energy enough to solve her own internal problems on rational and not sectarian lines. The Viceroy believed that in normal times federation would have been achieved by the summer of 1941, and he was not a man given to easy optimism. Once a central government had been formed, politicians of all races and creeds would have been thrown together willy-nilly, and there would have been a strong corrective to those disruptive trends which the 1935 Act had magnified by providing Hindu governments here, Muslim governments there, in provinces which had once all been subject to the overriding direction of the *Raj*. And the war did not only force the British to drop all ideas of federation until hostilities were over: it quickened, at the same time, the sense of urgency among Indian nationalists of all persuasions to get something quickly while the going was good from rulers whose defects in Europe, and far more importantly in Asia, on India's doorstep, showed them to be vulnerable in a way unsuspected since the mutiny of 1857.

On the surface, India's response to the outbreak of war in 1939 was very heartening. Two million volunteers served with the colours, and by doing so probably saved Egypt and Iraq, as well as their home country in the campaign in Assam. Even the Congress—a notably unwarlike body except where abuse of the British was concerned—felt its democratic kinship with the West; while Mr. Gandhi was prepared to try conclusions with the Japanese on his own well-tried basis of "non-violence."

However, this was not quite the spirit of 1914. Indians had not all leapt with enthusiasm into the struggle: the Viceroy's declaration of war without consultation with the political parties had deeply affronted Congress. How was it that "one man, and he a foreigner and a representative of a hated system" (in Pandit Jawaharlal Nehru's words) could plunge four hundred million people into war? And when Japan swept down through Burma and Malaysia in the winter of 1941–42, her victories could be seen by many as Asian victories against a white oppressor—perhaps even as the harbingers of Indian freedom.

In war as in peace the British remained stubbornly determined to provide that freedom themselves, but in their own time, at their own pace. Soon after the outbreak of hostilities in 1939 the Viceroy had declared that dominion status was Britain's pledge to India, but he set no date to it. He was really repeating what Edwin Montagu had said in 1917 at another time of crisis when Britain had been anxious to soothe Indian feelings with formulas. Surrounded by enemies and faced with deep divisions inside India, there was every reason to walk with care. "There remains to-day entire disagreement between the representatives of the major parties on fundamental issues," Lord Linlithgow complained to the Secretary of State in London. This slowness in reacting to the vagaries and ambitions of Indian statesmen nevertheless brought its penalties—Congress in disgust ordered all its ministries in the provinces to resign, and the Muslim League, not to be outdone in intransigence, responded a few months later with a call for its own national state of Pakistan.

The British reply to these clamorous politicians who were calling nations into being was to offer them a rather larger representation on the Viceroy's enlarged Council of State. As proof of what the French call British "phlegm" it sounds magnificent; but this was August 1940, in the days after Dunkirk, and it really *was* all that Britain could offer: she could hardly spare much effort for constitution-making in New Delhi when the Battle of Britain was about to begin. In any event, both Congress and League united in rejecting this "August Offer," and matters were restored to their thirties' norm, even to the extent of a new civil disobedience campaign on Mr. Gandhi's part which landed him back in gaol.

These ritual dances, undertaken by both the British and their Indian partners, were now rudely interrupted by the arrival of the Japanese in the war. In the months after Pearl Harbour their armies overran Burma and Malaysia, reaching out towards the frontiers of India in Assam. This was the background behind the mission of Sir Stafford Cripps to New Delhi in March 1942 as Churchill's emissary, offering an Indian Constituent Assembly to draft the future constitution of the country and full Indian representation in an interim government to see out the war. That Cripps on his government's behalf was prepared to concede India's ultimate right of secession from the Empire is proof enough of how reconciled even imperialists like Churchill had become to the ending of the *Raj*. Such realism and generosity met with no such response. To Mahatma Gandhi the Cripps offer was no more than "a postdated cheque on a failing bank," and at his urging Congress flatly rejected it on the grounds that it introduced no immediate constitutional change and left the defence of India still in British hands. The Muslim League rejected it because it did not provide for the creation of Pakistan. The sheer unreason of the politicians at this time was made even clearer in Congress's next step, which was to call on the British to quit India forthwith. During the ensuring disturbances in the country, which were easily suppressed, the Congress leaders were arrested and hauled off to gaol, where for the next three years they remained, passing the time in games of chess and badminton—so many Neros while the world burned around them.

With the end of the war in Europe they were released and invited to a conference at Simla with the new Viceroy, Lord Wavell. Once more they were offered an interim government, wholly Indian in form apart from the portfolios of Viceroy and Commander in Chief. This time they accepted. Mr. Jinnah for the League did not refuse. He merely raised his bid to 50 per cent representation for his 25 per cent holding, and predictably the conference broke down; to be followed after a decent interval by the appearance of a cabinet mission led by the Secretary of State for India in Mr. Attlee's newly elected Labour government, Lord Pethick Lawrence, but dominated, in fact, by Sir Stafford Cripps, no longer in bondage to a Tory Prime Minister but out on his radical own.

The constitutional scheme which emerged was a marvel of ingenuity. The 1935 Act had provided a two-tier structure of central and provincial government. Sir Stafford now suggested three: centre and provinces as before, but sandwiched between them room was made for "groups" of provinces which would reflect the desire of Hindus and Moslems to coalesce within their own majority areas. If there was ever to be a unitary India which also took account of racial divisions in the country, here was its blueprint. And for a time it almost seemed that the subtleties of the plan and the obvious goodwill and sincerity behind it had awakened an answering chord among the Indian political leaders.

Ten years, even five years earlier, agreement could have been had along such lines, but at a cost. The new Union government would have been at the mercy of its provinces and groups of provinces: it would have been too weak and divided to cope with the nation's enormous problems of poverty, illiteracy, famine, racialism and an exploding birth rate. Perhaps it was a blessing in the long run that the plan foundered within a matter of weeks under the mutual jealousies and ambitions that surrounded it like so many vultures on the Towers of Silence in Bombay, slicing off a proposal here, a proposal there, till nothing was left but the bones of an interim government picked over by Congress and League in "acrimonious association," to use the words of a distinguished expert on the period.

Of the parties at this stage, the League was certainly the more unyielding. Its declaration of a "Direct Action Day" in August 1945 in pursuit of its separatist aims brought five thousand dead in rioting in Calcutta alone; and when Lord Wavell announced the programme for the Constituent Assembly which was to plan for India's future, it was Mr. Jinnah and not Pandit Nehru who boycotted the proceedings. For the Muslims under his guidance had at last taken up a position irreconcilable with that of the other Indian parties.

It would be a bold man who would say whether or not the idea of Pakistan, of the separate Muslim nation within India's borders, had been inevitable all along. Sir Sayed Ahmad seems to have thought so, well over half a century before the thing happened, but there had been later trends suggesting quite the opposite: Mr. Jinnah's search for a share in coalition governments in 1937, to name only one. This could have been a mere tactical move; a wrecking ploy. Yet Jinnah himself had for many years been a member of Congress, and his revulsion against it was a very late development. On the other side, it should be remembered that the Emperor Akbar's humane attempt to conciliate and unite the two main races in sixteenth-century India had barely survived his death. The social and religious differences ran too deep. Indeed, it is possible to see all Indian history since that time as a series of sporadic Hindu attempts, under the Mahrattas, the Sikhs, and the Congress politicians, to reverse the Mogul conquest, and of Muslim resistance to such movements under the sheltering umbrella of the *Raj*. It was in such terms that Sir Sayed Ahmad had been thinking, and this had finally become Mr. Jinnah's viewpoint also:

> Hindus and Muslims have two different religious philosophies, social customs, literature. They neither intermarry nor even interdine. Indeed they belong to two different civilisations. . . . The Muslims are not a minority as the word is commonly understood. Muslims are a nation.

This was a claim whose implications ran counter to all British thinking and to the genuine idealism that underlay the *Raj*. To have found the country divided and to leave it divided would be a reproach, a "Vivisection of Mother India" in Gandhi's words which the heirs of Macaulay and Curzon were very reluctant to permit. Privately, however, they had begun to allow that such surgery might be necessary. Thus their "August Offer" of 1940, which the League as well as Congress had so contemptuously rejected, had included a pledge that power would not be handed over to any government whose authority was denied by "large and powerful elements in India's national life." At so late a stage this could hardly have been just another excuse for remaining in India for ever: it was a first admission that some kind of division of the country was on the cards. Similarly, in the spring of 1942 the first Cripps offer of an interim government and of a Constituent Assembly, designed to attract all interests towards the centre, had been accompanied by a saving clause which had provided that individual states or provinces could opt out of any future Indian union if they wished. If this was not an invitation to the Muslims to insist on Pakistan, it was at least a licence for them to do so. A fatalistic note had entered British thinking on this subject, though not for another five years was it finally spelled out in the Attlee government's declaration of February 20, 1947, announcing its "definite intention" to hand over power to "responsible Indians" by June 1948 at the latest. Since there was now no likelihood that any group of Indians "responsible" to the nation as a whole would or could be found in any foreseeable future, this meant in effect that the *Raj*, in giving itself its marching orders, was leaving the ground to two and conceivably more successors. As late as 1935 such a solution would have been unthinkable. In 1947 it seemed, if not the most natural thing in the world, at least the most inevitable.

* * *

To sweeten the pill, perhaps as much for themselves as for the Indians, the British government marked the occasion by sending out as its last Viceroy, Admiral of the Fleet Lord Louis Mountbatten.

No shrewder choice could have been made, for Lord Louis might have been designed from birth to appeal to everyone involved in the tragic tangle of Indian affairs—he was related to the King-Emperor, which gave him a *cachet* with the princes; he was sympathetic to socialism, which endeared him to the Congress; he was bringing Mr. Jinnah and the League the substance of their hopes; and as the commander who had accepted the Japanese surrender at Singapore he had avenged a disastrous defeat and was therefore qualified to wind up an empire with a show of dignity and self-respect.

These were personal advantages. But Lord Louis enjoyed others which arose out of the situation with which he had to deal. In the long Anglo-Indian dialogue which had begun at the turn of the century in the times of Morley and Minto it was the Indians who had called the tune or had, at least, always refused to pay the piper. They had made demands and had waited fairly confidently for the British to refuse them. Now the initiative had passed to the other side. The British were no longer making proposals but announcing decisions; they had nothing to offer except their own imminent departure. For the Indian leaders it was a sobering experience after fifty years of trumpeting around the walls of Jericho to see them actually crumbling.

Mountbatten had reached New Delhi in March 1947, officially charged to make one last attempt to find a unitary solution to a problem which he realised at once must mean partition. So partition of some kind it had to be. His first effort in the widely derided "Dickie Bird Plan" would have meant a Balkanisation of the country as bad as anything in the days of Clive, and speedily recovering from this false start, he proposed, and imposed by the force of logic and personality, a hand-over by the *Raj* to two dominions of "India" and "Pakistan." If he had had any doubts about the need for this, and for quick action, the communal rioting which was spreading through the North West Frontier Province and the Punjab would speedily have converted him, but, in fact, both he and the leaders of Congress and League needed little urging. The evidence was there for all to see; and so it happened that the last moves in a solution of infinite complexity were compressed into a matter of months.

No one and no party got exactly what it wanted. Congress and the British had to surrender their unitary dream. The Muslims did not achieve the grand six-province state they asked for, but only a truncated version, a "moth-eaten" Pakistan in Jinnah's words which came strangely from a man who had built himself a nation of seventy million people, the strongest Islamic state on earth. The princes were invited to accede to one side or the other—their days were numbered, and they, if any, were the losers in this final settlement, though not perhaps their peoples. The Sikhs, who had fought two resounding wars against the *Raj,* also had to submit to the harsh reality which proclaimed them a sect and not a nation.

Grim massacres, in which at least 200,000 died, and vast transfers of populations involving perhaps ten million people across the new frontiers of a divided Punjab marked this hand-over: "an orgy of murder and arson" was how Nehru himself described it. "Tomorrow the sun of Independence will rise for India, but for the Punjab it will be a cheerless dawn," wrote the *Civil and Military Gazette* of Lahore on the eve of the great day. And not for the Punjab alone, for divisions showed in even the minutiae of life across the whole of India, and when the British-owned *Statesman* of Calcutta (whose first editor had been among the honoured founders of the Congress) published photographs of Muslim leaders in its pages, it received a torrent of letters from outraged Hindus protesting against this desecration, including one unequivocal threat of violence, signed DEMON—"I am waiting here with my loaded pistol," this correspondent wrote.

It sounds and was horrific. But the civil war which many had expected between the two emergent states did not materialise, and among the leaders there was less recrimination and even regret than might have been expected. In Karachi Mr. Jinnah declared that the two Indias were parting as friends and would remain so. "Let us not be disheartened because freedom has not come in the full glory of a united India," said the Congress President, Acharya Kripalani; and the *Times of India* showed a similar acceptance of the inevitable:

However regrettable the partition may be, few will deny that thereby the greatest obstacle to the healthy growth of the body politic of the country has been removed.

It all has a resigned, pragmatical, rather middle-aged air. Indeed, few of the paladins of independence were any longer young, and after so many years of struggle most of them wanted to enjoy office and serve their people. They were glad to have attained what they had.

Similarly in Britain, relief at the shedding of an almost intolerable burden was the order of the day. There the spate of oratory over India in the past had been enormous—the trial of Warren Hastings, the speeches of Fox, of the younger Pitt and Macaulay had filled volumes, and the Government of India Act of 1935 was the bulkiest in British parliamentary history. Yet at the end hardly anyone in London had much to say, apart from the elementary courtesies. "With this transfer of power," ran the King's message, "comes the fulfilment of a great democratic ideal to which the British and Indian peoples alike are firmly dedicated." "It is our earnest wish" (ran Prime Minister Attlee's statement) "that India may go forth in tranquility and prosperity and in so doing contribute to the peace and prosperity of the world." There were good wishes from ex-Viceroys and other potentates. A few nostalgic expatriate sentiments were expressed—one was printed in the Calcutta *Statesman* and can stand for them all:

I shall always remember
Velvet Indian night's bejewelled firmament:
Jade with turquoise wisped in stippled monsoon sky:
Blue gardens aglow with pale moonlight,
By waxen frangipani lent
A heady, heavy fragrance, fleet to die.

I shall always remember
Bullocks yoked abreast and mud-caked buffaloes,
Golden sunflower and green glinting parakeet,
Dappled sails becalmed: the lilac flow
Of water hyacinth, and the rose
Of dusty plains adazzle in the heat.

But the London *Times* devoted only a couple of fairly perfunctory columns to the event, hoping that the British example in India had created in Indian minds a new conception of public service; and only at the end, taking heart from the Viceroy's praise of the spirit of co-operation and compromise he had met with among Indian leaders, did it break into a kind of elegy over the effects of three centuries of British rule:

> These are British qualities, and the political ideas and constitutional methods for reconciling liberty with order which are now guiding the deliberations of the Assemblies at Delhi and Karachi are of British origin, are indeed Britain's special gifts to mankind. That Indian minds are now enriched by them is the result of the quiet, persistent work, maintained for generations, of British men and women who under the Indian sun and at the sacrifice of domestic happiness did their duty unflinchingly before God and man.

These "adventurers from their gusty islands," *The Times* concluded, had built a bridge between East and West. But how strong a bridge, and for how long it would survive, were matters not dwelt on, still less the other lessons of that long experiment. In retrospect, the leader writer came back to the men who had administered the *Raj,* the British officials who had on the whole been very like the English weather—"more than trying at times but very healthy to live with."

* * *

In India there were rejoicings. After all, India—or rather the two Indias—had been victorious, just as Islam had won the Crusades (as the Emir Feisal is said to have reminded the Western statesmen assembled at Versailles in 1919). Medals, packets of sweets and free cinema shows were provided for the children, and in floodlit Delhi and Bombay huge crowds were out on the streets in scenes rivalling those of Mafeking Night in London. From Dublin, Mr. Eamon de Valera sent hearty congratulations and fervent hopes for India's welfare. The Chinese ambassador, Dr. Chia Luen-lo contributed a poem:

Be brave, forward riders on the chariot of time
While approaching the mountain peak, redouble
    your efforts to climb.
Unfailingly will you arrive at your ideal,
Lofty and beautiful, noble and sublime.

But on the whole the tone of the celebrations was muted because everyone remembered the violence which was erupting in the Punjab and would certainly have spread to Bengal but for Gandhi's presence in the province. "Few people in India to-day are in a mood of real rejoicing," wrote an observer in the special independence Supplement of the *Statesman.* Too much blood was already flowing. Also the astrologers had declared August 15—Independence Day—to be inauspicious.

In Karachi Mr. Jinnah presided as first Governor-General of Pakistan over the birth pangs of a nation which was largely of his own creation. It was a nation slighted at birth by the twin-dominion of India's determination to be known by that name of India and not by the pseudonym of "Hindustan": but in his oration in the presence of the last Viceroy on the lawns of Government House he said kind things of the *Raj.* Such a voluntary and absolute transfer of power was unknown in history, and he praised also Britain's gifts of order and a judicial system which was one of the "great bulwarks and safeguards" of people's liberties. "This is a parting between friends who have learnt to honour and respect one another, even in disagreement," he proclaimed.

At Delhi, India's new leaders had assembled amid the grandeurs of the Council House which they had inherited along with a population second only to China's. There, to an accompaniment of Indian lutes and zithers, the national song "Vanda Mataram," was sung by the wife of the Congress President. As the clock struck midnight the members of the Constituent Assembly pledged their loyalty to the motherland. Pandit Nehru made a short speech:

At the stroke of the midnight hour, while the world sleeps, India will waken to life and freedom. We end to-day a period of ill fortune and India discovers herself again.

Outside the hall a huge crowd celebrated the occasion with the blowing of conches and cries of "Mahatma Gandhi-Ki-jai." Mr. Gandhi himself spent the day fasting in Calcutta.

*   *   *

Thus was achieved what Macaulay had seen as Britain's "proudest day."

And the first and most obvious thing about it is that it was delayed too long. For all the compliments that had been lavished on the Viceroy, the invitation to him to stay in Delhi as India's first Governor-General, the tributes to British friendship and statesmanship, a sour note pervaded the final ceremonies—in his great speech to the nation Pandit Nehru paid not one grateful tribute to the *Raj*. While the ritual flags were being run up and down in Delhi and Karachi tens of thousands were dying and millions were being rendered homeless. The full story has never been told; probably never can be told; and no one to this day knows within ten thousand or so the tally of the dead.

Such horrors made a profound impact. There was a widespread feeling even among the ex-rulers that with more prescience, more generosity, they could largely have been avoided. In Mr. Gandhi's early days before civil disobedience, before the final breakdown between Congress and League, could not partition have been avoided and one India brought into existence in harmony and peace?

Of course no one could be sure. But the events of 1947 were a final disillusionment. The British had not been able to hold India against her will; they had not in the end been able to choose the kind of India they wanted to leave behind them or even to protect the Indian people. The British were still in form, if not in reality, an imperial power. They still ruled a colonial Empire of over seventy million people, and they had no immediate plans to hand over more than a fraction of it. But if the pressure for the secession of any part of it became too great, they were now conditioned to act in time. There had been the lesson of America, of Ireland, now of India, and it had been learnt at last. In the future the British would stay ahead of nationalist movements if they could.

XVII

Recessional

The haphazard spread of Britain's colonial possessions concealed an inner logic.

The West Indies were really remnants from her first expansion in the New World which had also created the thirteen colonies. But historically the growth and decline of these islands were also connected with the opposite shores of the Atlantic, with West Africa, via the nexus of the slave trade, in which English seamen had begun to interest themselves as early as 1562 with the voyages of John Hawkins to the Caribbean. By the Treaty of Utrecht in 1713, as a prize of victorious campaigns in Europe, Britain had acquired that most prestigious of commercial rights at the time, the *Asiento,* which gave her the monopoly of the carriage trade in slaves to the Spanish Americas—this was the genesis of her involvement along that malarial and inhospitable coast between the Gambia and the Niger. She had come there to export slaves: she stayed to root out slavery, and in the course of time to build up new trades in palm kernels, palm oil, gold dust, diamonds and cocoa.

The British Caribbean and West Africa were special cases, the legacies of a westward expansion which had also created Canada and Newfoundland. But if one excepts the Falkland Islands off the tip of South America, all the rest of the colonial Empire was directed

towards the East and owed its origin to the obsessive desire to protect India and the routes that led to her and towards the still larger
emporium of China.

The high-seas route to Calcutta needed its bases, and sure enough
they came to be marked red on the map: St. Helena, Ascension Island, Cape Colony, Natal, the Seychelles, Mauritius and Ceylon.
Within this category fell also the excellent port of Freetown in
Sierra Leone, though the colony had originally owed its existence to
the humanitarians who had founded a haven there for freed slaves.
It was a case of "Cast your bread upon the waters." Similarly, the
overland route to India—which became another and shorter sea
route with the opening of the Suez Canal—was a step-ladder of
British possessions: Gibraltar, Malta, Cyprus, Palestine, Egypt,
the Sudan, East Africa, Aden, the Gulf sheikdoms; and for better
protection and trade expansion on India's other wing, Burma, the
Malay peninsula, Singapore, parts of Borneo and Hong Kong. Even
the expansion into central Africa in the settlement of the Rhodesias
and Nyasaland, which were part of one man's neo-imperial dream,
has been seen by one modern writer as largely a move to curb the
Boers and keep the vital naval base of Simonstown in British hands.

Some of these territories were very large, some were minute specks
lost in the vastness of the oceans. Some of the subject peoples had
cultures far older than Britain's: others lived in the Stone Age. In
Barbados and Bermuda there were legislative assemblies venerable
in age; in Malta there were more "Counts" and "Honourables" in the
telephone directory than could easily be found in London; and at the
other end of the scale were Polynesian islanders in a state of nature.
In the Sudan, Britain shared sovereignty (theoretically) with Egypt,
though in fact the country was run by an *élite* civil service which had
no truck at all with Egypt, still less with the Colonial Office in
London, since it was a grand appendage of the Secretary of State for
Foreign Affairs. There were even four distinct kinds of colonial
territory: Crown Colonies, Protectorates, Protected States, and Mandates, these last being sub-divided into "A" Class Mandates, as in
Palestine (which by the terms of the League of Nations charter had
to be prepared for early independence) and "B" Class Mandates, as
in Tanganyika (which were of normal colonial status but for the
provision that they could not be permanently appropriated by the
mandatory power).

These complexities, however, were more academic than real, for apart from nearly independent Ceylon and Burma, and Palestine, which was in the pangs of a more painful birth of nationhood, the rest of colonial Empire was much of one political piece, and only the subtlest of constitutional lawyers could really appreciate the difference between Crown Colonies and Protectorates and the "B" Mandate in Tanganyika, though Protected States were more readily distinguishable as wards of court, satellites like the Indian princedoms. If one took them by and large, in fact, the vast mass of the colonial territories, great or small, sophisticated or savage, were all subject to one pattern of rule, a pattern both logical and flexible, based on the principles of trusteeship and of the Durham Report.

At the apex of the pyramid was the King in Parliament, whose wheelhorse in London was the Secretary of State for the Colonies and whose representative in the dependency was the Governor and Commander in Chief, a kind of minor Viceroy.

In the more primitive colonies the Governor would be an absolute ruler, assisted by an Executive Council of officials—he could not expect much at the ground roots from charges emerging in some cases with reluctance from a state of cannibalism. Similarly, in fortresses vital to Britain's defensive needs, like Gibraltar and Aden, there did not seem much room for constitutional experiment; and those that had been tried, as in Cyprus between the wars, had been far from encouraging.

But over most of the territories a limited kind of advancement had become the rule. The Governor and his Executive Council would call into being a Legislative Council or Assembly as a first step in the parliamentary nursery. Some of these legislatures, as in the West Indian territories, had been elective for a great many years and enjoyed very extensive powers, but the genesis in most of the colonial Empire was a modest chamber of notables and officials appointed by the Governor, though including a few indigenous representatives who were normally tribal chiefs.

As things developed, the "nominated" members of the assemblies would in time come to be outnumbered by representatives elected on a gradually widening franchise, and there would be appointments of such elected members to the Executive Council, though ultimate power would still rest with the Governor and his officials. This was the form of "representative" or advisory government which had existed in India before the Montagu-Chelmsford reforms, the next stage from which would be the formation of an elected native cabinet to advise His Excellency, as had occurred in the Indian provinces under Dyarchy—a form not far short of full "responsible" government, though still subject to certain reserved powers and vetoes residing in the Governor.

This was the escalator towards independence on which the colonial territories were embarked. But most of them were crowded near the bottom. It was hard to think of them in the same terms as India, since the scale was so vastly different. In fact, few of these territories were thought of in terms of pride, of that peculiar mixture of fascination and possessiveness which had always governed Britain's thinking about her *imperium* in the East. Many of them were frankly nuisances, burdens on the economy, handicapped children at best. The West Indies, in a permanent state of depression since the collapse of the slave trade and the price of sugar, were cases in point. In West Africa, "The White Man's Grave," it had been with considerable reluctance that the British government had been caught up in the humanitarian venture which had founded Sierra Leone or in the expansion along the Niger that had taken place under Sir William Goldie and his Chartered Niger Company. Cyprus had been a thorn in the flesh; Palestine was ungovernable; Burma in 1945 on the verge of secession.

But if she had not loved her colonies, had Britain exploited them? A case could be made either way, and in some respects the picture was dark. From good or bad motives the British had operated clumsily among the tribal communities in Africa which had fallen into her sphere of influence. In a delightful passage the traveller and writer Mary Kingsley explained how this had come about:

> I so often think of that improving fable of the kind-hearted she-elephant, who, while walking out one day, inadvertently trod upon a partridge and killed it, and observing near at hand the bird's nest full of callow fledglings, dropped a tear, and saying "I have the feelings of a mother myself," sat down on the brood. This is precisely what England, representing the nineteenth century is doing in West Africa. She destroys the guardian institutions, drops a tear and sits upon the brood with motherly intentions; and pesky warm sitting she finds it.

This was one kind of complaint: a more common one was that British rule was too paternalist, too inclined to pursue a "policy of woad" and leave the natives in primeval darkness instead of preparing them for the light. It was on this account that the system of "Indirect Rule" through tribal chiefs which was associated with the name of Sir Henry (later Lord) Lugard, the maker of Nigeria, was often condemned by progressives. But Britain was also guilty of more mortal sins. In Kenya she had allowed the best farm land in the White Highlands to be reserved for settlers of European stock. Even Lugard's famous principle of "The Dual Mandate," which defined the ruling power's role as being trusteeship both for the natives and for the world outside which needed their primary products, leaves one with an uneasy feeling of native needs and cultures sold short. What is more, in moving from free trade to protection, Britain had not considered colonial economies; and the quotas and tariffs in 1932 and 1934 had been widely resented. In Ceylon and the Straits settlements of Malaya these had only been imposed over the almost unanimous protests of the native representatives.

But there was another and better side to the story, which had found expression in relation to West Africa as early as 1816, in the aftermath of the abolition of the slave trade, when Grenville in the House of Commons had told the slavers to compensate themselves for the loss of their piratical profits by building up a "just and equitable traffic" with Africa. This had happened, and the fruits of it were evident a century and a half later in two booming economies in Nigeria and the Gold Coast. In overseeing this drive to prosperity the British had also managed to protect their charges from most of the evils of that "plantation" economy which had disgraced King Leopold's administration in the Congo; had protected them indeed to such a degree that even great and beneficent companies like the soap giant, Lever Brothers, had been warned off the premises. And if in much of this Britain had seemed more like a wet nurse than a mother to her colonial brood, it should be held to her credit that she introduced the cocoa bean to West Africa, the rubber tree to Malaya; that it was one of her scientists, Sir William Ross, who found the causes of malaria; and that it was in the dark days after Dunkirk, when her own survival was in the balance, that her government had passed the Colonial Development and Welfare Act, a gesture of purest faith in the whole ramshackle

organism—repeated five years later in an extension and enlargement
of the Act to the tune of £120 million over ten years at a time
when Britain herself was all but bankrupt. Whatever the mistakes
of the past, a clear realisation had been reached that it was not
merely by providing law and order and incorrupt government that
a ruling power fulfilled its obligations, but rather by providing for
the betterment of the governed over the whole field of political,
economic and social welfare: by an understanding, in fact, that the
work really began where the Victorians had left off. Trusteeship was
not just a word; it was a challenge that was being met; to some degree had *always* been met. "Within the British Commonwealth,"
W. K. Hancock had written in the early months of 1940, "there is a
story of Liberation which can already be told. An historian who has
rejected the complacencies and boasts must take care that he does
not also undervalue the achievements."

*   *   *

The achievements spoke for themselves. Vast areas of Africa
south of the Sahara which in Dr. Livingstone's time had been subject
to primitive tribalism and the ravages of the slave trade had been
brought seventy years later into the age of the bulldozer, not always
perhaps with the happiest commercial results, to judge from the fiasco
of the Overseas Food Corporation's attempts to grow groundnuts on
the virgin soil of the Tanganyikan bush. Freetown, Accra, Lagos,
Nairobi, were British creations. And so, to range further afield, were
Singapore and Hong Kong, the Rhodesian Copper Belt, the dock-
yards of Valetta, cricket in the West Indies, the spread of Rugby
Football to the Fiji Islands and Association Football everywhere,
Sandhurst trained cadets in local regiments, and even tropical variants of the British public school.

It was beneficent, tutelary. But what can easily escape the observer at this distance is the sheer boredom of it, the deadening
effects of a rule that seemed as traditional and hieratic as that de-
picted on the walls of Ancient Egyptian tombs. No one who did not
experience it can understand how stultifying it must have been to
embryo black nationalists—it was certainly bad enough for the
British administrators, soldiers and traders who came to live under
it, to sign the visitors' book at Government House on the Queen's

official birthday and wait for the invitation to the annual garden party on the proconsular lawn.

The tone was set by a Governor ranking "only just below the deity," as Colin Cross puts it in a piquant chapter in his book *The Fall of the British Empire*. The pompous uniforms, the salute of guns, the Union Jack ceremonially lowered at sunset, were all pure Victoriana, reflections of Kipling's Simla. The "Club" was Somerset Maugham country, as immortalised also in E. M. Forster's *A Passage to India:* so potent and necessary an adjunct to the *Raj* that it flowered even in territories where the British had only treaty rights, as in Cairo's splendid Gezira Club and Turf Club, and the Alwiyah Club in Baghdad, a perfect miniature of the species with its Sunday curry lunches, the weekly bridge drive and dance for members, who included a few carefully vetted Arabs of good social standing. Even the education offered to these satrapies conformed to the same rigid pattern—a very enduring one, for when a correspondent from the left-wing *New Statesman and Nation* visited the Gold Coast a few years after it had achieved its independence as Ghana, he was astonished to find the new university thoroughly Oxbridge in its habits, with dons dining at high table, students in red academic gowns (a great improvement on their tatty original), and grace said in Latin. It was a pattern which had been set by no less a person than Kitchener himself in his Gordon College at Khartoum.

When liberal-minded Governors tried to break out of this mould they usually encountered difficulties. Sir Ronald Storrs had tried to widen his administration on the social front in Cyprus in 1931, and had suffered a nationalist riot in which Government House had been burnt down. "If I might suggest, sir, no more mixed tea parties," was the recommendation of the officer commanding the British troops. To his mind it was a clear case of cause and effect. That was the way the *Raj* worked—it was a kind of idol which demanded worship and could not afford to be familiar. It stood on its imperial dignity, since it had little else to stand on except the prestige of the Royal Navy and a sprinkling of garrison troops.

In fact, there were great virtues in the system by and large. Backward and slow-moving it might be, but concealed under its rigid attention to discipline and order were the means by which a *new* order could be built. An excellent and devoted civil service provided the infrastructure of government: a working machine which could be handed over intact. Far more importantly it provided the political frame in which the colonies could liberate themselves, however gradually and painfully. An escape clause had been built into the social contract of British rule, and it was one which progressive opinion in London was aware of and willing to adopt. The war was hardly over before a correspondent in the *New Statesman and Nation* remarked on the speedy growth and spread of nationalism in West Africa and on the need for a "very substantial widening" of elective forms of government. The same was noted of Malaya; indeed, of Asia as a whole. "The political life of Asia no longer runs at a leisurely tempo," the same journal decided in January 1947. "The Western Powers . . . now face politically minded people who in many cases helped to win the war against Japan and now demand their independence. Nothing can stem the tide of their conscious maturity."

This was above all true of Ceylon, which had been occupied during the Napoleonic wars and after a century and a half of what *The Times* patronisingly called "tutelage" had been passing through rapid stages of constitutional advance in the thirties to the point where it was ready to follow India into independence within the Commonwealth. The smoothness of the transfer from colony into dominion was widely applauded in the British press, and the dignity and goodwill on both sides was noted as the Duke of Gloucester, making the first of several appearances in this role, read the King's speech at the opening of the new Parliament.

Burma, almost next door, was more troublesome. But then Burma had not been acquired without bloodshed: it had been forcibly occupied and its king deposed at the height of Jingo expansionism—the *Punch* cartoon of the time featuring a British soldier in the act of kicking the backside of the "Burmese Toad" was a period piece which most Englishmen were now anxious to forget. And whereas Ceylon had provided the headquarters for Admiral Lord Louis Mountbatten's command and a bastion of British power in the recent war against Japan, several Burmese leaders had actively collaborated with the enemy in the "Greater South East Asia Co-Prosperity Sphere" and in the aftermath of victory were demanding their freedom outside the Commonwealth.

What they asked, they were given. The Commonwealth, said Prime Minister Attlee, wanted no unwilling members. Even Mr.

Churchill, who in opposition thundered against this "fearful retrogression" in the East, had not pretended during the last years of his wartime coalition that such nations could be held against their will: and on Independence Day *The Times,* in its leader "Salute to Burma," spoke generously on behalf of the British people when it wished the Burmese people well in the course they had chosen for themselves. Two days later it reported the final ceremonies in Rangoon which had taken place at an hour carefully selected by Burmese astrologers, anxious not to repeat Indian mistakes:

> The Union Jack which had floated from the mast of the Assembly building, when the formal transfer of power took place in bright moonlight, was then stowed away on board the *Birmingham* on its way to Britain, where it will be kept in the British Museum.

And where better? The symbolism of the whole incident, even down to the use of a warship named after that arch-Imperialist Joseph Chamberlain's native city, is enough to evoke the ironic laughter of the gods.

*   *   *

In Palestine, the third of its most immediate post-war colonial problems, the ruling power could not even wait for the astrologers before hauling down the flag.

It was a problem the British had brought on themselves by quite gratuitously announcing in 1917 that they would "view with favour" the establishment in Palestine of a "national home for the Jewish people," and then in 1921 accepting a mandate from the League of Nations over this troublesome territory which they had conquered from the Turks and which two thousand years earlier had been a thorn in the Roman flesh.

The Balfour Declaration of 1917 that set the whole process in train had been one of those mixtures of humanitarianism and self-seeking which have always marked British imperial thinking. To help a small people find sanctuary in what had once been their historic homeland was compassionate and just. It was also very politic in terms of the sympathy and financial support it could attract for Britain among the powerful community of American Jews at a dark time in the struggle with the Kaiser's Germany. What exactly it all meant, whether it in fact meant anything, was concealed in Mr. Balfour's elegant phraseology—he was a great artist at definitions. No one then glimpsed the inherent contradictions which the Declaration itself contained when it went on to add that nothing in it should be taken as prejudicing "the civil and religious rights of the existing non-Jewish communities in Palestine." The vast majority of these, outnumbering the Jews already in the country by nearly ten to one, were of course Arabs, and what no doubt was in Mr. Balfour's and the government's mind was that no great harm would be done by allowing a small Jewish enclave to grow up in their midst. No one then foresaw—perhaps no one could reasonably have been expected to foresee—that the tightening of immigration quotas for entry into the United States and pogroms in Poland and in Hitler's Germany would turn the influx of Jewish immigrants from a trickle into a flood and then in 1945 into a torrent sweeping away all the barriers erected against it. That a cult of Zionism should turn into a mass migration was as shattering a surprise as the rapid spread of Arab nationalism throughout the Middle East.

By 1925, 34,000 Jews a year were coming to the Holy Land, an annual intake of more than half the total Jewish population there in 1918. Signs of the coming storm were not wanting, for in a burst of Arab chauvinism in 1929 over a hundred Jews were killed in three days of rioting and over three hundred were wounded. As the immigration pressures built up during the thirties and the British wavered over the quotas to be imposed, torn between compassion and their traditional fondness for the Arabs, both the main Palestinian communities became more and more incensed and militant, uniting only in their distrust of the mandatory power. The disturbances continued, rising to a new peak in 1936 with fresh Arab attacks and a general strike of dock workers in Jaffa: the embers were still burning when the world conflict broke out in 1939, revealing that the British had lost the sympathy of Arab popular opinion throughout the Levant and had come to be regarded not as liberators but as oppressors and betrayers of Arab rights. Thus the Mufti of Jerusalem, leader of the Palestinian Arabs, went over to the Nazis, as did Rashid Ali in the abortive "Golden Square" rising in Iraq, while

Egypt, though bound by her treaty obligations to give Britain a base, declared herself a non-belligerent.

Of the two warring races at the time, the Jews had by far the greater cause for dissatisfaction with the ruling power, for by the provisions of a British White Paper published in 1939 a quota had been set for Jewish immigration allowing them an entry of 75,000 over a five-year period, after which all immigration was to cease. A previous commission of enquiry had envisaged a small Jewish enclave within Palestine in treaty relationship with Britain, but under the White Paper provisions it was clear that Palestine was seen as basically Arab territory and the Jews must remain in one form or another as a permanent minority within it. One lesson of this was that Arab violence had paid, and it was a lesson not lost on militant Jewish circles.

In spite of this, throughout Hitler's war the Palestinian Jews behaved impeccably: they had even less to hope for from the Third Reich than from their lukewarm British protectors. A Jewish Brigade, attached to the British Army, served with distinction in the invasion of Sicily and Italy and later with the main forces in northern Europe. Their reward in the terrible condition of post-war Jewry was the British Labour government's implementation of the embargo on Jewish immigration into Palestine—an act which was not by intention inhumane, which was meant to be realistic in terms of the country, but which ignored both the huge social problem which Hitler's "Final Solution" had created, with its flood of tortured and anguished refugees, and also the physical fact that the Jews already in Palestine now amounted to half a million resolute, well-armed and able people, many of them trained in the use of modern weapons and techniques.

It took the British some time to realise the size and scope of the problem. National Home was one thing: the Jewish occupation of Palestine was quite another. It was not for this that the mandate had been created or accepted. A situation in which the British had tried to protect Jews from Arab terrorism was about to be transformed into one where Britons were subjected to a far more efficient and deadly terrorism by Jews. The Jewish Agency, which officially represented settler interests, remained diplomatic and correct, deploring each outbreak of violence. Not so the secret organisations of the Hagana and its associated force, the Palmach, boasting between them a sizeable field army of some 20,000 men, with more static units of perhaps double that number, or the still more secret terrorist splinter groups of the Irgun Zvai Leumi and the "Stern Gang," where quite different estimates had been made of Britain's will to override or her physical power to contain a really determined drive to create a Jewish state by force. The appeal to the world's compassion for the victims of the Nazi concentration camps was one wing of this offensive, the Gandhian one, and God knows it had merit in the light of what the European Jews had suffered. But the second arm owed more to the example of Ireland than to anything else. What British-administered Palestine was now to see was a return to the principles of Captain Moonlight, the killings in Phoenix Park, the "Troubles," the gradual process by which a ruling power could be driven first towards repression (as in the Coercion Acts and the employment of the Black and Tans), counter-productive in itself, and then by one violent stage after another to despair and ultimate surrender. It had worked in Ireland in the aftermath of one world war when Britain had seemed to most of the world invincibly strong: why should it not work in Palestine in the aftermath of a second war which had revealed Britain to be vulnerable and weak? No doubt this was as much in the minds of the extremist Jewish leaders in 1946 as Irish precedents had been in the minds of the Indian Congress two decades earlier—the Empire had always been, and was to remain, a kind of tutorial for self-government in which the Irish were the maverick professors.

The results on the ground had been grim in Ireland, and they were to be no better between Dan and Beersheba. But when observing them we must remember that the life and liberty of a small people was passionately felt to be at stake, just as to-day the plight of the exiled Palestinian Arabs lies at the root of Middle East unrest. We must understand the ideology that lay behind the violence: it was that that made it so formidable, so hard to resist.

Throughout 1946 the waves of terrorist attack built up. In mid-June, an armed Jewish commando raided the British Officers' Club in Tel Aviv and kidnapped five officers. In response, the British detained two thousand Jews for questioning. A number of secret arms dumps were uncovered—one most ingeniously hidden, where only the intrepid would have cared to look for it, in the bulls' stall of a village settlement.

These were mere preliminaries. On July 22 there took place in Jerusalem an event almost as shocking as any in the recent war. Just after mid-day a civilian truck drew up to the basement of the King David Hotel, which housed both the British military headquarters and the principal offices of the government Secretariat. From the truck emerged a small group of Jews dressed as Arabs on the normal milk delivery round. Forcing their way past the doorkeeper, they held up the kitchen staff at gunpoint, unloaded milk churns stuffed with high explosives under the Secretariat offices, and decamped. A British officer who heard suspicious sounds and came to investigate was shot dead on the spot. Some moments later a huge explosion ripped off a whole corner of the five-storey building destroying twenty-five rooms and killing well over a hundred people. "A dastardly crime" committed by "desperadoes" was the Jewish Agency's description of the act. "Insensate fanaticism, the product of a perverted propaganda," proclaimed The Times, but it neglected to draw the conclusion soon to be drawn by Chairman Mao that power comes from the barrel of a gun.

What stemmed from the atrocity was appeasement on the British side, the summoning of a conference in London to discuss the situation. When the conference was seen to be getting nowhere, there was simply a return to terrorism and an increase in illegal immigration by sea. Ten thousand a month was one estimate of immigrant numbers. An attempt was made to deport those caught to Cyprus: this caused violent demonstrations among the Jews of Haifa. In September a British major was killed in Tel Aviv in the ruins of his bombed home, and next day a British sergeant was shot in the back in broad daylight in the street. "In all its history," wrote The Times in a special article, "the British Army has seldom had duties so delicate and dissatisfying. . . . The Army is caught inevitably in a vicious circle of terrorism, curfews, searches, arrests, interrogations, detention, deportation, complaints of oppression, mutual personal hostility between citizen and soldier." During November, despite attempts at détente and the ending of the curfew, a railway station was blown up, six railway police were killed, and bombs were placed in the income tax offices in the centre of Jerusalem. Early in December Jews armed with hand grenades attacked the residence of the British G.O.C., and just after Christmas, to round up a year of savagery, a British major was kidnapped from a hotel in Natanya,

was given eighteen lashes with a rawhide whip and dumped in the
street in his underclothes, while two British N.C.O.s were given
similar treatment in the Zoological Gardens at Tel Aviv.

By 1947 the British had had enough.

> Despite Great Britain's arduous toil
> The Holy Land is barren soil,
> The awkward fact she cannot gloss
> That Palestine is Britain's cross,
> A heavy cross, a grievous care,
> A load almost too great to bear,

wrote that prolific versifier, "Sagittarius," in the radical *New Statesman.* As a committed Zionist, he went on to add that "Britain must
her path pursue" since the cross was carried by the Jew. This was
not, however, the general feeling among the British public at the
time as day after day they read of fresh atrocities. It was not what
"mandate" had been in the carefree days when such commodities
had been handed out like bonuses to deserving clients.

So the cheque was simply returned to drawer—to the United
Nations, the heirs and assigns of the League, for another commission
and report. When the British timetable for withdrawal was published
in the autumn of 1947 *The Times* remarked smugly with the satisfaction of a man handing over an intolerable burden: "The United
Nations will have in this hard task ahead of it no more loyal,
sympathetic and it may be added experienced supporter than Great
Britain." Supporter, yes: but in the wings. As with Pilate on another
occasion there was another public washing of hands, and some of
the spleen of wasted years was vented:

> It is not surprising that the British soldier, as he goes out to search
> for the murderers of his comrades, and the British parent, as he or
> she scans the casualty lists or reads of this country being denounced
> for imperialism and atrocities, feels that here is a burden equitably
> to be borne on international shoulders.

On May 18, 1948, at midnight, somewhat ahead of schedule, the mandate ended and the country was left to whatever salvation it could find. Perhaps the British had done a little better than their Roman predecessors: they had not themselves destroyed Jerusalem. "End of a Mission" ran *The Times* leader next day.

Confronted with a clash of world forces which they could not contain and with a schism which they could not close, the British might well have gone from Palestine sooner.

"Historic tragedy" . . . "melancholy tale" . . . and similar ejaculations made up the rest of the story. But essentially it was the simple lesson that Britain no longer had the power or the will to assert herself imperially in hostile conditions.

* * *

The decisions to give independence to Ceylon and Burma had really taken themselves, for clearly once the linchpin of British power in India was removed, the dependencies on her doorstep could not be held either. This went also for the patchwork of assimilated and semi-assimilated states in Malaya which, as a preliminary to full self-government, had been turned into a federation in 1948, the same year in which Burma and Ceylon achieved their freedom and Palestine was surrendered.

Towards the rest of the colonial Empire, however, British attitudes were more ambivalent and reserved. Even Churchill had accepted that large and advanced territories could not be retained against their wishes and that there must come a time when even Trusts had to be wound up, but what should one think of backward African territories, strategic fortresses in the Mediterranean and Red Sea, island chains like the West Indies and fragments in the Pacific? How fast should one go and how seriously could one take the notion of future "responsible" government in the bush?

Basically there were three viewpoints.

In the autumn of 1947 Sir Stafford Cripps had told a somewhat startled conference of Governors of African colonies called home to

London that Britain must be prepared to change attitudes and "force the pace" in the dependent territories. Clearly he was as much out of sympathy with the old traditionalist imperial thinking as any other left-wing intellectual who found his antipathy to "Colonel Blimp" echoed by the *New Statesman and Nation*'s ever-fertile "Sagittarius" in a poem entitled *The Old Buffer*.

> Some empires of antiquity collapsed without
>   declining
> While some declined at ease to break the fall,
> But Britain's ocean empire, where the sun is ever
>   shining,
> Has no idea of passing out at all.
> Unshrinkable, unsinkable,
> Its exit is unthinkable
> For Britain rules by her Imperial right. . . .

Intelligent people at home, wrote correspondent Rita Hinden in this same journal—meaning of course people of her own leftist political persuasion—had long felt "conscience stricken" about the Empire and the turgid, reactionary courses which to their eyes seemed to be followed even under a Socialist administration.

All those in this corner of the field cried "Forward!" finding the pace of advance abysmally slow. Not every Socialist would have agreed with them for one of Mr. Attlee's most powerful ministers, Herbert Morrison, had gone on record during the war as proclaiming that to give independence to backward tribal territories would be like giving a latchkey to a child of ten: and, of course, to the Tory right the rising pace of de-colonisation was deplored without reservations as an ill-considered experiment equally harmful to both rulers and ruled. Even the moderates shared some of these suspicions: a viewpoint well expressed in an article by Hugh Thomas in *The Spectator* in the summer of 1948:

> Now at what stage should self-government be granted and for what reasons, and after what preparation for so far-reaching a decision? Certainly not when a few persons discontented with their lot decide

that the time has arrived for them to take a hand in things. No; there must be a general advance in the social field to justify such an important step.

The third view, the official view held by Mr. Arthur Creech Jones, Attlee's Colonial Secretary, was that Britain must experiment, but not rashly—he left the extravaganzas to the Ministry of Food which in its White Paper was dreaming dreams of planting three and a quarter million acres of East African bush to provide 800,000 tons of groundnuts a year and bring margarine to every British breakfast table. Nevertheless, there were solid advances to which the Colonial Secretary could point with pride in the debates on the colonial estimates—new constitutions for Nigeria and the Gold Coast in particular which had brought representative government to both these important territories, the front runners of black Africa.

And in this viewpoint Mr. Creech Jones had support in unexpected and traditionalist places, for three years earlier, while the war with Hitler was still raging, the *éminence grise* of the Colonial Office, Sir Ralph Furse, who for years had been personally responsible for the selection of almost every official in the service, had written a memorandum in which he had suggested that perhaps Britain had been too intent on following the Roman model of promoting only the physical and material well-being of her colonies, and that more room should be found for the Greek spirit—for the spirit, in other words, of encouraging that intellectual enquiry which was likely to be manifested in the colonial territories not by tribal chiefs but by the increasing forces of educated native opinion. Furthermore, in a *Times* leader published before Sir Ralph Furse's memorandum actually saw the light of day, his message was underlined:

The system of indirect rule, however, with its policy on our part of *laissez faire* and "let them make their own mistakes" has led to some very serious consequences. In some countries where education has developed, largely outside the tribal system, an intelligentsia has grown up which has no part in the local government, often directed by illiterate and animist chieftains. . . . Agitators make capital out of such situations, while administrators, trying to be loyal to the principle of indirect rule, are surprised at this growing outbreak of hostility. Unless the policy is changed we shall be forced to grant self-government to colonial peoples, perhaps too soon, after repeated strikes, misunderstandings and exasperation. . . . In most of our colonies the people are being rushed from a pre-feudal, even from a pre-tribal, stage . . . into the modern world in a generation or two.

Here was the problem set fairly and inescapably. In the Ashanti country of the Gold Coast the village councils of elders were at precisely the same stage of development as had existed in the Saxon kingdom in King Alfred's time: and how could this be squared with the demands of an educated *élite* existing within the same country? Yet the trend from tribalism towards parliamentary conditions, as *The Times* pointed out in another article a year later, "was natural and inevitable."

But inevitable *when?* Gradualism seemed to be the answer. No one as yet who was not existing on the extreme radical left, well out of the radius of Mr. Attlee's moderate Social Democratic government, could see "responsibility" and independence just around the corner for territories whose hinterland had been revealed for the first time to the eyes of the white man by H. M. Stanley's epic crossing of the continent in 1877. In one of her lectures Margery Perham records the remark made to her by a senior official as late as 1939: "Well, at any rate in Africa we can be sure that we have unlimited time in which to work." Even ten years later it might have seemed a reasonable assumption. If this had not been the case, the British government would not still have been contemplating a vastly enlarged new Colonial Office, the site for which had been selected close to the mother of parliaments. It was never built.

*   *   *

Towards the African as a species the British attitude, for all its humanitarianism, still bore traces of traditional thinking about the innate racial inferiority of the black peoples and that still older dictum of Aristotle that some men are by nature free and others slaves.

The delight a civilised man could take in the vigour and colour of Africa has left its mark on English literature, from the journals of David Livingstone to Lord Lugard's *Dual Mandate,* and on another plane, the works of Rider Haggard and Edgar Wallace's *Sanders of the River.* It is a literature of affection which reflects the very real devotion of the rulers for the ruled, for the noble savage like Wallace's Bosambo.

For what were Africans but children? Children to be fed, encouraged, guarded, guided, and sometimes punished. Appealing little objects. And the more African, the more "bush" they were, the better. Take Blore, the District Officer in Joyce Cary's *Mister Johnson:* definitely a Lugardist with the principles of indirect rule through tribal chiefs graven on his heart:

> Blore, bald and pensive as Buddha, sits at the table watching Johnson through his small, gold spectacles. His expression is mild and benign, but the truth is that he dislikes all Negro clerks and especially Johnson. He is a deeply sentimental man, a conservative nature. He likes all old things in their old places and he dreads all change, all innovation. To his mind a messenger in a white gown, even if he speaks and writes English, is a gentleman; but a clerk in trousers, even if he can barely do either, is an upstart, dangerous to the established order of things.

Not all British administrators were Blores. Indeed, Cary's book contains the portrait of a much younger official, Rudbeck, far more sympathetic towards the aspiring Negro, far more prepared to accept him as a man. But significantly it is Rudbeck, who has encouraged and spoiled poor Mr. Johnson, who is called upon to condemn and execute him in the end. To such men, some of them barely out of their teens, administering huge tracts of territory in semi-savage conditions, the educated and westernised African was liable to be both an embarrassment and a nuisance. Whether the Empire produced the English public school or the public school the Empire remains a moot point, but certainly the product of those schools had been trained in a patriarchal tradition which made them far more at ease with Mohammedan emirs and the country-bred boys who made such excellent *askaris* and non-commissioned officers in the native army and police than with the "upstart" (in Blore's terms) products of the mission schools and the increasingly vocal bourgeois of the West African coastal towns. It was a reflection of what had happened in India, with the British admiration for princes and peasants and their contempt for the *babu* clerks who had really kept the wheels of the administration turning.

In fact, the British—which is odd in a nation of gamblers—had always backed, and were always to back, the losing horses in the colonial stakes. Mr. Johnson—an original, too original a soul—had lived out his pathetically short life in an up-country district among "bush" natives whom he despised, but in the big coastal towns of Nigeria and the Gold Coast he had a host of successors. The more humble served in the British forces in the war against Hitler— 30,000 of them from the Gold Coast alone—and found their griev- ances in a post-war world of rising prices and diminishing oppor- tunities common to ex-servicemen elsewhere. The more sophisticated and adventurous tended to go overseas, to universities and poly- technics in America and Britain, where they encountered for the first time both working democracy and the colour bar. It was an ex- plosive mixture. It would be untrue to say that Black Nationalism was born directly of such experiences, for it had been proclaimed in a sense by Toussaint l'Ouverture in Haiti in Bonaparte's time, but the West Indian Marcus Garvey's call of "Africa for the Afri- cans" was inspired by just this expatriate feeling, soon to be given greater point by African leaders like Kwame Nkrumah and Jomo Kenyatta who were not only to proclaim a slogan for a free Africa but to bring it about in their own lifetime. And inevitably the thing started—as all revolutions start—where a middle class had es- tablished itself and acquired grievances and ambitions: in African terms, in the big and prosperous capitals of Lagos and Accra.

*   *   *

The Gold Coast, which as Ghana was destined to become the first black African dominion and later the first African republic within the Commonwealth, had at one time been regarded as one of the most burdensome of British possessions. Though the "settler" colony on the coast had been transferred to the Crown as early as 1821, it was not till the first years of the new century, after a series of extremely hard-fought and sanguinary wars against the Ashanti tribes, that the British had established their rule inland over a territory no larger than Britain herself, cursed with one of the world's most killing climates. Sir Ronald Ross's researches into the cause of malaria and the introduction of the cocoa bean brought about a radical change in British attitudes, and by the time of the outbreak of the First World War the territory had built up an impressive economic position as a colony which actually paid its own way—almost the only one, Malaya apart, that did.

This economic advance, shielded from the worst vices of exploitation which had disgraced the Congo, brought about something quite new in Africa—a middle class of merchants, middlemen and entrepreneurs—and was mirrored, in turn, in political advances which had begun in the 1880s with the appointment of an unofficial African member to the Legislative Council and the introduction of the elective system at municipal level. Before the end of the First World War the Legislative Council of twenty included six Africans, three of them tribal chiefs, three of them representative of the coastal business community; and by the constitution granted in 1925 the pace of advance was stepped up to provide nine elected Africans in the Legislature. In 1946, under Mr. Attlee's government, the next stage was reached with the grant of representative government—of thirty members of the Legislative Council, eighteen were to be elected as against six officials and six "nominated" members. Additionally, the Governor's Executive Council of eleven now included three Africans.

Almost unremarked in the course of this steady constitutional advance towards self-rule, a very unofficial and unconstitutional body calling itself the Pan African Congress had met in 1945, not in Africa but in Manchester, and there assembled had given its *diktat* to the world in a demand for "autonomy and independence" in the whole of black Africa. One of the signatories was a young man from the Gold Coast by the name of Kwame Nkrumah, who was soon to be invited home by the doyen of black African politicians, Dr. Joseph Danquah, to become organising secretary of his United Gold Coast Convention party. It was like Kerensky asking Lenin to tea. Neither Dr. Danquah* nor his party were to figure for much longer in the

---

* Dr. Danquah was twice imprisoned by Nkrumah after independence. After being held on the second occasion for a year without trial, he died in gaol in February 1965.

political life of the colony, soon to be dominated by the rising star of Nkrumah and his breakaway Convention People's party.

In a sense it was strange that the Gold Coast should have been setting this trend in black nationalism and not the much larger and grander Nigeria next door. But then Nigeria included over a hundred tribal groupings and no fewer than 248 languages, whereas the Gold Coast was small and compact and there was not, as in the northern territory of Nigeria, the counterweight of powerful autocractic Islamic regimes deeply opposed to the pretensions of the Christian and pagan peoples of the coast.

In 1948, not long after Nkrumah's return, a massive demonstration of ex-servicemen was mounted in Accra against the cost of living. It was a real enough issue, skilfully worked on by propagandists with other ends in view. What resulted was a miniature Amritsar. By accident or design the procession strayed from the agreed route and appeared to be marching on the government headquarters in the castle of Christiansborg. The police, overwhelmed by the sheer size of the demonstration, failed to shepherd the marchers back on to their route; stones were thrown; the police opened fire; and there were casualties. The sequel was a major riot in which a mob of 50,000 ranged the streets of Accra; twenty-nine persons were killed and 237 injured; the Gold Coast Regiment had to be called out to restore order; and the trouble spread to other towns. Naturally enough the schools were in the forefront of the agitation. At Adisadel College the headmaster was appalled to see his three hundred boys, high on palm wine, occupying the campus where, according to one observer, they behaved "like a pack of wild beasts." Among the songs and slogans they chanted was Kipling's *Land of Our Birth*.

What had caused these disturbances in a hitherto peaceful colony? Most commentators at home put it down to the severe increase in the cost of living. But *The Spectator,* while agreeing that the outbreak was more economic than political, also ventured to think that the trouble had been part of a still-confused groping towards something new that was common to colonial peoples everywhere. Clearly, something would have to be done to look into the whole deplorable affair, and the natural British response was to set up a committee of enquiry, the Watson Committee, which sat under the chairmanship of the Recorder of Bury St. Edmund's, Mr. Aiken Watson, K.C.

From this body of modest status and competence emerged a quite shattering report which in effect rejected the whole concept of indirect rule by hinting "fairly bluntly" (in *The Times*'s words) that tribal chiefs should now be eliminated from the colonial system in favour of more literate and educated persons. The commission's recommendation was for a Legislature of forty-five to be chosen by elected regional councils and for an Executive Council of nine, five of whom would be African members of that Legislature, vested with powers to initiate policy instead of merely advising the Governor. The commission was, in fact, recommending government by a cabinet with a black majority. "This is going very far," noted *The Spectator* of these revolutionary suggestions—and it was certainly further and faster than the Labour government in London was prepared to go at the time. But one committee of enquiry always breeds another, and barely had the Watson Commission laid down the pen than another, the Coussey Commission, an all-African commission under a coloured judge of the Gold Coast High Court, took it up and produced something more revolutionary still. Its report is indeed a document of exceptional and historic interest: a blue-print for black African independence as remarkable in its way as the great Declaration made at Philadelphia on July 4, 1776.

Mr. Justice Coussey began by outlining constitutional developments in the Gold Coast and then referred to that quickening pace in men's aspirations which had come about as a result of global war.

Of the new forces at work perhaps the most important was the attitude of mind of the ex-Servicemen who now returned from the battlefields of the world. For the first time a relatively large percentage of the inhabitants of this country had travelled beyond its territorial limits and had seen new lands and other peoples. They returned in a knowledge of other nations, possessing no higher standards of cultural, social and intellectual development, who nevertheless are now ordering their own affairs. Moreover, having fought in defence of freedom, they considered it their right that they should have some share in the government of their own land.

Yet constitutional developments still lagged seriously behind these longings.

> To concede an African unofficial majority in the Legislature, without at the same time granting some measure of responsibility, represented a well-known constitutional defect. . . . This committee was composed of men of widely divergent political views. . . . The fact, therefore, that there is unanimity on most of the essential changes envisaged in our Recommendation is evidence enough, if any were needed, of the almost country-wide yearning for radical change.

Yet it was intended to be change within the British model—Mr. Justice Coussey, himself a product of the British system and heir to the principles of Burke and Coke, was insistent on this point. His radicalism was a British radicalism. The responsibility of the Executive to the Legislature was his guiding light and formed the major recommendation of his committee. And he was as cautious as any British constitutionalist in his suggestion that the universal adult suffrage which he now proposed for the Gold Coast should be qualified by the concept of "indirect election"—of electing in effect electors and not representatives at first—in order to do away with the dangers he foresaw of illiterate tribesmen falling victim to "the charlatan and the demagogue."

Had Mr. Justice Coussey foreseen the dictatorship to be erected in his country before many years were over? His proposed constitution certainly attempted to provide against it. But he had not been able to provide against the *"Führer"* concept which was to make its way into the Gold Coast in the shape of Dr. Nkrumah, certainly in his last phase a demagogue if not a charlatan. After the Coussey report, everything was set on the pattern now so familiar. Dr. Nkrumah still lacked one prerequisite of the fully fledged nationalist leader: he had not yet been to gaol. But this was easily remedied, and early in 1950, as a result of his activities in the "Positive Action" campaign, he was given the three years to qualify him. In the elections which followed under the Coussey provisions his Convention People's party swept to victory at the polls.

The British were left in their usual dilemma. They could keep Nkrumah in gaol or exile him to the Seychelles Islands—a course they had taken with the Shah of Persia during the Second World War and were to adopt again with another militant nationalist leader, Archbishop Makarios of Cyprus. They could outlaw the Convention

People's party as they had outlawed the Indian Congress. Or they could do a deal with it. The liberal-minded Governor, Sir Charles Arden Clarke, adopted this last solution: he released his prisoner and invited him to Christiansborg Castle to become leader of government business, which was the premiership in all but name. Huge rejoicings broke out among the people: a sheep was sacrificed; Dr. Nkrumah paddled the ritual seven times barefoot in its blood; and proceedings terminated with the singing by vast crowds of the hymn *Lead Kindly Light*—a truly African occasion.

So to the general astonishment the Gold Coast was launched on the last lap to independence, its way made smooth by the tact and avuncular kindness of the Governor and by his protégé's impressive restraint under the few remaining leading strings. March 6, 1957, was selected as Independence Day, and as the time drew near the *Ghana Evening News,* the Convention People's newspaper, watched it with rapt attention. "We have the right to govern ourselves" was the message it carried at its masthead. "We prefer Self-Government with danger to Servitude in Tranquility. We have the right to live as Men."

Its issues for that winter and spring make poignant reading. On January 7, 1957, to take one:

IT IS COMING
GHANA INDEPENDENCE DAY—MARCH 6th 1957
58 DAYS MORE.

This was the form repeated each morning—"Only 57 Days More." "Only 56." As the gap narrowed, an anxious concern began to be expressed as to whether the coming achievement might not somehow be marred by mistakes and misbehaviours unbecoming to Africa. Thus, on learning that certain members of the Legislative Assembly were talking of boycotting the last session under the *Raj,* the paper rounded on them with earnest exhortations to be good:

This is the time for us to demonstrate that we are not only nationalists but statesmen. . . . Mind you [it added], if you do not make hay while the sun shines, your star will never be seen anywhere anymore.

All the same, even the *Ghana Evening News* could not always remain patiently in full control of its emotions, and on the publication in London in February of a White Paper setting out the terms of the agreed dominion constitution, it burst into paeans of triumph a full month ahead of schedule:

> REJOICE. Ghana has achieved Self-government. . . . Independence—the inalienable right of the Ghana people—has at last been achieved and Ghana voices yell rapturous strains to enrich the symphony of an admiring world. Now onward to the future. . . . Watchman of the night, throw open the gates.

As February drew on the tempo mounted—one can sense the excitement not only in the content of the news pages but even in the increased inkiness of the paper's type. On February 12 (Only 22 days more):

> Everyone in this country is agog with eager expectancy to see March 6th 1957. . . . On March 6th this beloved country of ours will break the last fetters of imperial octopus amidst one terrific din of jubilation and spree. March 6th will see this country donning the toga of full nationhood. March 6th will mark the beginning of the Golden Age of Ghana.

Next day the headlines quoted Dr. Nkrumah as saying that they would make Ghana a paradise—and on the same day in smaller print the Minister of the Interior was reported as introducing a bill making it a misdemeanour to insult the Ghanaian flag.

Only a cynic, however, reading through these old files, could fail to be moved by the dominant effect, which was one of joy. For Saturday, February 23, a "Grand Picnic" was announced for Saltpond, a town on the coast west of Accra. Prices were not exorbitant—Gents 3/s, Ladies 2/s, Doubles 5/s—considering that the All Stars Band would be playing and all cabinet ministers would be taking part. "Saltpond will Quake," the paper prophesied with glee. No less natural was the sense of escape from the demon of imperialism, into

whose coffin the paper's cartoonist showed a black man hammering
in the last nail, exclaiming as he did so: "Lord grant that it may not
rise again even on the Resurrection Day."

This critical note was a little out of key—the *Ghana Evening
News* on the whole had come not so much to bury Caesar as to
praise the *patria*. And on Independence Day, that long awaited
March 6, the moment came:

> The Black Star is hoisted in
> Eternal Glory.
> Ghana is
> Born!!
> To-day We're Free.

"Jubilation ran riot," its chief reporter wrote. "With the cheerful din
of exploding enthusiasm and the universal exultation of five million
triumphant people died 113 years of imperialist dominion."

In London *The Times* took things more calmly. "To-day," ran its
leader, "Ghana is the first Black African State within the Commonwealth." But it did not elaborate on the achievement or the
message or moral of these events.

XVIII

Suez

In the Union of South Africa the message was duly noted and was followed almost at once in the fall of the pro-Commonwealth Smuts government before the forces of white Afrikaner nationalism.

The admittance to the Commonwealth of the brown Asian dominions had been accepted at the Cape with resignation, and when in 1949 Mr. Nehru's India had gone further and announced its intention of throwing off direct allegiance to the Crown and becoming a Republic, if possible within the Commonwealth, even this revolutionary concept had been swallowed without too much fuss. Was not India in South African eyes a bulwark against Communism? She was certainly too important a country to be rejected from the club without attempts being made to find a formula acceptable to all: and this was done by India's recognition of the British monarch as "Head of the Commonwealth."

The importance of the Crown, which had long been diminishing, was thus further whittled away. Even the loyalist Smuts had come to claim no more for it than that it was "something of a reality," but he was deeply troubled by thoughts of where this gradual and persistent weakening of the old "bonds" would lead. It had led to the erection on African soil of the black Dominion of Ghana, which everyone could see would soon be the Republic of Ghana, and for

South Africa this was the last straw, the beginning of the white "backlash" which was to lead by stages to the doctrine of *Apartheid* and the Union's own departure from the Commonwealth.

In Britain, however, Ghana's independence raised hardly a stir. The silence was almost deafening. Few cared. Empire and Commonwealth had both ceased to interest the public. The intellectual weeklies like the *New Statesman* and *The Spectator* were committed and concerned, lamenting each setback and applauding each advance. But to the successors of those who had wept for Gordon and danced in the streets on Mafeking Night, the whole thing had become a bore. Very few ex-servicemen had served in West Africa or seen anything of it beyond a view of Freetown from the sweltering decks of a troopship on convoy round the Cape. Burma, Malaya and Singapore were places best forgotten, symbols of defeat. But in one area—in the Middle East—a heroic tradition had been built up in the exploits of the Eighth Army, and this was something which had entered the national consciousness as no other event had done apart from the Battle of Britain, because it was there in the Western Desert that victory over Hitlerism had begun.

The "Desert Rats" had been based in Egypt. The spiritual home of the British staffs, the "Gaberdine Swine" and "Short Range Desert Group," had been in Cairo's famed mausoleum of Shepherds' Hotel, on the "fish slab" of the Gezira swimming pool and on the Turf Club roof. The troops from the fighting front on a night out at Dolls' or the Cairo brothels, like their support troops in the verminous barracks of Abbasiyah and the camps along the Canal, had a strong emotional attachment to the country which they both derided and enjoyed. Some writers have supposed a natural antipathy between the British and their Egyptian hosts—this is an error, for on the whole British troops and Egyptian waiters, chowkidars, taxi drivers, dragomen, hostesses and whores got on extremely well. But there remained a strong undercurrent of resentment of Egypt's self-chosen role as a non-belligerent in the struggle against Hitler and of her sullen refusal to show proper gratitude towards her deliverers.

Much of this ill-feeling on both sides arose out of the peculiar relationship which had existed between Britain and Egypt since the occupation of the country in Gladstone's time. The British had never incorporated Egypt directly into the Empire, because to have done so would have grossly offended the French with their own cultural and economic ties with Cairo. But just as certainly they had never been able to leave Egypt alone. It was too strategic a site. From 1919 onwards there had been a sequence of riots, repressions, attempts to govern the country without actually appearing to be doing so, and finally a solemn treaty in 1936 by which Egypt was recognised as fully sovereign and independent, subject to a continuing British presence in the Canal Zone for a further twenty years.

Blessed are not the benefactors. Apart from saving the country from the Axis in 1940 and 1942, Britain had largely created modern Egypt by the reforms of Lord Cromer's time. All she earned was a hatred which became more obsessive as the years passed and she persisted in staying on. In 1951 even the corrupt regime of King Farouk found it politically necessary to wave the nationalist flag and denounce the 1936 treaty—it did not prevent the monarchy's fall or the accession of more militantly nationalist rulers, who in 1954 managed to effect the complete withdrawal of British combat troops from the Suez base at the mere cost of re-affirming the Convention of Constantinople of 1888 which guaranteed freedom of navigation in the Canal.

Was not this enough? The British had provided Egypt not only with a viable economy and a sound financial system but also with a standing grievance of the kind so helpful to nationalist leaders. Colonel Nasser would not have established his power so quickly if the Suez Canal Company had been an Egyptian and not an international body and if the ghost of the British presence had not still lived on. The real affront to Egypt's pride was to come from Washington, where the American Secretary of State, Mr. John Foster Dulles, suddenly declined to sponsor any longer a grandiose scheme for building a new dam across the Nile at Aswan. But it was on British heads that Nasser's fury exploded. He had learned of Dulles's rejection of his cherished scheme while on a visit to another "Third World" leader, President Tito of Yugoslavia, and his response, which was to nationalise the Suez Canal and seize the resources of the Suez Canal Company, was exquisitely timed to embarrass not Mr. Dulles, a man of notably thick skin, but the British Prime Minister, Sir Anthony Eden, who at the very moment when the news reached London was entertaining the King of Iraq, an Arab satellite, to dinner in Downing Street.

Sir Anthony himself, as his memoirs clearly show, regarded this *coup* as an event similar in kind to the assassination at Sarajevo which had taken him to the trenches in the First World War and the activities of the Axis dictators which had brought him back to the Foreign Office in the second. This was a personal and excessive view. Yet Mr. Gaitskell for the Labour opposition was not far behind him in his denunciation of Colonel Nasser's "high handed and totally unjustifiable step" which threatened to interfere with that international freedom of navigation through the Canal, guaranteed by the Convention of 1888 and renewed by Egypt's solemn pledge to respect it in the treaty of 1954. One third of the fourteen and a half thousand annual transits of ships through Suez were British; 75 per cent were those of the ships of NATO powers; more than half of Britain's supplies of oil came through that channel. Was not Eden right when he claimed that a new dictator had placed his hand on the "windpipe" of the nation?

To the public, and particularly the ex-servicemen, the wogs were simply at it again—worse than King Farouk and the extortions of "gyppo" taxi drivers and tarts. Opinion polls make it clear that a majority of the country—though not an overwhelming one—supported Eden and were resentful of being pushed too far. "Time for Decision" ran *The Times* leader of July 28. Interference with Britain's free use of the Canal would cut at the roots of her domestic economy and of her chances of survival as a great power, the paper thought. It would mean the severance of stategic sea links with Asia and the Far East. "The situation," it concluded, "is certainly not one that can be left to be dealt with by an exchange of Notes of protest." And on August 1 it elaborated on this stand:

> When the Commons take up Suez to-morrow there is one thing they can be sure of. If Nasser is allowed to get away with his *coup,* all the British and other interests in the Middle East will crumble. . . . The great oil works and fields of the Middle East are one of the main foundations of Britain's and Western Europe's industry and security. Anyone who thinks that victory for Nasser will not encourage other extremist deeds against the oil fields—and against strategic bases—should confine himself to tiddleywinks and blind man's buff. . . .

The paper ended:

> The spirit of giving in is the most fatal disease to which nations
> are subject, and it is apt to attack them like a cancer when they
> have arrived at the meridian.

Alas, no one at the editorial desk in Printing House Square or in
the cabinet room in Downing Street had yet realised that the
meridian had been passed. On the Tory right this knowledge was
necessarily hidden. In the House of Lords, Lord Killearn, who had
himself imposed a new government on Egypt during the war by appearing at the gates of King Farouk's palace with an escort of tanks
behind him, had more advice of the same kind to offer in face of
this international "piracy." "I think when you catch a fellow at it he
deserves short shrift. Get after him. Treat him as a pirate."

And at first the attitude of some members of the Labour "shadow
cabinet" did not seem so very dissimilar. In the big debate in the
Commons Mr. Gaitskell had compared Nasser's actions to those of
Hitler and Mussolini. "It is all very familiar," he said, recalling those
appalling days of the rape of Czechoslovakia and Poland. Unnoticed
at the time were the qualifications in his speech in which he pointed
out that Egypt's cause had supporters in the world and that as a signa-
tory to the charter of the United Nations Britain must act in ac-
cordance with that charter and not get herself into a position where
her legitimate complaints might be denounced by other nations as
aggression. When Lord Hinchingbrooke from the Tory benches demanded that Egypt be sent an ultimatum to stand back, Mr. Warbey
for the opposition replied that in such event Britain would find
three fifths of the world against her. It was a considerable underestimate.

The Prime Minister's public attitude was still that of "firmness
and care." "We do not seek a solution by force but by the broadest
possible international agreement," he told the nation in a BBC
broadcast on August 8. The only trouble was such agreement was
simply not to be had. On August 7 *The Times* had reported "Asian
misgivings" over the mere calling of a conference to discuss the
crisis; the Soviet Union and Third World opinion were definitely on

Egypt's side; and still more importantly Mr. Dulles was soon seen to be back-pedalling furiously away from any talk of force. His view was shared by the bulk of Labour members in the House of Commons, concerned over possible Tory misinterpretation of Mr. Gaitskell's speech, which it was now stressed had given Eden no blank cheque to take to arms unilaterally and without the sanction of a United Nations resolution. "Nearly in step," noted *The Times* of this opposition attitude which it took some comfort in regarding as not having ruled out force entirely: but of course the truth was that the Eden government was now out of step with everyone except its French ally, a watchful Israel and *The Times* itself.

What followed for the British cabinet was a diplomatic nightmare in which acceptable solutions made their appearance one by one over the horizon, only to vanish without trace. On August 16 a conference of twenty-two powers, the main users of the Canal, met at Lancaster House in London, eighteen of whom were prepared to advocate a new convention and a new board to ensure continued international control. Since India and the Soviet Union were determined to make this at best a purely advisory body without teeth, it was predictable enough that Colonel Nasser would refuse to entertain any international interference with his sovereignty and that this line of approach must break down. On September 4 the fertile mind of Mr. Dulles proposed the formation of a "Users' Club" to hire pilots and manage the Canal. From the first the French were suspicious of the scheme. So were the British, but anxious above all to keep the goodwill of the United States, Eden forced an acceptance of the Dulles plan on his reluctant cabinet. Even this modest move was received with outrage on the Labour left as provocative of Egypt, and Eden was repeatedly urged to renounce force in advance, a pledge he refused to give. No such doubts or hesitations troubled the United States administration. As early as September 3 President Eisenhower had told Eden that public opinion in America altogether rejected force, and on September 13, the same day as that on which the Labour opposition harried poor Sir Anthony in the Commons, Mr. Dulles remarked of his own brainchild, the Users' Club, "We don't intend to shoot our way through." It was almost an invitation to Colonel Nasser to denounce the whole harebrained scheme which for a while he had seemed resigned to accept in some form or another.

On October 1 the ill-fated infant was officially brought to birth in London. "Escapers' Club" *The Times* had dubbed it in advance, in a leader castigating the general retreat that had been sounded by the Labour leaders, once hot enough for action. Had not Mr. Herbert Morrison, the deputy leader of the party, called Nasser "this pocket dictator in Cairo" and begged the government not to be too nervous in standing up for Britain's rights? What had come over everyone? What was happening to the fibre of the nation? "Doubtless it is good to have a flourishing tourist trade," the paper fumed, "to win Test Matches and to be regaled by photos of Miss Diana Dors being pushed into a swimming pool.* But nations do not live by circuses alone. The people in their silent way know this better than the critics. They still want Britain great."

Whether this was true or not—and it probably *was* true where the confrontation with Egypt was concerned—the British government undoubtedly felt it had a mandate for firmness in defence of what it conceived to be the nation's vital interests: the protection of the oil fields and of friendly Arab regimes which might be toppled in turn if Nasser won. Diplomacy had visibly failed. The Canal Users' Association was a dummy. A case existed for direct action.

Mystery still surrounds much of what followed and will probably continue till the archives are opened, for no British cabinet minister in the course of his memoirs has yet admitted what is now generally accepted as the truth: that despairing of international action, the British and French governments, at a series of secret meetings in the absence of their interpreters and advisers, had worked out the details of a plan to launch Israeli forces in an attack on Egypt, which they themselves would follow up by an ultimatum to both sides to keep a ten-mile distance from the Canal while Allied forces landed to protect it (an ultimatum which Egypt was bound to reject), then by the bombing of Egyptian airfields, and finally by sea-borne landings at Port Said to occupy the Canal Zone and "separate the combatants."

Whatever the provocation—and here one must admit that the provocation had been great—Britain's attack was aggression on the same terms as the bombardment of Alexandria in Gladstone's time. The hypocrisy with which the action had been dressed up was glee-

* Miss Dors (as one ought not to have to remind anyone) is a movie star who was encountering domestic difficulties at the time.

fully seized on in a satirical extravaganza printed by the *New Statesman and Nation* under the title *Edebras Furioso*. Take the third canto:

> Sir Edebras was round the bend
> But Molly, his fair female friend,
> Whispered: "Just leave the thing to me:
> Something is going to start—you'll see."
> And so it was—Nass was attacked,
> Biffed, pummelled, bitten, scratched and hacked.
> Then Molly said: "What can we do,
> To save the peace, *but hit him too?*
> *Mon ami,* 'tis no time for wasting—
> We too must give young Nass a pasting.

And this does seem to represent exactly what happened during those extraordinary Suez days when the nation suddenly found itself involved in a war which had not only not been declared but which the government was reluctant to admit had even started. The whole process was greeted in opposition circles at Westminster with a mixture of astonishment, fury and derision. In the debate in the Commons on October 31, when the Prime Minister rose to justify himself he could hardly make himself heard above a continuous barrage of interruptions and abuse. And as the crisis developed, the total estrangement of the left found expression in a torrent of speeches and articles, each more indignant than the last, culminating in a stormy scene in the Commons when the Speaker had to suspend the sitting. A deep sense of shame filled all the liberally minded, the *New Statesman* wrote, at the "crime" being committed in their name.

The government still got a comfortable majority of 67 when it came to a vote. If the job could have been done quickly and Egypt had been overwhelmed at a stroke, on the lines of Soviet Russia's brutal repression of the Hungarian rising which was almost exactly contemporaneous with Suez, Britain and France might have got away with their own intervention. But to be successful, as *The Times* was to point out sadly when all was over, the operation had to be a *coup,* not a long drawn-out struggle. In retrospect it now seems strange that Attlee in the Lords should have accused the government of carrying out a Pearl Harbour against Egypt, since that was exactly what the government had *not* done in the course of its slow, laborious, clumsy campaign which had been spread over a week, from the first bombings of Egyptian airfields on October 31 to the assault by parachute troops near Port Said on November 5 and the final arrival of the seaborne armada at the northern end of the Canal on the 6th. Britain had not possessed the means for a lightning strike: her nearest deep-water port to the Nile had been in Malta, six days' steaming away.

In the interval between bombings and landings the forces of world opinion had time to mobilise. The British had counted on Russian hostility, which was to culminate in one of the stiffest and most bellicose notes a government ever received and in a Russian call at the United Nations for the aggression against Egypt to be halted, if necessary by force. It had probably been assumed in London that Russia's own aggression against Hungary had put her out of court and that she would be seen as Satan rebuking sin. This in itself was a mistake on Britain's part, but no grosser one than her misunderstanding of how deeply her actions would shock American opinion and that of the Asian members of the Commonwealth, who regarded her performance in Egypt (as was remarked at the time) with the pained horror and dismay of nephews and nieces who see a favourite uncle being publicly exposed as a rapist—and of a near relative at that. "A strange way of guarding the peace!" exclaimed India's elder statesman, Mr. Rajagopalachari, who also dubbed the invasion "a scandal to be permanently inscribed in imperial black." "Wanton brutality" was the verdict of the Minister without Portfolio, Mr. V. K. Krishna Menon; a gamble by "fevered brains," that of the *Hindustan Times;* while the *Times of India* thought Britain had exposed herself to charges of deceit and treachery unmatched since the days of Hitlerite Germany.

The whole Indian press was unanimous in its hostility; even the British-owned *Statesman* called the adventure "this disastrous course." "You will have few friends left," an Indian Socialist leader told the *Manchester Guardian*'s correspondent. In Bombay a motion was passed demanding withdrawal from the Commonwealth, a move with which the much respected Rajagopalachari agreed. "Clear and naked aggression which self-respecting and independent

nations of Asia and Africa are not going to tolerate" was the judgment of the most powerful Asian of all, the Prime Minister, Pandit
Nehru, whose part in the Suez story (much misunderstood in some
circles at the time) should always be seen in the light of his continuing support for the idea of Commonwealth and his firm resistance
to Communist moves to end it.

This condemnation of Suez was total throughout the East. "The
stupidest blunder of the century," wrote the *Straits Times* of Singapore. The *Times of Ceylon* declared that Britain, like France, had
returned to her "historic occupation of murder, massacre and pil-
lage." The more balanced *Ceylon Observer,* agreeing that Britain
was up to her old tricks again, asked more in sorrow than in anger
whether there was any point in continuing with such a Commonwealth. In Pakistan (a soul torn between her Islamic ties with Egypt
and her treaties with the West) the government kept cool, but the
press and public were in a state of frenzy, with the Urdu daily
Imroze calling Suez "the most unholy story of the twentieth century,"
while an editorial in *Jung* chimed in with cries of "Ignorance, folly
and madness." "How long," demanded *Dawn,* "can we continue this
association with Britain 'red with tooth and claw'?" According to the
London *Observer,* November 3 was Hate Britain Day in Pakistan.
Ten thousand rioters set fire to the British Information Service building in Dacca in East Bengal: next day another ten thousand demonstrated in Karachi carrying a coffin with "EDEN MURDABAD" inscribed on it. Indeed, in the East only the splendidly commercial
government and citizens of the colony of Hong Kong really kept
their heads. Asked by Egypt for a shipment of fifty thousand steel
helmets, they declined to supply them, "on advice from London."
Instead they sold 38,000 steel helmets—to the Lebanon!

In what had once been the old white dominions, public opinion
was more divided, but Britain could take small comfort from that.
Even in New Zealand, where both government and labour opposition dutifully rallied to the call with "Ready? Aye, ready," the
Auckland Star raised awkward doubts in a leader headed "It Doesn't
Look Right," and there were many who felt only dismay at the
strange course the motherland was following. In Australia the
federal Prime Minister, Mr. R. G. Menzies (as he then was), proved
a stauncher Edenite than Sir Anthony himself, and he had many
supporters in the press. "This is more like the old Britannia!" en-
thused the Sydney *Telegraph,* while the Sydney *Sun* found the opera-

tion "heartening" after the locust years of "giving way to idealists and selling out to opportunists." But it was a close run thing, and according to a survey in the London *Observer*, of eleven leading Australian dailies, four fully supported Britain, four were mildly critical, three "trenchantly hostile," as were certainly Dr. Evatt's Labour Opposition in the federal parliament and most of the academics and intellectuals.

In Canada, opinion tended as always to split along the old cleavage line between the French- and British-speaking peoples. In Quebec the adventure was deplored—odd in a way, since in Egypt on this occasion France and Britain were acting together. But even in the loyalist areas there were voices raised against agression, and in the heart of the citadel, in Toronto itself, the *Star* could speak of the "incredibly reckless and arrogant conduct" of the Eden government —conduct, in fact, so obviously troubling to Canadian consciences that the Egyptian ambassador in Ottawa was encouraged to appeal publicly for volunteers to fight by Egypt's side: an extraordinary demonstration of how far, in some foreign eyes, Canada seemed to have strayed from Britain. And not Canada alone. South Africa simply took refuge behind the formula: Not consulted, Not involved. "It is best to keep our heads out of the bee-hive," her Prime Minister had remarked very early in the crisis and he adhered to this principle to the end.

So what did Suez really amount to?

It brought a series of humiliations for Britain—a Security Council Resolution which but for her use of the veto would have branded her as an aggressor; an appalling moment in the full Assembly of the United Nations when the only support she and France could muster against sixty-five hostile voices and an abstention from Canada came from Israel, Australia and New Zealand; a temporary breach with the United States; the ultimate horror (revealed by the Chancellor of the Exchequer) that the pound sterling was on the verge of collapse. Some of the most poignant moments occurred at home, at Westminster, when the United Nations call for the ending of hostilities was accepted by the government and waves of cheering on the opposition benches greeted the Prime Minister's lame and belated surrender.

The Commonwealth itself was not the casualty that had been feared at the height of the crisis when eager voices in Asia had been trumpeting its demise. They had found little support among the cautious, sensible rulers then in power in Delhi, Karachi and Colombo. The very fact that the Commonwealth, in *The Scotsman*'s happy phrase at the time, was "a club without rules" helped it to survive. Nevertheless, it had not emerged unscathed or unchanged. Suez had emphasised differences and divergences which up till then had only been half expressed—India's neutralist position; the intense parochialism of Boer-dominated South Africa; the growing awareness in Australia and New Zealand of their individuality as Pacific powers on the borders of Asia and not as mere extensions of far-off Atlantic islands; the realisation in Canada (which for a few nightmare moments seemed to have fallen headlong into the sudden rift between Britain and the United States) that she had a role to play on the world stage wholly independent of these two embarrassing neighbors. From this viewpoint, her initiative in proposing a peace-keeping force for the Canal was one of the most significant of all the by-products of Suez.

Finally, what was the effect on Britain herself? On most counts a sharp and salutary one. When eventually the Cease Fire came, *The Times* noted that it had brought general relief. Had the whole venture in its timing and conception, it wondered, been ill-advised and impossible from the beginning? When all was over, the *New Statesman* was to list some of the risks Britain had run in her defiance of the forces of world opinion—50,000 Indonesians had apparently registered as volunteers to fight at Egypt's side: the Chief Nawab of Baluchistan had offered Nasser the services of his tribesmen.

It would be easy to laugh at this solemn and ludicrous catalogue, particularly at the Nawab's tribesmen, who would certainly have spoiled the Egyptians if given half a chance. But in a wider sense the Nawab had the root of the matter in him: he was far more of a realist than Sir Anthony: he knew the new balance of forces in the world. At Suez, Britain had acted as though she were still an imperial power. She was not. The Commonwealth, apart from Australia and New Zealand, had not supported her; had indeed rejected and judged her. She was not even a Great Power in the terms of the Cold War. What the Russians could do in the streets of Budapest, Britain could no longer do in the bazaars of Port Said or along the salt waters of the Canal, once her lifeline. She was simply one medium power among many, and the realisation was to play its part in leading her away from the concept of Commonwealth in search of an older identity in Europe.

XIX

Insubstantial Pageant

I believe one eminent scholar has recently propounded that a bird's eye view of history is strictly for the birds, and from the purely academic point of view he may well be right.

Nevertheless, I suspect that when some time in the second milennium some future Gibbon comes to write the definitive story of the rise and fall of Britain's empire, he will treat everything after Suez as an epilogue and may conceivably remove it to a footnote.

The basic facts are certainly remarkable. In the autumn of 1956 the British had only a toe-hold left in Asia, but the rest of their colonial Empire was much as it had been in 1939. In was now in Africa that the centre of the Empire lay, and apart from the loss of the Canal Zone and the Sudan, every position in that continent was intact. In the west, Britain held the Gold Coast, Nigeria and Sierra Leone; in the east and centre, British Somaliland, Kenya, Tanganyika, Zanzibar, Uganda and the Federation of Southern and Northern Rhodesia and Nyasaland; in the south, the large desert territory of Bechuanaland, and the two enclaves of Basutoland and Swaziland, the one wholly, the other partly, within the borders of the Union of South Africa. Twelve years later London administered no single African territory; the Central African Federation had broken up; white-dominated Southern Rhodesia (a quasi-dominion since 1923) had made its Unilateral Declaration of Independence; and the Union of South Africa had left the Commonwealth.

Whether this was cause and effect must forever remain uncertain. Probably not. Even if Suez had not happened, or had ended differently with Nasser's defeat and victory for the old colonial powers, it is hard to think that decolonisation throughout Africa could have been long delayed, given the irresistible forces of nationalism at work. But Britain's and France's *débâcle* at Suez undoubtedly hastened (if it did not raise) that "Wind of Change" which was to sweep the continent from Egypt and Algeria to the Zambesi. It did more. For after Suez the British people, as indeed their government, had no longer any desire to stand in the eye of the storm. Immersed in the joys of the affluent society and the Welfare State, they had few energies or thoughts to spare for a colonialism which radical thinkers had for years been telling them was evil and profitless and which (after humiliation at the hands of an Egyptian pocket dictator) had evidently to be accepted as such. If subject peoples wanted their freedom, let them have it. Whether they were ready for it or not no longer seemed Britain's concern. After Suez it was clear that no one could stop them anyway without recourse to physical repression on a scale no sensible man could contemplate and which the country could no longer afford. Had not British rule always been dependent on the consent of the governed? If that consent was now withheld, then British rule itself must cease. It was a viewpoint accepted even by those sections of the upper-middle and middle classes which had really cared about Imperialism and had run the Empire. Milked by high taxation, no longer encouraged to strive or save, their *mores* derided, they too were prepared to abandon Imperialism and even trusteeship as a bad job and see what could be saved from the wreckage of the old regime by a timely accommodation with the new emergent Africa.

The appearance of the dominion of Ghana in 1957, only a few months after Suez, was the first experiment in shedding such colonies without pain. Three years later the much larger and more important Nigeria evolved along the same lines to a general and deserved chorus of praise. In east and central Africa most of the colonies were much less advanced than these, and the very notion that such torn, backward and impoverished states could become self-governing dominions would have taxed Mr. Balfour's famous philosophic detachment to the utmost if it had been suggested to him when he was working out his definition in 1926:—"autonomous communities . . . equal in status . . . in no way subordinate to one another . . ." To equate Kenya, Tanganyika, Uganda or the island of Zanzibar with Canada or Australia required a very striking exercise of the imagination. With the few honourable exceptions of Julius Nyerere, Jomo Kenyatta, Tom Mboya, Milton Obote, Dr. Hastings Banda and Kenneth Kaunda, there was no black politician of any stature in the whole vast area as large as western Europe, and barely a handful of trained African doctors, lawyers, scientists or administrators to serve them. Nevertheless, during the 1960s, dominions they became, and in due course fully independent republics within the Commonwealth. So did Northern Rhodesia (as Zambia) and Nyasaland (as Malawi) after the break-up of a white settler attempt at federation with white-dominated Southern Rhodesia. "I say that Britain has lost the will to govern in Africa," declared the federal Prime Minister, Sir Roy Welensky, as he surveyed the wreckage of his hopes, and it was no more than the truth.

In 1962, the year of Welensky's outburst, Britain gave independence also to the Caribbean islands of Jamaica and Trinidad with Tobago, fragments of that other federation of the West Indies which also collapsed about this time. Malaya had reached dominion status in 1957, Cyprus in 1960; Sierra Leone on the West African seaboard followed in 1961. Jamaica and Trinidad were sophisticated westernised societies with experience in democratic ways—the same could hardly be said of Sierra Leone, where the independence celebrations were somewhat marred by the fact that most of the "minority" "opposition" leaders had been put in gaol. In 1965 independence within the Commonwealth was given to The Gambia, a sliver of land in West Africa three hundred miles long by thirty miles wide, a "geographical absurdity," in the words of one modern expert. In 1966 Basutoland achieved its independence as Lesotho. In the same year Bechuanaland became the Republic of Botswana: it was at least larger than Swaziland which reached the goal two years later, another hostage of the white racialist Union.

Whether all these acts of liberation were really of service to Africa or the Africans remains to be seen. But the trend had become irreversible. Colonial demand and British acquiescence had created a run on the market which no one could any longer resist. "Those who really want independence, get it," declared the Colonial Secretary, Mr. Anthony Greenwood, in 1965. What he said was indisputably true and sensible and adapted to a time when delaying actions, even pauses for reflection, had lost validity. However, it was not quite what Fox and Burke or even Mr. Greenwood's Socialist predecessors had had in mind when they had talked of "Trusteeship." Was anything left? A Commonwealth? Or was it no more than a "project" for one, to adapt Adam Smith's phrase about the "Empire" of his time? The fact that in 1965 and again in 1971 two Commonwealth states, India and Pakistan, went to war with one another hardly commends it, either practically or ideologically.

*   *   *

Three and a half centuries before these events occurred, Shakespeare had provided an epitaph for another island:

> Our revels now are ended. These our actors,
> As I foretold you, were all spirits, and
> Are melted into air, into thin air:
> And, like the baseless fabric of this vision,
> The cloud-capped towers, the gorgeous palaces,
> The solemn temples, the great globe itself,
> Yea, all which it inherit, shall dissolve,
> And, like this insubstantial pageant faded
> Leave not a wrack behind.

The cloud-capped towers of Simla, the gorgeous palaces of Lutyens' grandiose New Delhi, are now inhabited by others; the solemn temples of the *Raj*, like the Gateway to India on the Bombay water-front, built for the reception of King-Emperors and their Viceroys, have no evident use except to be gaped at by tourists; and the pigeons roost on those statues of the Great White Queen that have not been blown up by nationalists or removed by municipal councils to museum or scrap-yard. Even the British "Club" has been infiltrated by the natives; and though in Malta's sister island of Gozo you may still find a "Royal Lady Hotel" and "Lord Kitchener

Bar," most of the traces of a once triumphant culture are being over-laid by the glass and ferro-concrete of our age faster than the grass grew over the ruins of the Roman Forum or the sands drifted over Aknaton's Tel-el-Amarna. Indeed, if the legendary man from Mars were to come down to earth and look around him, it is doubtful if on the material evidence alone he could deduce that the British Empire had ever existed.

If it had not existed, would it have been necessary to invent it? And why did it decline and fall?

Primarily because such is the fate of all organic things. It came in with the rise of sea power and had to go out with its eclipse. For a significant period of time it wielded in the Royal Navy a force which made it important in Europe and overwhelmingly predominant on the sea routes, along which passed also the products of an industrial revolution in which for half a century it led the world. These were advantages that could not last for ever. While they lasted, it was necessary that the Empire, if it were to survive, should create for itself an organic cultural and economic unity, a sense of common purpose and a joint policy of defence.

However the British were not by nature an imperially minded people.* Such political ideologies as they had were directed more towards disposing of the estate than of developing it. During their first phase they had a theory of mercantilism which was at least logical and matched their needs. Unfortunately its practice affronted others and its foundations were swept away by the broadsides of Adam Smith and the rebellion of the thirteen colonies. In the self-questioning and the great economic debates in the aftermath of that disaster the experiment of a tightly run empire was abandoned and the Navigation Acts, which had provided the cordage, were re-pealed.

What followed under free trade was the greatest era in British history. Not in British *imperial* history, however, for this period saw also the growth of separatism among the white colonists overseas and of disinterest and Little Englander feeling at home. It was all too easy to draw the wrong conclusions from this unparalleled pros-perity and expansion. The success of free trade seemed to suggest that this was the universal panacea and that the doctrines of *laissez*

---

* As admirably demonstrated by Professor Max Beloff in his recent *Imperial Sunset*.

faire were a good enough way to run an empire. In fact, that success owed everything to Britain's industrial and naval lead over her competitors and nothing to the intrinsic virtues of Cobdenite doctrines. It was a lead that had to be short-lived, as larger and more soundly based industrial powers began to overtake Britain's productivity while at the same time acquiring colonial empires of their own.

When towards the end of the 1870s the British realised what was happening they turned back towards methods which for three decades they had discounted: they began to assert themselves in Africa and in the excesses of Jingoism, which for a short while made imperialism a genuinely popular movement. Yet even then, they still had no clear theory of Empire. It was a shallowly based imperialism with the flavour of the music-hall about it, a fact which was commented on by the sober minded and those whose conscience was outraged by aggression in South Africa, Egypt and the Sudan. The cruelties and sufferings of the Boer War seemed like a judgment on iniquity, and by the early 1900s Jingoism was a creed which had been rejected by the intellectuals and bored the man in the street. Even in professedly imperialist circles, among the Tories and their Liberal Unionist allies, there was no really consistent thinking about Empire. The pressure groups for imperial federation carried no weight, and even when this last belated attempt to make an economic unit of the Empire was taken up by a man of force and genius in Joseph Chamberlain, it was defeated as much by apathy at home as by separatism among the colonists abroad.

As a working organism the British Empire died with that failure. There was to be no *Zollverein* such as had made the fortunes of Imperial Germany and to-day is re-making the fortunes of Europe in the Common Market. Neither was there to be a *Kriegsverein,* a formal defence pool. Even if twice within a quarter of a century Britain had not been called upon to spend herself for civilisation in two ruinous world wars, so loose, widespread and untidy an entity must inevitably have slipped from control of the motherland to dissolve into its component parts. The effects of those wars merely hastened the process. They strained an economy already declining in relative terms and destroyed Britain's financial leadership of the world, her great international role. They led to the emergence of the super-power in America and Soviet Russia. But still more importantly they unleashed the forces of nationalism which a weakened Britain was powerless to resist, was indeed ideologically committed *not* to resist once a certain point was reached. For, in fact, Britain had long been preparing her own abdication. It is a pleasing irony that it was this moral disarmament, not the armies and navies of the *Raj,* which ultimately preserved the ghost of it and extended long beyond its normal term the prestige and influence of the small group of islands from which the impetus of Commonwealth came.

What to do with an *imperium* was a question that had never troubled the Romans, a very practical and self-confident people. It had not greatly troubled the British either until the loss of the thirteen American colonies, but thereafter the heartsearchings were poignant. If colonists of British stock could not be coerced, then obviously they would have to be wooed. The inhabitants of Quebec and Montreal must be assured of their liberties in Canada in the hopes of encouraging them to regard themselves as Englishmen abroad. By the time this illusion was revealed for what it was, it was too late to go back—the liberal conscience had been aroused and great state papers like the Durham Report had extended the doctrine of Responsibility across the Atlantic. No other empire in history ever prepared the way so thoroughly for its own demise. Step by step, under governments that tolerated imperialism, under governments that abhorred the very concept, and even under governments that professed to practise imperialism, the British people prepared for the liquidation of their own inheritance. Not at all stages did they admit even to themselves where these theories were leading; not all the statesmen who mouthed them always meant them seriously. Even in Macaulay's great speech on future Indian independence a cynical ear may detect more than the hint of a suggestion that it might never happen, and indeed until the early 1900s such thoughts were fairly widespread among the less idealistic of ministers and viceroys, just as until the 1950s few could find it in themselves to believe in the independence of colonies in Africa. All the same, the work of decolonisation went steadily on, and "Trusteeship" became not just a grand word in a parliamentary oration but a charter for liberation. What made the whole thing more remarkable was that many of the British leaders and civil servants who brought western ways to India were working against their better judgment;

themselves profoundly convinced that without India their own small islands would sink to the status of a second-rank power.

The gift of freedom to India was one of the most magnanimous, most sensible, as it was in many ways one of the most important events in world history, and alone would justify the existence of the Empire. Having failed to assimilate their own kith and kin in America and Canada, the British deliberately set out in India to anglicise by the force of education and example a whole spectrum of peoples of quite alien culture and traditions, and to some degree succeeded and left the Indian parliamentary democracy as their memorial. In Pakistan their political example failed to find takers, as it has largely failed in Africa, where the preparations for independence were too rushed, too ill-prepared and perhaps too insensitive to African traditions. But it was not Britain's fault that they were rushed. Two world wars and the mushroom growth of nationalism took her unawares—the very success of Indian independence played its part in arousing a too great impatience in others waiting in the queue. The British Empire made many mistakes and was guilty of many shortcomings, but one should no more blame its failures in the face of irresistible natural forces than one should judge Rome for her inability to tame the new world that had been building up behind the lines of the Danube and the Rhine. Even the failures of such empires fertilise: their successes are in the realm of the spirit as much as of substance. Like old soldiers in the barrack-room ballad they never die; they only fade away.

*　　*　　*

What other legacies did Britain leave?

Cities where before her coming there was often nothing but bush or swamp or huts in a clearing of the forest. Many of the sites are splendid but few of the towns are memorable as Paris and Venice and New York are memorable—if we except Sydney on its incomparable harbour graced by its jewel of an opera house in the shadow of that monstrous coat hanger of a bridge. Only one set out to be consciously imperial: Lutyens' New Delhi, which is Versailles in a hot climate and every bit as uncomfortable. It is probably only a rumour that officials and their messengers take to bicycles when travelling to and fro along its interminable corridors, but if the

Indians have not yet demolished it, they do not love it. British colonial architecture was not lovable architecture: most of it was of a bad period, and it shows.

But then most Britons, if called to account to God for their stewardship, would not have based their apologia on such material things, though they might have put in a good word for the ports and harbours, the trunk roads and railways, the irrigation schemes which had transformed huge areas of desert and bush. They would have ventured a modest claim for having provided their charges with law and order during most of their period of occupation. Was this, as many critics have said, a negative virtue at best and little but the dead hand of repression and reaction? Events in the Punjab during the partition of 1947 and more recent holocausts in Biafra and East Bengal make one wonder whether peace and the rule of law were quite such insignificant gifts and the *Pax Britannica* quite the blimpish joke that superior people once supposed. Three hundred and seventy-five people died at Amritsar, and it provoked an outcry in Britain louder than has accompanied a whole world's protest at the killing, mutilation, rape and exile of a thousand times that number in territories once administered in tranquility by a handful of British officials and police.

Those officials would not perhaps have made any great claims for the gift of parliamentary democracy, for it brought them an infinity of trouble. But they might have added that such government as they did provide was incorrupt government answerable to an incorrupt judiciary. It was something that even their enemies did not deny— even if you could bribe an English magistrate, one of the characters in E. M. Forster's *A Passage to India* complains, he would still infallibly defeat you by finding for the other side; and there is hardly an Indian writer who does not somewhere pay tribute to this inscrutable fair-mindedness. Here British administration greatly surpassed its Roman predecessor, for almost to a man, in the generations after Clive, the proconsuls returned home to tea rooms in Cheltenham without any of those spoils of office which procurators had brought back from Judaea and senators from Egypt. And the legal system they administered throughout most of the territories was basically the same as that which had been so carefully built up by precedent and statute since the time of Bracton. Like Rome, Britain did not fail to offer one common legal heritage to her successors.

Even many of the faults which marked the *Raj*—the Club, the colour bar, the racial exclusiveness—arose to some degree out of the need of administrators and judges to stay aloof from those they had to tax and try, though it owed perhaps more to the invincible prejudices of their wives.

The creation of a Christian empire is something none of them would have dreamed of claiming. Even in Victorian times, when the Christian ethic was at flood tide, the British made no attempt to impose it on their Hindhu, Muslim or Buddhist subjects whose religions they scrupulously respected. They leaned so much the other way that for years they had tolerated *Suttee* and painstakingly fired off ceremonial guns at festival time to honour Hindhu gods whom the militant Christian subjects of the Queen regarded as so many Baals. Missionaries were distrusted politically and looked down on socially even in Africa where genuine triumphs for the missions were achieved. And since Britain herself can hardly claim to-day to be a Christian country, this attitude is much in sympathy with modern thought.

What other legacies?

A common monetary system? It would certainly be typical if the sole relic of the *Raj* were to prove to be the Sterling Area—a fitting gift from shopkeepers! But the Sterling Area has never been synonymous with either Empire or Commonwealth, and seems at present in a fair way to being dismantled.

A common British culture? On this point visiting businessmen, writers, soldiers, scientists and diplomats are all agreed. Nigeria is Nigerian and Jamaica is Jamaican, but both are unmistakably British, and this goes for almost everywhere the British trod—the same uniforms for the armed forces, the same moustaches and rather dated service slang, the sundowners in the Club, the government tea party on the lawns, the same sports on the oval or maidan. Canada, one must admit, being something of an apostate in this, has never taken to cricket. On the other hand, in Singapore even some Chinese play it, as do a number of Egyptians and inhabitants of the Greek island of Corfu, who were taught the game by the ubiquitous Royal Navy. In fact, apart from baseball and polo, which the British picked up in India, there is hardly a game or sport from mountaineering to boxing, from lawn tennis to golf, which the English or

Scots did not first develop and then export via their old Commonwealth and their ex-colonial partners in America to the world.

Here, as in the realm of fashion and pop culture, for which London is now the undisputed global capital, is proof of a neo-colonialism which finds few objectors among the young on the campuses and in the discothèques in every continent. Out of the ashes of the *Raj* arises, phoenix-like, another paler, more evasive but still potent spirit appealing to generations to whom imperialism itself is an evil dream.

Another Athens? That might be to set the sights and certainly the achievements of modern Britain unduly high. But the prestige she has won so recently may rank among the bonuses of Empire. It has not been earned by devotion to duty in the Niger swamps or in the villages of Bengal. But an ex-Empire is surely entitled to some luck in the days of its decline. And one is left, finally, with an intriguing thought. Perhaps it may be chiefly for this—for the froth and frolic which are in a sense a backlash against the old imperialist creed—that the British Empire will be remembered and honoured. But then the Roman Empire is popularly remembered to-day not for Augustus, Hadrian, Horace, Seneca, Livy, Scipio Africanus, Vergil and Marcus Aurelius, but for Mark Antony's dalliance with Cleopatra, for the chariot races between the Blues and the Greens, and the lions in the Colosseum.

BIBLIOGRAPHY

The following were consulted:

UNITED KINGDOM NEWSPAPERS

Daily Chronicle
Daily Mail
Daily News
Daily Telegraph
News of the World

The Scotsman
The Standard
The Sun
The Times
The Observer

UNITED KINGDOM JOURNALS AND MAGAZINES

Blackwood's
Economic History Review
The Economist
Edinburgh Review
English Historical Review
Fortnightly Review
Fraser's Magazine
Graphic
History
The Historical Journal
Illustrated London News
John Bull

Journal and Proceedings of the
   Royal Colonial Institute
National Review
New Statesman and Nation
Nineteenth Century
Pall Mall Gazette
Punch
The Round Table
The Spectator
Truth
Vanity Fair
Westminster Gazette
Westminster Review

ASIAN NEWSPAPERS

Amrit Bazar Patrika
The Bengalee
Ceylon Observer
Civil and Military Gazette
Dawn
The Hindu
Hindustan Times
Imroze
The Indian Patriot

Jung
The Madras Mail
The Statesman
The Statesman Weekly
The Straits Times
Times of Ceylon
The Times of India
Young India

DOMINION AND COLONIAL NEWSPAPERS

Auckland Star
The Bulletin
Cape Times
The Daily Times (Lagos)
The Daily Telegraph (Lagos)
Ghana Evening News
Mail and Empire (Toronto)
Montreal Gazette
Montreal Daily Star
New Zealand Herald

New Zealand Times
Ottawa Free Press
Quebec Daily Telegraph
Sydney Daily Telegraph
Sydney Morning Herald
Sydney Sun
Toronto Globe
Toronto Star
Wellington Independent

BOOKS

AMERY, L. S., ed. *The Times History of the War in South Africa.*
ANDREWS, C. F. and MOOKERJI, G. *The Rise and Growth of Congress in India.* (1938.)
ASHWORTH, W. *An Economic History of England, 1870–1939.* (1960.)
———— *A Short History of the International Economy, 1850–1950.* (1952.)
AUSTIN, ALFRED. *Collected Poems.*

BARKER, SIR E. *Ideas and Ideals of the British Empire.* (1951.)
BASSETT, J. R. *The Nineteen-thirty-one Political Crisis.* (1958.)
BEARCE, G. *British Attitudes Towards India.* (1961.)

BECKETT, J. C. *The Making of Modern Ireland, 1603–1923.* (1966.)

BEER, G. L. *The Origins of the British Colonial System, 1578–1660.* (Rep. 1933.)

——— *The Old Colonial System, 1660–1688.* (Rep. 1933.)

——— *British Colonial Policy, 1754–1765.* (Rep. 1933.)

BELL, K. N. and MORRELL, W. P. *Select Documents on British Colonial Policy, 1830–1860.* (Rep. 1969.)

BELOFF, MAX. *Imperial Sunset: Britain's Liberal Empire, 1897–1921,* Vol. 1. (1970.)

BEN-GURION, DAVID. *Recollections.* (1970.)

BENHAM, F. C. *Great Britain under Protection.* (1941.)

BENNET, G. *The Concept of Empire: Burke to Attlee, 1774–1947.* (1953.)

BENTHAM, JEREMY. *Works of.,* ed. Bowring.

BEVERIDGE, SIR W. *Social Insurance and Allied Services: A Report.* (1942–43.)

——— *Full Employment in a Free Society.* (1944.)

BLAKE, ROBERT. *The Unknown Prime Minister: The Life and Times of Andrew Bonar Law.* (1955.)

——— *Disraeli.* (1966.)

BODELSON, C. A. *Studies in Mid-Victorian Imperialism.* (Rep. 1960.)

BOSE, S. C. *The Indian Struggle, 1920–1934.* (1935.)

BOURRET, F. F. *Ghana.* (1960.)

BOWLEY, A. L. *Some Economic Consequences of the Great War.* (1930.)

BRADY, A. *William Huskisson and Liberal Reform.* (1928.)

BRIGHT, JOHN. *Select Speeches of the Rt. Hon. John Bright, M.P. on Public Questions.*

BUCKLAND, C. T. *Sketches of Social Life in India.* (1884.)

BULLOCK, ALAN. *Life and Times of Ernest Bevin.* (1960.)

BURKE, EDMUND. *Speeches and Letters on American Affairs.*

BURN, W. L. *The Age of Equipoise: A Study of the Mid-Victorian Generation.* (1964).

BURNS, SIR A. C. *History of Nigeria.* (1963.)

BUTTERFIELD, H. *George III, Lord North and the People.* (1949.)

CAIRNCROSS, A. K. *Home and Foreign Investment, 1870–1913.* (1953.)

CAMBRIDGE HISTORY OF THE BRITISH EMPIRE. (8 Vols., 1929–63.)

CAMBRIDGE ECONOMIC HISTORY.

CAMBRIDGE HISTORY OF INDIA.

CAMPBELL-JOHNSON, A. *Mission with Mountbatten.* (1953.)

CARY, JOYCE. *Mister Johnson.* (1939.)

CARRINGTON, C. E. *The British Overseas—The Making of the Empire.* (Rep. 1968.)

CHURCHILL, SIR W. S. *The World Crisis.* (1928.)
———— *The Second World War.* (1948.)
CLAPHAM, J. H. *Economic History of Modern Britain, 1926–1938.*
CLARK, G. *Balance Sheets of Imperialism.* (1936.)
COBDEN, RICHARD. *Speeches on Public Policy.* ("Cobden Club Essays," 2nd series, 1862.)
COLE, G. D. H. *History of the Labour Party from 1914.* (1948.)
COUPLAND, R. *The American Revolution and the British Empire.* (1930.)
———— *The Indian Problem, 1833–1935.* (1942.)
———— *Indian Politics, 1936–1942.* (1943.)
———— *The Future of India.* (1943.)
———— *The Durham Report.* (1945.)
———— *Wilberforce.* (1945.)
COURT, W. H. B. *British Economic History, 1870–1914—Commentary and Documents.* (1965.)
CROMER, LORD. *Modern Egypt.* (1911.)
CROSS, COLIN. *The Fall of the British Empire.* (1968.)

DANGERFIELD, G. *The Strange Death of Liberal England.* (1936.)
DAWSON, R. M. *Development of Dominion Status, 1900–1936.* (1967.)
DAWSON, R. M. and NEATBY, H. B. *William Lyon Mackenzie King* (2 Vols.), *1874–1923, 1924–1932.* (1958, 1963.)
DILKE, SIR CHARLES. *Greater Britain.* (1885.)
DODWELL, H. H. *The Nabobs of Madras.* (1926.)
DOW, J. C. R. *The Management of the British Economy, 1945–1960.* (1964.)
DUTT, R. C. *The Economic History of India in the Victorian Age.* (1916.)
DWIVEDI, R., ed. *Life and Speeches of Pandit J. Nehru.* (1929.)

EAYRS, J. *The Commonwealth and Suez.* (1964.)
EDEN, SIR A. *Full Circle.* (1960.)
EDWARDES, M. *Glorious Sahibs, 1799–1838.* (1968.)
———— *British India.* (1967.)
ENSOR, R. C. K. *England, 1870–1914.* (1936.)

FAGE, J. D. *An Introduction to the History of West Africa.* (1955.)
FEILING, KEITH. *Life of Neville Chamberlain.* (1946.)
FIELDHOUSE, D. K. *The Colonial Empires.* (1966.)
FLINT, J. E. *Sir George Goldie and the Making of Nigeria.* (1960.)
FORSTER, E. M. *A Passage to India.* (1924.)

GANN, L. H. and DUIGNAN, P. *Burden of Empire*. (1968.)
GARDINER, A. G. *Pillars of Society*. (1913.)
GARRET, G. T., ed. *The Legacy of India*. (1931.)
GARVIN, J. L. and AMERY, JULIAN. *Life of Joseph Chamberlain*. Vol. III, 1895–1900, by Garvin; Vols. IV, V, VI by Amery.
GLENDEVON, JOHN. *The Viceroy at Bay*. (1971.)
GRAHAM, MARIA. *Journal of a Residence in India, 1809–1811*. (1813.)
GRAVES, R. and HODGE, A. *The Long Weekend: A Social History of Great Britain, 1918–1939*. (1941.)

HAILEY, LORD. *An African Survey*. (1957.)
HALÉVY, ELIE. *A History of the English People in the Nineteenth Century*, 6 Vols. trans. by E. I. Watkin.
HALL, H. L. *The Colonial Office: A History*. (1937.)
HANCOCK, SIR W. K. *A Survey of British Commonwealth Affairs*. (2 Vols., 1937, 1942.)
———— *Argument of Empire*.
———— *Smuts*. (2 Vols., 1962, 1968.)
———— and GOWING, MARY M. *British War Economy*. (1949.)
HANNA, A. J. *The Story of the Rhodesias & Nyasaland*. (Rep. 1965.)
———— *European Rule in Africa*. (Hist. Assoc., 1961.)
HANSARD. *Parliamentary Reports*.
HARLOW, V. T. *The Founding of the Second British Empire, 1763–1793*. (1952.)
———— and MADDEN, F. *British Colonial Development, 1774–1834*. (1953.)
HARROD, ROY. *The Life of John Maynard Keynes*. (1951.)
———— *Free Trade and the Manchester School*. (1951.)
HAVINGHURST, A. F. *Twentieth Century Britain*. (1962.)
HICKEY, WILLIAM. *Memoirs*. (3 Vols., 1913, 1925.)
HOBSBAWN, E. J. *Industry and Empire*. (1968.)
HOBSON, J. A. *Imperialism: A Study*. (1902.)
HODSON, H. V. *Slump and Recovery, 1929–1937*. (1938.)
HOLLAND, B. H. *The Fall of Protection, 1840–1850*. (1913.)
HOSKINS, J. L. *British Routes to India*. (1966.)

IMLAH, A. H. *Economic Factors in the* Pax Britannica. *Studies in Foreign Trade in the Nineteenth Century*. (1958.)
INDIAN NATIONAL CONGRESS. *Reports of Annual Sessions, 1885–1928*.

JACQUEMONT, VICTOR. *Letters from India, 1828–1831*. (1936.)
JEANS, J. S. *England's Supremacy*. (1885.)
JENKINS, ROY. *Asquith*. (1964.)

JONES, J. H. and others. *The Coal Mining Industry.* (1939.)

JONES, THOMAS. *Lloyd-George.* (1951.)

—— *Whitehall Diary, 1916–1925.* (1969.)

KAHN, A. E. *Great Britain in the World Economy.* (1946.)

KAYE, SIR J. W. and MALLESON, G. B. *History of the Indian Mutiny of 1857–58.* (6 Vols., 1908–09.)

KEITH, A. B. *Speeches and Documents on Indian Policy, 1750–1921.* (2 Vols., 1922.)

—— *Select Speeches and Documents on British Colonial Policy, 1863–1917.* (1953.)

—— *Speeches and Documents on the British Dominions, 1918–1931.* (1932.)

KENDLE, J. E. *The Colonial and Imperial Conferences, 1887–1911.* (1967.)

KEYNES, J. M. *Economic Consequences of the Peace.* (1919.)

KIEWIET, C. C. DE. *The Imperial Factor in South Africa.* (Rep. 1965.)

KIMBLE, D. *A Political History of Ghana, 1850–1928.* (1963.)

KIPLING, RUDYARD. *Collected Works.*

KIRKMAN, W. P. *Unscrambling an Empire.* (1966.)

KNAPLUND, P. *The British Empire, 1815–1839.* (1942.)

—— *Britain, Commonwealth and Empire, 1901–1955.* (1957.)

—— *James Stephen and the British Colonial System, 1813–1847.* (1953.)

KNORR, R. *British Colonial Theories, 1570–1850.* (1963.)

KNOWLES, L. C. A. *The Economic Development of the British Empire, 1763–1914.* (1924.)

KOEBNER, R. *Empire.* (1961.)

—— and SCHUTT, H. D. *Imperialism . . . A Political Word, 1840–1960.* (1964.)

LAWRENCE, T. E. *Seven Pillars of Wisdom.* (1935.)

LAWRENCE, SIR W. *The India We Served.* (1928.)

LENIN, V. I. *Imperialism: The Highest Stages of Capitalism.* (1917.)

LIDDELL-HART, SIR B. H. *Foch: Man of Orleans.* (1931.)

LLOYD, T. O. *Empire to Welfare State, 1906–1967.* (1968.)

LLOYD-GEORGE, DAVID. *War Memoirs.* (1938.)

LOCKHART, J. G. and WOODHOUSE, C. M. *Rhodes.* (1962.)

LOWE, C. J. *The Reluctant Imperialists.* (1967.)

LUCAS, SIR C. P. *Lord Durham's Report on the Affairs of British North America.* (3 Vols., 1912.)

LUGARD, LORD. *The Dual Mandate in British Tropical Africa.* (1929.)

MACCOBY, S. *English Radicalism*. (2 Vols., 1935, 1955.)

MACELWEE, W. *Britain's Locust Years, 1918–1940*. (1962.)

MAGNUS, SIR PHILIP. *Gladstone*. (1963.)

MANSERGH, P. N. S. *Documents and Speeches on British Commonwealth Affairs, 1931–1952*. (1953.)

—— *Survey of British Commonwealth Affairs: Problems of External Policy, 1931–1939*. (1953.)

—— *The Multi-racial Commonwealth*. (1955.)

—— *South Africa, 1906–1961: The Price of Magnanimity*. (1962.)

—— *The Commonwealth Experience*. (1969.)

—— and others. *Commonwealth Perspectives*. (1958.)

MAWS, N., ed., assisted by LUMBY, E. W. R. *Transfer of Power, 1942–1947*. Vol. 1: *The Cripps Mission*. (1970.)

MANTOUX, E. *The Carthaginian Peace*. (1946.)

MARJORIBANKS, E. *The Life of Lord Carson*. (1932.)

MEHROTRA, S. R. *India and the Commonwealth*. (1965.)

MELLOR, G. R. *British Imperial Trusteeship, 1783–1850*. (1951.)

MILLER, J. D. B. *The Commonwealth in the World*. (1959.)

MILLIN, S. G. *Rhodes*. (1952.)

MILWARD, A. S. *Economic Effects of the World Wars on Britain*. (1970.)

MOON, PENDEREL. *Divide and Quit*. (1961.)

MORLEY, JOHN (LORD). *Life of William Ewart Gladstone*. (1903.)

NAMIER, SIR LEWIS B. *England in the Age of the American Revolution*. (1930.)

NEHRU, PANDIT J. *Autobiography*. (1942.)

—— *Letters*.

NEVILL, LADY DOROTHY. *Reminiscences*. (1906.)

NICHOLSON, SIR HAROLD. *King George V, His Life and Reign*. (1952.)

OFFICIAL HISTORIES. (First World War.)
Statistics of the Military Effort of the British Empire. (1922.)
Gallipoli. (1929–32.)
France and Belgium. (1922–48.)

OXFORD HISTORY OF MODERN INDIA. (1964.)

OXFORD HISTORY OF EAST AFRICA.

PAKENHAM, LADY ELIZABETH. *Jameson's Raid*. (1960.)

PARLIAMENTARY HISTORY

PELLING, H. *The Origins of the Labour Party, 1880–1900*. (1954.)

PERHAM, MARGERY. *Lugard*. (2 Vols., 1956, 1960.)

—— *Colonial Sequence*. (2 Vols., 1970.)

"PEREGRINE PULTNEY." *Life in India*. (3 Vols., 1844.)

PLATT, D. C. M. *Finance, Trade and Politics in British Foreign Policy, 1815–1914.* (1968.)

PORTER, B. *Critics of Empire.* (1968.)

ROBINSON, R., GALLAGHER, J., and DENNY, A. *Africa and the Victorians.* (1961.)

ROGERS, J. E. THOROLD. *Cobden and Political Opinion: The Colonial Question.* ("Cobden Club Esays," 2nd series, 1871.)

RONALDSHAY, EARL OF. *The Life of Lord Curzon.* (3 Vols., 1928.)

RUSSELL, W. H., ed., M. EDWARDES. *My Indian Mutiny Diary.* (1957.)

SAIYID, M. A. *M. A. Jinnah.* (1945.)

SCHLOTE, W. *British Overseas Trade from 1700 to the 1930s.* (1952.)

SCHULL, J. *Laurier.* (1965.)

SCHUYLER, R. L. *The Fall of the Old Colonial System.* (Rep. 1966.)

SEELEY, J.R. *The Expansion of England.* (1883.)

SEMMEL, B. *Imperialism and Social Reform.* (1960.)

SITARAMAYYA, B. P. *The History of the Indian National Congress.* (2 Vols., 1946, 1947.)

SLEEMAN, W. *Rambles and Recollections of an Indian Official.* (1844.)

SMITH, ADAM. *An Enquiry into the Wealth of Nations.* (Rep. 1904.)

SMITH, GOLDWIN. *The Empire.* (1863.)

SPEAR, T. S. P. *History of India.* (2 Vols., 1965.)

——— *The Nabobs.* (1932.)

STOKES, E. *The Political Ideas of English Imperialism.* (1960.)

STORRS, SIR RONALD. *Orientations.* (1937.)

SYMONS, JULIAN. *The General Strike.* (1957.)

TAYLOR, A. J. P. *English History, 1914–1945.* (1965.)

TAYLOR, DON. *The Years of Challenge, 1945–1958.* (1959).

TAYLOR, MEADOWS. *Seeta.* (1877.)

TENDULKAR, D. G. *Mahatma: Life of Mohandas Karanchand Gandhi.* (8 Vols., 1951–54.)

THORNTON, A. P. *The Imperial Idea and its Enemies.* (1959.)

TITMUSS, R. M. *Essays on the Welfare State.* (1958.)

TREVELYAN, G. M. *Life and Letters of Macaulay.*

TREVELYAN, SIR G. O. *The Competition Wallah.* (1864.)

WALPOLE, HORACE. *Letters.*

WEAD, EUNICE. *British Public Opinion of the Peace with America, 1782.* (American History Review, Vol. 34.)

WHEARE, K. C. *The Constitutional Structure of the Commonwealth.* (1960.)

WHEELER-BENNET, SIR J. *King George VI.* (1958.)
WOODRUFF, PHILIP. *The Men Who Ruled India.* (2 Vols., 1953, 1954.)
WRAXALL, SIR N. W. *Historical Memoirs of My Own Times.* (1815.)

YOUNG, G. M. *Victorian England. Portrait of an Age.* (1960.)
YOUNG, K. *Arthur James Balfour.* (1963.)
YOUNGSON, A. J. *Britain's Economic Growth, 1920–1966.* (1967.)

ZIMMERN *The Third British Empire.* (1926.)

INDEX

DATE